INTERNATIONAL PERSPECTIVES ON SUPPORTING AND ENGAGING ONLINE LEARNERS

INNOVATIONS IN HIGHER EDUCATION TEACHING AND LEARNING

Senior Series Editor: Patrick Blessinger, St John's University and Higher Education Teaching and Learning Association, USA

Associate Series Editor: Enakshi Sengupta, Higher Education Teaching and Learning Association, USA

Published Volumes:

Volume 23	University–Community Partnerships for Promoting Social Responsibility in Higher Education – Edited by Enakshi Sengupta, Patrick Blessinger and Craig Mahoney
Volume 24	Leadership Strategies for Promoting Social Responsibility in Higher Education – Edited by Enakshi Sengupta, Patrick Blessinger and Craig Mahoney
Volume 25	Integrating Community Service into Curriculum: International Perspectives on Humanizing Education – Edited by Enakshi Sengupta, Patrick Blessinger and Mandla Makhanya
Volume 26	International Perspectives on Improving Student Engagement: Advances in Library Practices in Higher Education – Edited by Enakshi Sengupta, Patrick Blessinger and Milton D. Cox
Volume 27	Improving Classroom Engagement and International Development Programs: International Perspectives on Humanizing Higher Education – Edited by Enakshi Sengupta, Patrick Blessinger and Mandla Makhanya
Volume 28	Cultural Competence in Higher Education – Edited by Tiffany Puckett, and Nancy Lind
Volume 29	Designing Effective Library Learning Spaces in Higher Education – Edited by Enakshi Sengupta, Patrick Blessinger and Mandla S. Makhanya
Volume 30	Developing and Supporting Multiculturalism and Leadership Development – Edited by Enakshi Sengupta, Patrick Blessinger and Mandla S. Makhanya
Volume 31	Faculty and Student Research in Practicing Academic Freedom – Edited by Enakshi Sengupta and Patrick Blessinger
Volume 32	International Perspectives on Policies, Practices & Pedagogies for Promoting Social Responsibility in Higher Education – Edited by Enakshi Sengupta, Patrick Blessinger and Craig Mahoney
Volume 33	International Perspectives on the Role of Technology in Humanizing Higher Education – Edited by Enakshi Sengupta, Patrick Blessinger and Mandla S. Makhanya
Volume 34	Humanizing Higher Education through Innovative Approaches for Teaching and Learning – Edited by Enakshi Sengupta, Patrick Blessinger and Mandla S. Makhanya
Volume 35	Humanizing Higher Education through Innovative Approaches for Teaching and Learning
Volume 36	Integrating Research-based Learning across the Curriculum
Volume 37	International Perspectives in Social Justice Programs at the Institutional and Community Level
Volume 38	The Role of External Examining in Higher Education: Challenges and Best Practices

INNOVATIONS IN HIGHER EDUCATION TEACHING AND LEARNING   VOLUME 39

INTERNATIONAL PERSPECTIVES ON SUPPORTING AND ENGAGING ONLINE LEARNERS

EDITED BY

JAIMIE HOFFMAN
Noodle Partners, USA

and

PATRICK BLESSINGER
International Higher Education Teaching and Learning Association, USA

Created in partnership with the
International Higher Education Teaching and Learning Association

https://www.hetl.org/

United Kingdom – North America – Japan
India – Malaysia – China

Emerald Publishing Limited
Howard House, Wagon Lane, Bingley BD16 1WA, UK

First edition 2021

Copyright © 2021 Emerald Publishing Limited

Reprints and permissions service
Contact: permissions@emeraldinsight.com

No part of this book may be reproduced, stored in a retrieval system, transmitted in any form or by any means electronic, mechanical, photocopying, recording or otherwise without either the prior written permission of the publisher or a licence permitting restricted copying issued in the UK by The Copyright Licensing Agency and in the USA by The Copyright Clearance Center. Any opinions expressed in the chapters are those of the authors. Whilst Emerald makes every effort to ensure the quality and accuracy of its content, Emerald makes no representation implied or otherwise, as to the chapters' suitability and application and disclaims any warranties, express or implied, to their use.

British Library Cataloguing in Publication Data
A catalogue record for this book is available from the British Library

ISBN: 978-1-80043-485-1 (Print)
ISBN: 978-1-80043-484-4 (Online)
ISBN: 978-1-80043-486-8 (Epub)

ISSN: 2055-3641 (Series)

INVESTOR IN PEOPLE

CONTENTS

List of Contributors   vii

Series Editors' Introduction   ix

PART I
IN PRACTICE

Introduction to Supporting and Engaging Online Learners
Rachel Scott and Jaimie Hoffman   3

Transforming the Practice of Student Affairs Professionals: Creating an Ecosystem of Support that is Inclusive of Online Learners
Jaimie Hoffman and Autumn Willinger   13

Reshaping the Online Student Experience
Molly A. Mott, Kristyn Muller and Michele Forte   29

Beyond Instruction: Scaling Support for a Large Online Master's Program
David A. Joyner   43

PART II
INNOVATIVE APPROACHES

Connecting with Online Learners: Case Studies from A Scottish University
Lorraine Syme-Smith, Louise Campbell and Lynn Boyle   59

Facilitating Co-curricular Connections among Millennial and Generation Z Students in Digital Environments
Shelley Price-Williams and Pietro A. Sasso   73

Promoting Student Engagement with Data-Driven Practices
Jeremy Anderson, Heather Bushey, Maura Devlin and Amanda J. Gould   87

One University: An Interdepartmental Collaboration Model to Enhance Online Student Engagement
Roland Nuñez   *105*

Engaging Students in Asynchronous Advising Using The Dynamic Student Development Metatheodel: Toward a Critical Approach
Pietro A. Sasso and Tyler Phelps   *119*

Engaging with Online Graduate Students Through Writing Support and Employment
Jessica J. Jones   *135*

Student Transitions: Academic Support for Postgraduate Online Distance Students
Louise Connelly and Donna Murray   *149*

Supporting Online Students in US-Based Professional Doctoral Programs
Melora Sundt and Leslie Wheaton   *163*

Medical Versus Social Models of Disability: Increasing Inclusion and Participation of Students in Online and Blended Learning in Higher Education
Nathan Whitley-Grassi, Bryan J. Whitley-Grassi, Shaun C. Hoppel and Melissa Zgliczynski   *181*

About the Authors   *195*

Name Index   *203*

Subject Index   *209*

LIST OF CONTRIBUTORS

Jeremy Anderson	Dallas College, Dallas, TX, USA
Lynn Boyle	University of Dundee, Dundee, UK
Heather Bushey	Bay Path University, Longmeadow, MA, USA
Louise Campbell	University of Dundee, Dundee, UK
Louise Connelly	The University of Edinburgh, Scotland, UK
Maura Devlin	Bay Path University, Longmeadow, MA, USA
Michele Forte	The State University of New York, New York, NY, USA
Amanda J. Gould	Bay Path University, Longmeadow, MA, USA
Jaimie Hoffman	Noodle Partners, New York, NY, USA
Shaun C. Hoppel	State University of New York, Empire State College, New York, NY, USA
Jessica J. Jones	Arizona State University, Tempe, AZ, USA
David A. Joyner	Georgia Institute of Technology, Atlanta, GA, USA
Molly A. Mott	The State University of New York, New York, NY, USA
Kristyn Muller	The State University of New York, New York, NY, USA
Donna Murray	The University of Edinburgh, Scotland, UK
Roland Nuñez	Lake Sumter State College, Leesburg, FL, USA
Tyler Phelps	Southern Illinois University, Edwardsville, IL USA
Shelley Price-Williams	University of Northern Iowa, Cedar Falls, IA, USA
Pietro A. Sasso	Southern Illinois University, Edwardsville, IL USA
Rachel Scott	Noodle Partners, New York, NY, USA
Melora Sundt	Noodle Partners, New York, NY, USA
Lorraine Syme-Smith	University of Dundee, Dundee, UK

Leslie Wheaton	Noodle Partners, New York, NY, USA
Bryan J. Whitley-Grassi	Niagara University, Buffalo, NY, USA
Nathan Whitley-Grassi	State University of New York, Empire State College, New York, NY, USA
Autumn Willinger	Noodle Partners, New York, NY, USA
Melissa Zgliczynski	State University of New York, Empire State College, New York, NY, USA

SERIES EDITORS' INTRODUCTION

The purpose of this series is to publish current research and scholarship on innovative teaching and learning practices in higher education. The series is developed around the premise that teaching and learning is more effective when instructors and students are actively and meaningfully engaged in the teaching–learning process.

The main objectives of this series are to:

1) present how innovative teaching and learning practices are being used in higher education institutions around the world across a wide variety of disciplines and countries;
2) present the latest models, theories, concepts, paradigms, and frameworks that educators should consider when adopting, implementing, assessing, and evaluating innovative teaching and learning practices; and
3) consider the implications of theory and practice on policy, strategy, and leadership.

This series will appeal to anyone in higher education who is involved in the teaching and learning process from any discipline, institutional type, or nationality. The volumes in this series will focus on a variety of authentic case studies and other empirical research that illustrates how educators from around the world are using innovative approaches to create more effective and meaningful learning environments.

Innovation teaching and learning is any approach, strategy, method, practice, or means that has been shown to improve, enhance, or transform the teaching–learning environment. Innovation involves doing things differently or in a novel way in order to improve outcomes. In short, innovation is positive change. With respect to teaching and learning, innovation is the implementation of new or improved educational practices that result in improved educational and learning outcomes. This innovation can be any positive change related to teaching, curriculum, assessment, technology, or other tools, programs, policies, or processes that leads to improved educational and learning outcomes. Innovation can occur in institutional development, program development, professional development, or learning development.

The volumes in this series will not only highlight the benefits and theoretical frameworks of such innovations through authentic case studies and other empirical research but also look at the challenges and contexts associated with implementing and assessing innovative teaching and learning practices. The volumes represent all disciplines from a wide range of national, cultural, and organizational contexts. The volumes in this series will explore a wide variety of teaching and learning topics such as active learning, integrative learning, transformative learning, inquiry-based learning, problem-based learning, meaningful learning, blended learning, creative learning, experiential learning, lifelong and lifewide learning, global learning, learning assessment and analytics, student research, faculty and student learning communities, as well as other topics.

This series brings together distinguished scholars and educational practitioners from around the world to disseminate the latest knowledge on innovative teaching and learning scholarship and practices. The authors offer a range of disciplinary perspectives from different cultural contexts. This series provides a unique and valuable resource for instructors, administrators, and anyone interested in improving and transforming teaching and learning.

Patrick Blessinger
Founder, Executive Director, and Chief Research Scientist,
International HETL Association

Enakshi Sengupta
Associate Editor, International HETL Association

PART I
IN PRACTICE

INTRODUCTION TO SUPPORTING AND ENGAGING ONLINE LEARNERS

Rachel Scott and Jaimie Hoffman

ABSTRACT

This chapter unpacks the unique characteristics of online students, research that exists pertaining to support of online students in American higher education, and reviews the subsequent chapters in this volume. The chapters in this book focus on research, theoretical foundations for supporting the success of online student. Authors present case studies in various context including a large state university system, a large and increasingly growing public master's degree, two private institutions, and a Scottish institution. Various theoretical constructs are provided to help inform practices for supporting online students including "communities of practice" (Wenger, 2000) or "communities of inquiry" (Garrison, 2007) and the Dynamic Student Development Metatheodel (DSDM). The final chapters of this book unpack the experiences of specific populations including post-baccalaureate, students, and doctoral students, understanding that each subset of students encounters different challenges throughout their online experiences. Finally, this book closes with a focus on a very important topic for all professionals: accessibility discussing the importance of inclusion, participation, and engagement for students with disabilities no matter the modality of learning. The last chapter compares two models of support (medical and social) and offers recommended changes for implementation of best practices to enhance literacy supports in online learning environments.

Keywords: Online education; higher education; student support; student engagement; retention; student support.

INTRODUCTION

There is no doubt that online education is increasing as a learning modality in higher education. This growth is not limited to a single institution type within the United States, the expansion is prevalent in the private and public sectors of higher education and encompasses both for-profit and not-for-profit institutions, with the largest growth of online education enrollments at two years, private not-for-profit institutions (Seaman, Allen, & Seaman, 2018). Large institutions of higher education (enrolling over 15,000 students) have educated the largest portion of online students, totaling 46–66% of the enrolled students in online education (Seaman et al., 2018; Wladis, Hachey, & Conway, 2014). Online students encompass 30% of all college students and 60% of all community college students (Wladis et al., 2014) in the United States. In the fall of 2018 (National Center for Education Statistics (NCES), 2018), there were nearly 7 million students taking online courses; 5.7 million online students were undergraduates and about 4.9 million enrolled at a public institutions. Enrollment of online students at institutions of higher education is growing faster than on-campus student enrollment, with a compound annual growth rate from 2002 to 2012 of 16.1% and 2.5%, respectively (Allen & Seaman, 2013).

With such significant growth it makes sense to turn our attention to supporting and engaging this emerging population. We also cannot ignore that at the time (2020 during the coronavirus pandemic) this chapter was authored, we were in the midst of a global pandemic, causing universities around the world to move to exclusively distance learning for their entire student population. This drastic shift caused universities to make quick decisions with the safety of their students in mind but unveiled that many universities were not able to (and likely remain unable to) provide the same level and quality of student support in a distance format. This chapter unpacks the unique characteristics of online students, research that exists pertaining to support of online students in American higher education, and reviews the subsequent chapters in this volume.

CHARACTERISTICS OF ONLINE STUDENTS

Online college students share a variety of characteristics; they often do not take online courses exclusively – in fact, only 14.9% of the total student population enroll in a fully online program, while 16.7% of the total student population enroll in some form of an online course alongside their on-ground courses (Seaman et al., 2018). In addition, 56.1% of fully online students took courses from institutions located in their same state, and most online students enroll at institutions of higher education located within a 100-mile radius of their home (Aslanian & Clinefelter, 2012; Seaman et al., 2018).

From a demographic standpoint, 40% of online students are under the age of 30 years old (Aslanian & Clinefelter, 2012) and women make up 70% of the distance learning population (CollegeAtlas.org, 2017). The online student population is juggling more than just schoolwork, with 79% of undergraduate online students reported being employed, either part-time or full time while pursuing their degree (Radford, 2011). Research has also found that students with mobility disabilities enroll in a distance education course more often than students without a disability (Radford, 2011). Online students also vary in their pursuit of degree type and in the credit hour consumption. Of students enrolled in online courses, 60% (of both undergraduate and graduate students) study full time and 73% of exclusively online students pursue a degree, compared to 19% pursuing a certificate and 8% pursuing a license (Aslanian & Clinefelter, 2012). The literature is not clear on the most popular courses and degree programs for online students. Aslanian and Clinefelter (2012) reported that business degrees dominate the field of study, while Radford (2011) found computer and information sciences to hold the highest enrollment percentage of online students.

Online students choose distance education for a variety of reasons. The most commonly reported reasons for taking an online class included accommodation of work schedules, family obligations, a students' distance from their campus, financial reasons, the ability to take a course not offered on campus, the availability of fast-track courses, and the ability to study anytime, anywhere (Aslanian & Clinefelter, 2012; Dare, Zapta, & Thomas, 2005). Online courses have opened up a new world for the student looking to further their education while continuing to work full time, for the parent juggling family responsibilities on top of their studies, for the student who has dreamed of having a degree from a university across the country. Simply put, online education gives students new opportunities they may not have in a traditional classroom setting.

With the foundational understanding of who online students are, their enrollment preferences, and their motivation for pursuing online education, we can turn our attention to the unique support services online students need.

STUDENT SUPPORT IN HIGHER EDUCATION

This leads us to a conversation on the types of support that our online student population needs. Online students expect a range of services, transactions, and communication to be performed online (McCracken, 2005) with administrative services (such as online registration and online bill payment) being their most significant support service need (Dare et al., 2005). While online students identify administrative services as their top need, this could be the result of a lack of exposure to other support services; Jackson-Boothby (2017) found a significantly lower number of institutions of higher education providing non-academic student support services to online students. Currently, sparse literature exists that explores the potential effect that access to additional support services may have on online students.

Despite the sparse literature exploring the effects of additional support services for online students, higher education experts note the need for online students to receive support services. Brindley, Walti, and Zawacki-Richter (2008) found that due to online students having more responsibility to manage their own learning and that online learning requires more competency and skills to build, student support services for online learners should take added importance in the student affairs profession. Further, Crawley and Fetzner (2013) found a general agreement that online students require the same support services as on-campus students. Yet, despite this apparent need for online students to have access to online support services, institutions of higher education have offered online support services at a slower rate and on a more limited basis (Smith, 2005). The slow pace of offering online student support services in higher education is met with an additional barrier of a variance in expectations for faculty and administrators pertaining to online student support (Bailie, 2014). Together, the literature showcases a disconnect between an identified need for online student support services, and the current state of institutions of higher education meeting that need. Even when online students are invited to participate in opportunities, they are not necessarily created for this population specifically; 76% of student affairs professionals in a study (Jackson-Boothby, 2017) identified student engagement opportunities (e.g., events, workshops, and trainings) for online students offered at their college or university, but many of those opportunities were for on-campus students that online students were invited to attend. As student affairs professionals, we see this often; universities will host speakers, or events and invite online students via a livestream, but forget to engage with them or acknowledge them in the event. We also find that events sponsored by the university specifically for online students are also sparse and, in our experience, are left to the individual programs to design, market, and fund.

BARRIERS FOR PROVIDING SERVICES TO ONLINE STUDENTS

Reviewing the research unpacked in the previous pages may leave you wondering: if distance education enrollment is increasing, and students have a clear need for support services, why are universities not delivering on this need? One of the top barriers to institutions providing effective student support services to online students is that campuses do not cater to online students (Hoffman, 2018). Specifically, institutions of higher education offer office hours and schedules that do not consider different time zones in which students may reside, host events exclusively on campus, do not adopt additional services, such as counseling or health services in an online environment, and levy fees to online students that do not apply to their off-campus status (Hoffman, 2018). Institutions of higher education are also not in a practice of displaying readily available resources for online students (Jones & Meyer, 2012).

In addition to the overall structural barriers to providing effective student support services to online students, Bailie (2014) found a variance of expectations for online students. The variance noted relates to communication with online students (whether faculty should be required to initiate email contact with each new student or host a welcome phone call), instructor presence and engagement in the online classroom (how frequently faculty should respond to discussion posts and maintain office hours), and online instructor's timeliness and response time (how quickly to respond to emails). The author argued this variance could possibly signify that administrative expectations are less for faculty when working with their online students and courses (Bailie, 2014).

Crawley and Fetzner (2013) noted that the challenge for institutions of higher education is not just to provide the student support services but to do so in a way that fosters a meaningful connection back to the institution. Milman, Posey, Pintz, Wright, and Zhou (2015) took Crawley and Fetzner's recommendation one step further, noting that students with marginalized identities (such as first-generation students and students of color) are often overlooked in online student support and suggested that institutions of higher education should be focused on online student support at an individual basis. In the recent months of the publication of this book (2020), we have seen an increase in support of students from marginalized identities, including town hall events to provide students with a safe place to share experiences and hear from university leaders about how they are addressing key issues related to racism on their campuses. We have also seen universities expand their counseling center availability for students (where licensing allows) to provide students with more opportunities to connect with professionals in support of their academic pursuits and personal challenges. While these efforts benefit all students, it is particularly impactful for students from marginalized backgrounds who have experienced an uptick in violence and polarizing legislation in the recent months.

Identifying the barriers that prevent universities to provide effective support services for online students is one step in the direction toward making services available and accessible to online students. The more we can highlight to university leaders the priority of online students and the importance of providing these services in a manner that meets online students where they are at, the better chance we have at enacting real change in higher education; a change so desperately needed for higher education to continue to thrive in the future. This volume provides a series of best practices and research for successfully supporting online students, each chapter is briefly summarized below.

CHAPTER OVERVIEWS

In "Transforming the Practice of Student Affairs Professionals: Creating an Ecosystem of Support That Is Inclusive of Online Learners," by Jaimie Hoffman and Autumn Willinger discuss the importance of supporting and engaging online students such that all students feel valued, welcomed, and supported. They provide recommendations on ways campuses can transform the existing ecosystem of support services and engagement opportunities to be inclusive of online learners. A systematic review of the current ecosystem of support is provided to analyze the ways in which access is provided remotely to online learners and to ensure that the language and engagement opportunities shared with students are inclusive of online learners. The authors suggest that campuses create and implement specific initiatives for their online population including online orientation, success coaching, library support services, and the use of predictive analytics for student success.

In "Reshaping the Online Student Experience," by Molly A. Mott, Kristyn Muller, and Michele Forte discuss structure and strategies that institutions can use to transform the experience of students learning at a distance. They provide details on how one of the largest educational systems in the United States, the State University of New York (SUNY), reshaped the student online learning experience via the "Open SUNY" model. Specific strategies for infusing existing models of support with new ways of thinking are explained. Attention is paid to the infrastructure of the Open SUNY model of collaboration, the use of the Open SUNY Readiness Approach for preparing colleges to deliver quality online programming, and the unique Open SUNY + Signature Element program for assessing the quality of online programming and support structures. Finally, this chapter also highlights the efforts of one campus, the SUNY at Canton, to leverage Open SUNY and take its signature element on student engagement to the next level.

In "Beyond Instruction: Scaling Support for a Large Online Master's Program," by David Joyner examines the program- and institute-level infrastructure to support learners in Georgia Tech's online Master of Science in Computer Science program (launched in 2014). The program is novel due to its cost and size: total tuition for the entire degree is around $7,000, and to date, it has enrolled over 15,000 total students with 9,000 enrolled in fall 2019. This chapter examines administration at the program level, including its academic advisers, career counselors, and alumni relations, and at the institute level, where it integrates with on-campus infrastructure for academic integrity, student advocacy, and disability accommodations. The author concludes with three guidelines for implementing similar programs at other schools, taking into consideration the full range of experience in building Georgia Tech's program.

In "Connecting with Online Learners: Case Studies from a Scottish University," by Lorraine Syme-Smith, Louise Campbell and Lynn Boyle share some of the key ideas that impact the creation of online learning environments. This chapter explores some aspects of Connectivism and its relation to wider ideas of community-building, heutagogy, and motivation and articulates some of the factors that have influenced the authors' practice in creating online learning. Examples of how theory influenced practices are brought to life in three case studies – each looking at a course the authors were part of creating. The case studies illustrate how these theoretical foundations fostered the development of learning communities, encouraged students to have autonomy over the direction of their learning, and engaged students to maintain their motivation for learning.

In "Facilitating Cocurricular Connections among Millennial and Generation Z Students in Digital Environments," by Shelley Price-Williams and Pietro A. Sasso focus on the online learning experience for two specific populations: Millennials and Generation Z students. In order to build relationships and community, the authors encourage consideration beyond technology toward creating a higher value aspect of learning by developing models closely aligned with "communities of practice" (Wenger, 2000) or "communities of inquiry" (Garrison, 2007). This chapter examines how to engage Millennial and Generation Z traditional undergraduate students through distance learning approaches in ways that support student learning and development.

In "Promoting Student Engagement with Data-driven Practices," by Jeremy Anderson, Heather Bushey, Maura Devlin and Amanda J. Gould encourage readers to anchor their work around supporting online learners in an intentional way that is attentive to student needs. This chapter focuses on American Women's College (TAWC) at Bay Path University's Social Online Universal Learning (SOUL) model to promote degree completion through a constellation of evidence-based practices that cultivate student engagement in a personalized online learning environment. SOUL employs an innovative adaptive technology approach with universal design for learning (UDL) principles to promote accessibility and affordability. Foundational to these frameworks is a commitment to leveraging technology to gather data that drive action-oriented analytics, triggering interventions by faculty and staff, and generating predictive models to inform wrap-around support. SOUL's high-tech, high-touch attributes give students agency over their unique learning paths and provide instructors and administrators the meaningful insights needed to target efforts in a personalized yet scalable way, to promote and positively impact student success. Lessons learned in the process of developing data-driven "high-tech, high-touch" practices are presented in this chapter.

In "One University: An Interdepartmental Collaboration Model to Enhance Online Student Engagement," by Roland Nuñez presents an in-depth case study of the steps that one private American university took, following the Kezar model (2005), to improve online student engagement. The first phase involved buy-in from leadership and creating a valid justification for the collaboration efforts. The second phase involved taking the first steps to create a culture of collaboration across the institution. The third phase involved the development of programs that continued collaboration efforts through various campuses and departments to create tangible products promoting student success. The institution focused more on the *process* of collaboration than the results in an effort to create a foundation that could outlast staff changes and restructuring of departments. Early results indicate a potential for other universities to examine their processes used for collaboration between colleges and departments.

In "Engaging Students in Asynchronous Advising Using the Dynamic Student Development Metatheodel: Toward a Critical Approach," by Pietro A. Sasso and Tyler Phelps explore challenges to distance education student retention and persistence, share the theoretical construct of the Dynamic Student Development Metatheodel (DSDM), and discuss how to apply specific student success strategies to distance education. These strategies include intrusive advising and asynchronous advising techniques. This chapter concludes with how these advising techniques and strategies can facilitate increased student persistence through engagement with academic advisors using asynchronous approaches that move beyond the traditional temporal, didactic strategies employed by most higher education institutions.

In "Engaging with Online Graduate Students Through Writing Support and Employment," by Jessica J. Jones unpacks the experience of a specific population, graduate students. This chapter provides a review of the theory and research to show that there is a need for academic support for graduate-level students while also discussing how institutions have worked to create meaningful connections for students. Drawing on Astin's theory of student involvement, this chapter discusses three ways that the University Academic Success Programs department at Arizona State University has worked to address that need and provide academic support to online graduate students: online graduate writing centers, online dissertation writing camps, and employment of online graduate students. Using interview examples from former student tutors, this chapter shows how these opportunities helped online graduate students feel valued, supported, and connected to the institution. This chapter concludes by addressing limitations, areas for program growth and future research, and recommendations for practitioners to apply in their own institutions.

Continuing in the vein of more mature students, in "Student Transitions: Academic Support for Postgraduate Online Distance Students," by Louise Connelly and Donna Murray unpack the academic needs of postgraduate online distance students. Typically, the students will be over 35 years old and studying part-time, while juggling other commitments, such as family or employment. Therefore, providing academic support which is targeted and meets their needs is paramount for enhancing the student experience and ensuring that they have the best possible chance of succeeding at the postgraduate level. This chapter presents an academic transition roadmap (ATR) that can be used by institutions, in order to provide targeted academic support that is aligned with the three stages. By implementing the ATR, there is the potential for enabling students to become more confident while on their academic journey, and ultimately, this contributes to enhancing the student experience.

In "Supporting Online Students in US-based Professional Doctoral Programs," by Melora Sundt and Leslie Wheaton narrow in on a subset of the graduate student population: doctoral students. This chapter focuses on the factors that contribute to professional online doctoral student success (in the United States). The online doctoral student occupies two underserved categories of higher education students: doctoral students and online students, both of which have historically low graduation rates (Bawa, 2016; Stone, 2017). A number of US online doctoral programs have significantly higher graduation rates than normal, demonstrating that it is possible to create highly successful online doctoral programs. In this chapter, the authors apply the Clark and Estes (2008) conceptual framework of human performance to understand the factors contributing to doctoral student success in online programs. Looking at three stakeholder groups, faculty, staff, and students, the authors review the factors and solutions that could allow each group to contribute to doctoral student success. This review of the literature is informed by examples drawn from two online professional doctoral programs for which the authors either designed and taught courses, and chaired dissertations, or were enrolled in as a student.

In the final chapter, "Medical Versus Social Models of Disability: Increasing Inclusion and Participation of Students in Online and Blended Learning in Higher Education," by Nathan Whitley-Grassi, Bryan J. Whitley-Grassi, Shaun C. Hoppel and Melissa Zgliczynski examine the challenges associated with supporting higher education students with disabilities in an online learning environment.

They discuss and recommend delivering literacy support to online students by embracing the social model of disability and universal design principles as opposed to the typical medical model of disability that is pervasive in educational systems. Under the Americans with Disabilities Act of 1990 (ADA), educational institutions are required to promote auxiliary aids and services. Broadly defined, these aids are meant to enhance communication, inclusion, and participation of people with disabilities. The discussion of the resources put forth in this chapter begins with an exploration of the evolving consensus on the nature of disability and the standard (medical) model for providing accommodations and supports for students with disabilities, which was developed before the rise of online and blended learning environments. Next, the authors explore the problems inherent in the use of the medical model and highlight how the social model and UDL can be utilized to empower learners and enhance their learning experiences in online and blended learning environments. The discussion returns to the importance of inclusion, participation, and engagement for students with disabilities no matter the modality of learning. This chapter concludes with a comparison of two models of support and recommended changes for implementation of best practices to enhance literacy support in online learning environments.

CONCLUSION

With an evident need for change in the higher education sector and a clear gap in services offered to online students, coupled with increasing enrollments and the long-term unknown impact of a global pandemic on higher education, it is now more important than ever for this book to exist. The experiences of the professionals, the programs developed and implemented, and the subsequent impact on online students as a result of their work demonstrate that when higher education can shift its focus and resources on to distance education and online students, the impact is immeasurable, and the return on investment far exceeds the initial cost. We encourage you to not only read this book but to be inspired by the ideas and challenge yourself to see how you can better serve your online students and adapt to the new wave of student support.

REFERENCES

Allen, I. E., & Seaman, J. (2013). Grade change: Tracking online education in the United States. Retrieved from http://www.onlinelearningsurvey.com/reports/gradechange.pdf

Aslanian, C. B., & Clinefelter, D. L. (2012). Online college student 2012: Comprehensive data on demands and preferences. Retrieved from https://www1.udel.edu/edtech/e-learning/readings/Online-College-Students-2012Survey.pdf

Bailie, J. L. (2014). What online students want. *Online Journal of Distance Learning and Administration*, *17*(2). Retrieved from https://www.westga.edu/~distance/ojdla/summer172/bailie172.html

Brindley, J. E., Walti, C., & Zawacki-Richter, O. (2008). Learner support in open, distance, and online learning environments. Retrieved from https://uol.de/fileadmin/user_upload/c3l/MDE/Download/asfvolume9_ebook.pdf

CollegeAtlas.org. (2017). 41 Facts about online students. Retrieved from https://www.collegeatlas.org/41-surprising-facts-about-online-students.html

Crawley, A., & Fetzner, M. (2013). Providing service innovations to the students inside and outside of the online classroom: Focusing on student success. *Journal of Asynchronous Learning Networks, 17*(1). Retrieved from https://files.eric.ed.gov/fulltext/EJ1011382.pdf

Dare, L. A., Zapta, L. P., & Thomas, A. G. (2005). Assessing the needs of distance learners: A student affairs perspective. *New Directions for Student Services, 112*. Retrieved from https://onlinelibrary-wileycom.libweb.uwlax.edu/doi/epdf/10.1002/ss.183

Hoffman, J. (2018). Best practices for student affairs supporting online learners. Retrieved from https://drive.google.com/file/d/1-1QQsCDt-JVDQ6usCsFh9UlIJaNQES2r/view

Jackson-Boothby, C. (2017). Supporting online learners in higher education: The role of academic advising and student development in the new frontier of online learning: The professionals' perspective (Order no. 10271052, University of Southern California). ProQuest Dissertations and Theses, *145*. Retrieved from https://libweb.uwlax.edu/login?url=https://search-proquest-com.libweb.uwlax.edu/docview/1911698956?accountid=9435?q=Florida+State+College&s=all&id=133702#programs

Jones, S. J., & Meyer, K. A. (2012). The "virtual face" of distance learning at public colleges and universities: What do websites reveal about administrative student support services? *Online Journal of Distance Learning Administration, 15*(5). Retrieved from https://www.westga.edu/~distance/ojdla/winter154/jones_meyer154.html

McCracken, H. (2005). Web-based academic support services: Guidelines for extensibility. *Online Journal of Distance Learning Administration, 8*(3). Retrieved from https://www.westga.edu/~distance/ojdla/fall83/mccracken83.htm

Milman, N. B., Posey, L., Pintz, C., Wright, K., & Zhou, P. (2015). Online master's students' perceptions of institutional supports and resources: Initial survey results. *Online Learning, 19*(4). Retrieved from https://content.ebscohost.com/ContentServer.asp?T=P&P=AN&K=110721396&S=R&D=ehh&EbscoContent=dGJyMNHX8kSeqK44zdnyOLCmr1Cep7BSrqy4TLCWxWXS&ContentCustomer=dGJyMPPt6nnhset55%2BS5febl8YwA

National Center for Education Statistics. (2018). Fast facts: Distance learning. Retrieved from https://nces.ed.gov/fastfacts/display.asp?id=80

Radford, A. W. (2011). Learning at a distance: Undergraduate enrollment in distance education courses and degree programs. Retrieved from https://files.eric.ed.gov/fulltext/ED524625.pdf

Seaman, J. E., Allen, I. E., & Seaman, J. (2018). Grade increase: Tracking distance education in the United States. Retrieved from http://onlinelearningsurvey.com/reports/gradeincrease.pdf

Smith, B. (2005). Online student support services. *Community College Journal, 76*(2). Retrieved from https://web-b-ebscohost-com.libweb.uwlax.edu/ehost/pdfviewer/pdfviewer?vid=1&sid=78704b2c-dc75-4d01-aba3-cef17d185479%40sessionmgr102

Wladis, C., Hachey, A. C., & Conway, K. (2014). The role of enrollment choice in online education: Course selection rationale and course difficulty as factors affecting retention. *Journal of Asynchronous Learning Networks, 18*(3). Retrieved from http://www.cwladis.com/papers/JALN%20enrollment%20choice%20FINAL%20accepted%20version%20for%20sharing.pdf

TRANSFORMING THE PRACTICE OF STUDENT AFFAIRS PROFESSIONALS: CREATING AN ECOSYSTEM OF SUPPORT THAT IS INCLUSIVE OF ONLINE LEARNERS

Jaimie Hoffman and Autumn Willinger

ABSTRACT

As institutions forge forward with creating online learning experiences for college and university students, student affairs professionals should seek to create an experience that anticipates and supports their needs from expression of interest in the program to graduation. The term "student affairs" encompasses administrative and management functions created to meet the needs of students including extracurricular activities as well as academic and emotional support. Student affairs departments may be involved in residence life, advising, leadership development, career services, advocacy and support services, and more. All students, including online students, excel both academically and emotionally when they feel valued, welcomed, and supported. The following chapter provides recommendations on ways campuses can transform the existing ecosystem of support services and engagement opportunities to be inclusive of online learners. A systematic review of the current ecosystem of support has been made to analyze the ways in which access is provided remotely to online learners and to ensure that the language and engagement opportunities shared with students are inclusive of online learners. In addition to this expanding of current support systems, it is recommended that campuses should consider specific initiatives they can create and implement for their online population including online orientation, success coaching, library support services, and the use of predictive analytics for student success.

Keywords: Online education; student support; student services; cocurricular; engagement; library services

INTRODUCTION

Few would argue that online learning is transforming the higher education landscape and the student experience of college students around the globe. While enrollment in American higher education may be decreasing, students are enrolling in online courses at an increasing rate: in fact, as of 2015, almost 30% (29.7%) of undergraduate students in higher education are taking at least one online course, and among the 30%, 14.3% are taking all courses at a distance. Growth is seen across the board; public, private for-profit, and private not-for-profit institutions have grown their distance learning enrollments (Allen & Seaman, 2017). Additional access to higher education proves to be one of the benefits of online education.

In the United States (US Department of Education, National Center for Education Statistics, 2016), the attainment of an advanced degree has been shown to increase the lifetime earning potential of individuals without such a degree, by over two million dollars. Even with the creation of the community college system, which allows flexible and affordable associates degree (AA) completion as well as the relative ease of borrowing funds for college, there still exists a large disparity in who is actually obtaining those degrees. Among parents in the lowest 25% of income in the United States, 1 out of 10 children obtain a college degree by the age of 25 compared to 7 in 10 of those families in the highest 25% of income. Students from lower income families may not be able to stop working for four years, move to a different part of the country, and live independently while attending college.

One way to decrease the disparity between 1 of 10 and 7 of 10 students obtaining a college degree is to address the practical issues faced by students from the lower income brackets who may simply not able to participate in the traditional style education requiring regular attendance at a particular site due to the need to work, support family, or move away from home. Online learning is beneficial in terms of equalizing access to education, allowing a far greater number of students to receive a college degree, which is proven to result in significantly greater earning potential than workers without a college degree (Burnsed, 2011).

In addition to creating opportunities for increasing income, online programs demonstrate positive learning and student satisfaction-related outcomes. While there may be some universities or colleges who retain a stigma associated with online education, most students feel that online instruction is as good or better than on-ground instruction. According to Clinefelter, Aslanian, and Magda (2019), majority of online students say their skills such as critical thinking and problem-solving, writing, time management, teamwork, and oral communication improved through their education. Along those lines, online programs are helping build students' future; 81% of online college students report that they graduate with the skills and knowledge they need to be successful in their careers and thought their courses were interesting.

Although online learning and advances in technology can greatly improve access to education by providing pathways to many subjects in diverse settings, there remains concern among some university community members and students that online education may be of a lower quality than face-to-face learning (Baum & McPherson, 2019). A common refrain among those who are not proponents of online learning is that the lack of personal connection with the instructor or university personnel depersonalizes the education process (Jacobs & Hyman, 2013).

In traditional learning environments, the teacher–student relationship is seen as crucial to student engagement and success (Bejerano, 2008; Bernstein, 2015). The chance encounters that come with membership in a diverse intellectual community cannot be underestimated. Whether a guest lecture, an unplanned conversation with a peer majoring in a different field, or the experience of befriending someone from a different background during a lunch break, place-based encounters can spark new interests and set students on fulfilling paths they might never have traveled otherwise (Aoun, 2012). Additionally, the friendships developed at a traditional college often lead to both personal and professional networks that continue long past graduation.

The benefits of knowing and being in a relationship with one's teachers, support staff, and fellow students are implicit, and the loss of those face-to-face relationships can also lead to the feeling that online learning institutions are inferior (Bowen, Chingos, Lack, & Nygren, 2013). It is therefore very important to mitigate this potential lack of connection using methods such as synchronous sessions in which faculty and students are interacting in real-time for their weekly or biweekly class time, as well as ad hoc meetings for students to schedule video chats or phone calls with faculty, staff, and other students.

Understanding the unique needs of online learners and creating a campus ecosystem that is inclusive of the online population is paramount for fulfilling our duty of meeting the needs of all students. In addition to facilitating meaningful learning experiences in an online environment, other university support teams need to create an experience for online students that both anticipates and supports their needs. Creating more supportive environments should increase student efficacy, retention, graduation rates, earning power, and eventually a strong alumni community (Bowen et al., 2013). The following chapter provides recommendations on ways campuses can transform the existing ecosystem of support services and engagement opportunities to be inclusive of online learners as well as specific support mechanisms or programs specific to online students.

ONLINE STUDENT SUPPORT SERVICES: TRANSFORMING THE EXISTING CAMPUS ECOSYSTEM

Most university campuses provide a wide range of student services to complement and support the academic offerings. University Student Support offices now have the opportunity to reconsider delivery models which support online learners as well as those students for whom access to on-campus services is possible. Student Affairs stakeholders and leaders should begin to think of ways to support their online student population by creating a vision for the kind of community the campus needs for its online ecosystem and how it would like to support online learners to be successful members of the university community. From there, each functional unit should consider how it can contribute to the vision by transforming its services to operate in this ecosystem's broader vision. There are six key elements of transformation the student service offices on college and university campuses can activate to embrace and support online learners:

1. *Provide remote access to campus services.* Students need to have access to services which support their academic success. Campuses should conduct an audit of on-ground processes to ensure they are inclusive of online students and do not present unnecessary barriers to access these services. An online student should not be expected to travel to another state (or country) to complete administrative processes or to receive services. Services typically offered on campus should be repurposed so that they are accessible online. Examples of administrative services may include judicial hearings and associated forms/documentation, Title IX allegation and hearings, obtaining identification cards, technology support, financial aid forms, processes and services, Family Educational Rights and Privacy Act (FERPA) records, and release requests. Personal support services may include student orientation, health services, disability support services, counseling services, veteran's services, career counseling, and success coaching support. Academic support services may include writing support, tutoring, access to textbooks, degree completion tracking, academic advising, library, and alumni services.
2. *Ensure all languages are inclusive of online learners*: Campuses should check websites and other documents provided to students to make sure language is inclusive of online learners. For instance, if an online student visits a campus website that says, "come to building X, Y, Z, you're welcome here" – the opposite message of what is intended is communicated; online students do not feel welcome, in fact, they could feel invisible as they are unable to access these on-campus services. Campuses should undergo a systematic review of the materials including mission statements and policies with which students review or have access to ensure language includes online learners (Appendix 1).
3. *Anticipate and establish protocols for addressing student support needs*: Campuses should document all frequently asked questions they anticipate online students may ask about their varied logistical/administrative needs and determine responses and protocol that are appropriate for remote learners (Appendix 2).
4. *Respond to students in a timely manner*: Since online students can often feel isolated and are unable to walk into a campus office due to their distance from campus or inability to have meetings during regular office hours, it is important that their questions are answered in a timely manner. Also, online students do expect quick response times – typically anywhere from 24 to 48 hours depending on the priority of their concern (Getzlaf, Perry, Toffner, Lamarche, & Edwards, 2009; Mupinga, Nora, & Yaw 2006) (Appendix 3).
5. *Use multiple modalities in providing support*: Ideally, online students should be able to schedule appointments with campus personnel online, get their questions answered via email, chat, phone, and video and have someone available to support them nights, weekends, and holidays (when they are working on their schoolwork). To achieve this, staff needs to have an understanding of the needs of online learners, how to use technology for varied modality connections, and the hardware/software to support remote connectivity (e.g., webcams and headphones) (Appendix 4).
6. *Identify and implement engagement opportunities*: Online learners want to feel engaged in, and part of, the virtual campus community, so it is important to

identify engagement strategies that will be created specifically for online learners or existing strategies that can be inclusive of online learners. This core element also comes with the most opportunity for innovation. For instance, campuses can work with student organizations to create online student representatives, brainstorm unique virtual events that draw in alumni or career professionals from miles away, or innovate ways to engage students in on-campus events through livestreaming, tweeting, etc. Peer-to-peer and faculty-to-student engagement can also be fostered through the creation of a virtual hub possibly called a "Virtual Student Union" (known on ground as the "living room of the campus"). Faculty presentations or a guest alumni lecture series can be hosted using videoconference technology. "Meetups" between students who live in close proximity to each other can be scheduled by staff to leverage the synergy of face-to-face meetings (Appendix 5).

ONLINE STUDENT SUPPORT SERVICES: UNIQUE SUPPORT MECHANISMS AND PROGRAMS

Earlier, we described core ways in which campuses can adjust their existing ecosystem to be inclusive of online learners. However, the reality is that there are some very specific support mechanisms or programs that should be created for online learners given their unique needs and experiences. Below we discuss the importance and relevance of creating new programs which support the unique needs of online learners including online orientation, success coaching, library services, and predictive analytics for student success.

Online Orientation

Students need to be prepared for both the transition to the college environment and to be successful online learners. Some students already have experience with technology and possibly online learning, but others need to be introduced to all elements of the university experience from expectations of being a student to how to access and use the technology in courses. Orientation or onboarding programs foster a seamless transition to college, which is essential for student success. Student orientation helps to foster student success, and those who participate in orientation programs generally perform better than those who do not (Busby, Gammel, & Jeffcoat, 2002) and persist to graduation at a higher rate (Boudreau & Kromrey, 1994).

Research demonstrates that most new students benefit from an introduction to their new academic community, particularly those from historically marginalized populations who are less familiar with the higher education experience (Hollins, 2009; Pascarella & Terenzini, 2005; Robinson, Burns, & Gaw, 1996). The best mechanism to inform online students of those resources available to them and to welcome them to the campus community is through orientation. When creating orientation programs for online students, campuses should consider what information can be provided in an online orientation to introduce resources and services to students. Engaging a broad group of stakeholders to determine the desired learning outcomes of the orientation program lays an important foundation. Often, a good starting point is reviewing the existing on-ground orientation to see what similarities or differences in content may exist. Typically, online orientations should introduce students to the university community; boost student confidence for being successful online learners; help to develop a sense of community between students, faculty, and staff; offer some academic preparedness skill-building (e.g., time management, study skills, etc.); provide support and engagement resources; and give students a thorough introduction to the technology they will use in their courses.

Students who are less familiar with technology are shown to have less satisfaction with online courses, feeling that the need to master technology is equally challenging if not more so than the course content itself (Jonassen, Howland, Moore, & Marra, 2003). More experienced users of the Internet and technology display higher levels of satisfaction with online learning. To make the most of their online learning environments, students need to have familiarity with the use of computer hardware, software, and basic Internet navigation skills. Lacking the required skills and technology can become a barrier to learning, leading to feelings of disconnectedness and dissatisfaction (Jonassen et al., 2003; Rodriguez, Ooms, & Montañez, 2008). Giving students information about the technology they will encounter during the college experience and the opportunity to use those skills during the orientation process is important for student success.

In addition to course content, other logistics associated with the program design should be considered starting with the modality of the experience (e.g., fully synchronous, asynchronous, or blended/hybrid). Presuming some elements will be asynchronous, the orientation would ideally be housed in the existing learning management system to provide a central location through which the student accesses all campus resources. Other considerations during the course design process involve determining what content requires interactivity to achieve the learning outcomes, if the course will be moderated or facilitated by a quasi "instructor" or entirely self-paced/independent. Finally, it is important to consider how the orientation experience will be assessed on an ongoing basis to ensure it is achieving all desired outcomes and is meaningful to students.

Kirkpatrick and Kirkpatrick's (2005) four levels of evaluation can serve as a framework with which to assess the program. These four levels include consideration regarding how students felt about the experience; what students learned through the course (e.g., assessing the achievement of the stated learning outcomes); how what was learned at the student orientation was applied once they began their courses; and, finally, how the student orientation affects overall student success. Another step in this stage is to determine if the program/course will be required, how students will be informed of the completion expectation, and how they will verify completion.

Online Student Success Coaching

One such strategy for retaining online students is ensuring they feel connected and supported through proactive (sometimes called intrusive) success coaching.

This kind of support is beyond the scope of what is typically offered to on-ground students who usually have the ability to drop into an office to receive support elsewhere when visiting campus or can more easily connect with their faculty members or peers during a face-to-face class (Bettinger, Fox, Loeb, Taylor, 2017; Boerner, 2015; Cannon, 2013). Some schools are making the shift from student advising which focuses on information provision and course registration, to a more holistic model in which students have a dedicated advisor or coach who is able to connect them to services. The services commonly offered may include financial aid and registrar as well as other services offered across the institution such as institutional research, counseling, veterans' services, etc. For online students in particular, this type of advising must leverage technology and become ingrained as part of the campus culture of support. There are a number of elements to consider when creating a success coaching program for online students:

1. *Key Performance Indicators (KPIs)*. As with all initiatives, it is important to "begin with the end in mind" (Covey, 2004) by thinking through what the goals are for your success coaches and how you will measure their success. Consider creating KPIs around the following: response time, time to resolve student issues, community/student engagement expectations (e.g., number of meetups facilitated, number of students with similar interests connected), outreach expectations to students (e.g., percentage of students with whom the coach held a welcome meeting), student retention and communication tracked in one system or platform.
2. *Tracking Communication for Seamless Support*. Coach-to-student communication should be tracked in one system or platform. This allows for tracking and assessing against KPIs, reviewing data for themes during program evaluation processes, and fosters a seamless support process for students. For instance, students will be more seamlessly supported if students talk with a coach and then with a financial aid counselor who has reviewed the coach's notes in the same support platform.
3. *Coach Communication Plan*. Many universities have hired dedicated student success coaches for online learners. This role may be filled by someone already familiar with or working for the university, but it may also be outsourced to a company which specializes in online support coaching. To foster consistency and empower coaches with the tools to support students, it is important to create a coach communication plan. This plan should provide a general set of communication templates or outlines and a cadence which coaches should follow when working with students. Elements of a coach plan could include information about a seamless handoff from enrollment advisor to the coach, coach introductions/outreach to faculty, protocol for following up with students on a leave of absence, and a proactive outreach cadence. Proactive outreach communication should be structured such that it aligns with the arch of the student experience, likely including more frequent touch points early on to support the students' transition. Coaches should be empowered to adjust the plan based on student preference and use of predictive analytics to inform the frequency of outreach (e.g., students with specific pre-entry characteristics or in certain disciplines) might benefit from more frequent outreach.

4. *Coach-to-Student Ratio.* Ideally, coaches will maintain a low enough student load that they can develop a rapport with each student and understand their goals, challenges, and potential strategies for success. We recommend a ratio of 65 students to a part-time coach (20 hours per week) and 130 students to a full-time coach (40 hours per week). Of course, all universities are not the same, and AB testing can be completed to determine if the ratio of students to coaches can increase while still maintaining KPIs.
5. *Availability of Coaches.* Success coaches need to be available at night, on weekends, and even at times the campus might be closed since that is when students complete their work. Additionally, coach supervision should be available during these times to support coaches as issues arise. These expectations should be made clear during the hiring process.
6. *Mode of Communication.* Student success coaches should be able to communicate with students in their preferred modality (including chat, text, email, phone, and video conferencing). Coaches should seek to hold at least some meetings via videoconference to foster greater connectivity.
7. *Trained as Concierge.* Online students have very busy lives and schedules. Having coaches making it as easy as possible to get questions answered is essential (Clinefelter et al., 2019). The student success coach should be trained to be the "concierge" for students and have as many responses to anticipated questions regarding university and faculty policies as possible.
8. *Retention Risk Triggers/Predictive Analytics.* The student success coaches should monitor student performance to identify potential triggers that might pose a challenge or risk for student success. Such triggers might include missing synchronous class sessions, earning a grade below average (e.g., B for graduate students, C for undergraduate students), missing assignments, and low activity/participation in asynchronous conversations. Additional insight into the use of predictive analytics for supporting online students is provided later in this chapter.
9. *Community Facilitation.* The student success coach may also facilitate community between students and other members of the academic community (e.g., faculty). Coaches could schedule "meetups" between students (e.g., in person meetings between students who live near each other, virtual faculty research presentation/discussion, etc.), match students with similar interests or challenges for a virtual meeting, and post-asynchronous engagement in a Virtual Student Union.

Online Library Services

In order to serve online students, particularly at the graduate level, it is vital that library resources are available for research and other projects. While the same online resources are often available to both on- and off-campus students, the discrepancies of the service (interlibrary loan, reference, and library instruction) available to the on-ground population versus remote students can be significant (Dalal & Lackie, 2014). In order to create library services that are inclusive of online students, campuses should consider the role of the librarian, remote access of physical materials, incorporating online learners into activities and events, and marketing library services to online students.

A digital library is often defined by a heavy emphasis on resources and less emphasis on librarians and the service they provide. The focus of services to online students tends to be more about the technology and information resources with little discussion of the service aspects of the digital library. Promoting not only library materials but also services to online students is important in maintaining equity for both online students and those who are studying on ground and more able to avail the services of a librarian. When library search support is not utilized by online students, students typically replace it by basic internet searches, decreasing the users' ability to search digital scholarly resources properly. The role of the librarian as facilitator of research and obtaining of relevant articles and databases is of undeniable importance to students, thus campuses need to consider ways to avail this support to online learners (Koenig, 2019).

Accessing physical materials can present a barrier to online students. Students who are studying online should not be placed at a disadvantage because they are unable to access hard copies of materials and books at the college or university library. While a great deal of research material is available online, there are still some sources that exist only in a physical copy which librarians typically assist in locating and obtaining. Respondents from a survey conducted by the Brooklyn Campus Library of Long Island University's remote graduate campus shared that a key issue for remote users was the lag time in receiving physical library resources. This challenge was addressed in several ways from delivery of articles via email or fax to delivery of books via United States Postal Service, which was more costly but cut delivery time in half (Tremblay & Wang, 2008).

Determining how to incorporate online students into activities and events attended by on-ground students needs to be explored by university libraries. In 2011, one university, the Full Sail University Library in Winter Park, Florida, implemented programs to more effectively support online students by using chat reference to provide real-time answers to students online questions, a resource-mailing program, interlibrary loan, website updates, online workshops, and tutorials. Emails and announcements were delivered via social media and the library webpage (McCallister & Peuler, 2016). Additionally, media-savvy library work-study student employees were recruited to create tutorials about services, write on the library blog, and lead/create library events. One event included an open-mike and karaoke contest night that was offered via video conferencing, and on-campus screens and projectors allowed distance learners to "see" on-campus students. Another library event inclusive of online learners was Graduate Launch (GL) which was an orientation for graduation. Attendance was mandatory for GL and included on-ground students meeting in the library with representatives from various university departments and vendors and online students participated FaceTime, GoToMeeting (McCallister & Peuler, 2016).

In addition to the creation of library support services to online learners, one must not overlook how these services are marketed to potential users. As online learners are rarely, if ever, on the actual campus space, they may be simply unaware of the resources and services available to them; this puts them at a disadvantage as most graduate students are required to search, find, and use professional journals. Equity among all students must include the ability of remote students to be able to access research tools and training to make the library experience relevant and support their academic success (Dalal & Lackie, 2014).

While databases are typically available to remote students, their existence is not always promoted to online students. Librarians can support their online students by updating their training sessions to cover more relevant resources and services such as the use of the library catalog, interlibrary loan services, reference chat, and remote database access. Online students should be taught how to obtain full-text articles from citations, as well as further training in subject and keyword searching in order that they are able to conduct meaningful research and obtain data remotely. This proactive support from college and university library staff will give online students the tools they need to successfully obtain needed resources for both research and writing.

Predictive Analytics for Online Student Success

Using predictive analytics to proactively affect retention is another important area in online student support. Data has been used by many schools to assess prior behavior such as the likelihood of persistence and success in classes based on attendance, time spent on assignments, and length and quality of discussion posts. Colleges and universities should use this data to create actionable items in supporting students: foresight rather than hindsight. Student information such as grades, attendance, class participation, number of holds on student records, use of library resources, and other data points could be used to predict outcomes and suggest pivots in teaching, learning, and student support which would foster student success. Interventions could be triggered automatically which would indicate to faculty and staff members which students need intervention at what time and in what area (Pelletier, 2015).

Data analytics of online students' behavior can be used as a lever for cultural change on the campus asking "what if" questions that can lead to new practices that can help drive transformational change. Data can help answer specific operational questions such as "Are we offering classes for which there is a demand? How well are we managing tuition revenue? How can we optimize space utilization?" At an even more practical level, data about operations like help desks and completing purchase orders can help improve student services and campus efficiency for both online and on-ground students (Pelletier, 2015).

Access to student data for predictive purposes has the potential for greatly benefiting student support and retention. However, this data must be treated with great care. Data security is frequently a concern shared by both university staff and faculty as well as the students. Randomized algorithms and the use of digital security keys are being used by many institutions to protect student data. Involving the school's Institutional Review Board (IRB) can also be helpful in determining the best and most ethical way to collect and use the data at that particular institution. Adherence to privacy laws such as FERPA and Health Insurance Portability and Accountability Act (HIPAA) is vital and provides a framework or the minimum amount of protection needed in student records such as social security numbers, student records, medical records, and more (Pelletier, 2015).

CONCLUSION

Preparing for the future of higher education means embracing online education. Further, we have an obligation to adjust our practices to meet the needs of our student population, specific online learners. A systematic review of our current ecosystems of support is needed to analyze how access is provided to online learners and that the language about engagement opportunities is inclusive of online learners. In addition to this, campuses should consider specific initiatives they can create for this population including online orientation, success coaching, and using predictive analytics for student success. Qualities important in online student support should focus on engagement and connectivity. Some research suggest that students who are in online courses are at a higher risk of dropping out because they are not physically present with college or university staff and faculty, nor are they participating in on-campus experiences.

The ongoing examination of student support to adult online learners is crucial. The importance of a college degree to American's financial well-being cannot be overstated. Adults without a college degree often find it difficult to return to a traditional institution of higher education due to work, family, and other responsibilities. Online learning, with the ability to study anytime anywhere, is often the only viable solution for adults wishing to obtain their college degrees.

Determining how to best support this population in persisting in obtaining a college or university degree online, therefore, has significant implications for our national economy as well as individuals and their families who benefit from the ability to earn more income and have more flexibility in choosing a career. It is vital, therefore, to create opportunities for non-traditional and adult learners to obtain a college degree and remove unnecessary barriers to education. In addition to building online courses for colleges and universities which are pedagogically sound, other college and university support systems such as staff who support student success coaches, student registration, and the library services have both the opportunity and the responsibility to utilize existing methods of student support as well as use data and experience to envision and implement new ways of supporting this very important student population.

REFERENCES

Allen, E., & Seaman, J. (2017). *Digital learning compass: Distance education enrollment report 2017*. Digital Learning Compass. Babson Survey Research Group, e-Literate, WCET.

Aoun, J. (2012). Learning today: The lasting value of place. *The Chronicle of Higher Education*. Retrieved from http://chronicle.com/article/In-Learning-the-Lasting-Value/127378/

Baum, S., & McPherson, M. (2019, Fall). The human factor: The promise and limit of online education. *Daedalus, 148*(4), 235–254. Retrieved from https://www.amacad.org/sites/default/files/publication/downloads/Daedalus_Baum%20McPherson_Fall2019.pdf

Bejerano, A. (2008). Face to face or online instruction? Face to face is better. *Communication Currents: Knowledge for Communicating Well, 3*(3). Retrieved from https://www.natcom.org/CommCurrentsArticle.aspx?id=884

Bernstein, E. (2015). How active learning makes both participants feel better. *Wall Street Journal*. Retrieved from http://www.wsj.com/articles/how-active-listening-makes-both-sides-of-a-conversation-feel-better-1421082684

Bettinger, E. P., Fox, L., Loeb, S., & Taylor, E. S. (2017, September 1). Virtual classrooms: How online college courses affect student success. *American Economic Review*, *107*(9), 2855–2875.

Boerner, H. (2015, August 1). Predicting success: How predictive analytics are transforming student support and success programs. *Community College Journal*, *86*(1), 14–18.

Boudreau, C. A., & Kromrey, J. D. (1994, November 1). A longitudinal study of the retention and academic performance of participants in freshmen orientation course. *Journal of College Student Development*, *35*(6), 444–449.

Bowen, W., Chingos, M., Lack, K., & Nygren, T. (2013). Online learning in higher education. *Education Next*, *13*(2). Retrieved from http://educationnext.org/online-learning-in-higher-education

Burnsed, B. (2011). How education affects lifetime salary. *U.S. News & World Report*. Retrieved from http://www.usnews.com/education/best-colleges/articles/2011/08/05/how-higher-education-affects-lifetime-salary

Busby, R. R., Gammel, H. L., & Jeffcoat, N. K. (2002). Grades, graduation, and orientation: A longitudinal study of how new student programs relate to grade point average and graduation. *Journal of College Orientation and Transition*, *10*(1), 45–57.

Cannon, J. (2013, March). Intrusive advising 101: How to be intrusive without intruding. *Academic Advising Today*, *36*(1). Retrieved from http://www.nacada.ksu.edu/Resources/Academic-Advising-Today/View-Articles/Intrusive-Advising-101-How-to-be-Intrusive-Without-Intruding.aspx

Clinefelter, D. L., Aslanian, C. B., & Magda, A. J. (2019). *Online college students 2019: Comprehensive data on demands and preferences*. Louisville, KY: Wiley Edu, LLC.

Covey, S. (2004). *The 7 habits of highly effective people: Restoring the character ethic*. New York, NY: Free Press.

Dalal, H. A., & Lackie, R. J. (2014). What if you build it and they still won't come? Addressing student awareness of resources and services with promotional videos. *Journal of Library & Information Services in Distance Learning*, *8*(3), 225–241. doi:10.1080/1533290X.2014.945841

Getzlaf, B., Perry, B., Toffner, G., Lamarche, K., & Edwards, M. (2009). Effective instructor feedback: Perceptions of online graduate students. *Journal of Educators Online*, *6*, 2.

Hollins, T. (2009). Examining the impact of a comprehensive approach to student orientation. *Inquiry: The Journal of the Virginia Community Colleges*, *14*(1). Retrieved from https://commons.vccs.edu/inquiry/vol14/iss1/3

Jacobs, L. F., & Hyman, J. S. (2013). *The secrets of college success*. San Francisco, CA: Jossey-Bass.

Jonassen, D., Howland, J., Moore, J., & Marra, R. (2003). *Learning to solve problems with technology: A constructivist perspective* (2nd ed.). Upper Saddle River, NJ: Prentice Hall.

Kirkpatrick, D. L., & Kirkpatrick, J. D. (2005). *Evaluating training programs*. San Francisco, CA: Berrett-Koehler Publishers.

Koenig, S. (2019). Creating libraries for online students is harder than you think. *Edsurge*. Retrieved from https://www.edsurge.com/news/2019-11-14-creating-libraries-for-online-students-is-harder-than-you-think

McCallister, K. C., & Peuler, M. (2016). Behold the power of the donut: A successful case study of a DE library, departmental, and faculty & student collaborations. *Journal of Library and Information Services in Distance Learning*, *10*(3–4), 340–348. doi:10.1080/1533290X.2016.1221626

Mupinga, D. M., Nora, R. T., & Yaw, D. C. (2006). The learning styles, expectations, and needs of online students. *College Teaching*, *54*(1), 185–189. doi:10.3200/CTCH.54.1.185-189

Pascarella, E. T., & Terenzini, P. T. (2005). *How college affects students: V. 2*. San Francisco, CA: Jossey-Bass.

Pelletier, S. (2015). Taming "Big Data": Using data analytics for student success and institutional intelligence. *AGB Association of Governing Boards of Universities and Colleges*, *23*(7), 24–40.

Robinson, D. A. G., Burns, C. F., & Gaw, K. F. (1996, December 7). Orientation programs: A foundation for student learning and success. *New Directions for Student Services*, *75*, 55–68.

Rodriguez, M. C., Ooms, A., & Montañez, M. (2008). Students' perceptions of online-learning quality given comfort, motivation, satisfaction, and experience. *Journal of Interactive Online Learning*, *7*(2), 105–125.

Tremblay, P., & Wang, Z. (2008). We care – Virtually and in person: A user-centered approach to assessment, implementation and promotion of library resources and services to a remote graduate campus. *Public Services Quarterly*, *4*(3), 207–232. doi:10.1080/15228950802100545

US Department of Education, National Center for Education Statistics. (2016). Digest of Education Statistics, 2014. Retrieved from http://nces.ed.gov/pubs2016/2016006.pdf

APPENDICES

Appendix 1: Inclusive Language Checklist

- ☐ Read website and note needed revisions for inclusivity.
- ☐ Put hard copy handouts or brochures online in an accessible format.
- ☐ Review mission/purpose statements and policies.
- ☐ Get approval from an authority on website revision.
- ☐ Make revisions toward inclusive language.
- ☐ Determine digital form submission and digital signature process.

Appendix 2: Student Support Needs Checklist

- ☐ Ask all support services to document the questions they are asked most frequently.
- ☐ Work with support services to create responses for remote students.
- ☐ Aggregate questions and responses into a central repository.
- ☐ Regularly review and revise questions and responses for accuracy.

Appendix 3: Response Timeliness Checklist

- ☐ Train campus personnel assigned to supporting online students on the questions they anticipate being asked.
- ☐ Hire and train staff with clear expectations around response times.
- ☐ Identify a notation system for personnel to track student contacts.
- ☐ Monitor timeliness of responses via notation system.
- ☐ Survey students about their perceptions of and satisfaction with, timeliness.

Appendix 4: Multiple Modalities Checklist

- ☐ Ensure all relevant staff have access to webcams and headphones.
- ☐ Determine videoconferencing and chat platforms to be leveraged for communicating with remote students.
- ☐ Train staff on the use of applicable technology.
- ☐ Review and revise campus human resource policies around night, weekend, and holiday work to ensure they work for flexible scheduling.
- ☐ Hire and train staff with clear expectations of flexible work hours.

Appendix 5: Engagement Opportunities Checklist

- ☐ List all events and engagement strategies.
- ☐ Discuss if goals could still be achieved by adding online learners and list events that would be accessible to online learners.
- ☐ Invitation for online students to on-campus events (but acknowledge they may not live here) and post in orientation and/or Virtual Student Union.
- ☐ Gather or list resources or announcements to add to Virtual Student Union.
- ☐ List student groups and think about how to include online students in these groups or create similar groups for online learners.

- Discuss the inclusion of online learners with student organization leaders.
- Advise student leaders of potential bylaw changes (e.g., if adding a voting member representing online students).
- List student group involvement opportunities in orientation or Virtual Student Union or send to students.

RESHAPING THE ONLINE STUDENT EXPERIENCE

Molly A. Mott, Kristyn Muller and Michele Forte

ABSTRACT

The purpose of this chapter is to share the structure and strategies that institutions can use to transform the experience of students learning at a distance. Details on how one of the largest educational systems in the United States, the State University of New York (SUNY), reshaped the student online learning experience via the "Open SUNY" model will be described. Specific strategies for infusing existing models of support with new ways of thinking will be explained.

In particular, this chapter will explore the infrastructure of the Open SUNY model of collaboration, the use of the Open SUNY Institutional Readiness approach for preparing colleges to deliver quality online programming, and the unique Open SUNY+ Signature Element program for assessing the quality of online programming and support structures.

This chapter will also highlight the efforts of one campus, SUNY Canton, to leverage Open SUNY and take its signature element on student engagement to the next level. A case study on Canton will show how the campus incorporated online students in all aspects of campus life to reduce student isolation. Specific online student engagement strategies will be provided.

Keywords: Concierge model; distance learning; early alert monitoring; online education; online student readiness; online tutoring; student engagement; student services; student success; student preparedness; SUNY Canton; technical support; virtual fairs.

INTRODUCTION

Online learning continues to expand across institutions of higher education in the United States (Seaman, Allen, & Seaman, 2018). A recent report from the Education Department's National Center for Education Statistics shows that the number of students taking at least some of their courses online grew by 350,000 between fall 2016 and fall 2017 (Ginder, Kelly-Reid, & Mann, 2018). As more students seek to enroll in online programs, online course delivery is becoming more prevalent and increasingly accepted as part of higher education (Lederman, 2018). With this growth comes the need to ensure high-quality instruction and support services. To prepare campuses to meet this demand, the State University of New York (SUNY) System launched Open SUNY, a comprehensive suite of online learning support resources and services designed to assist SUNY campuses deliberately and effectively expand their online learning offerings.

The first half of this chapter describes the SUNY System's efforts to promote quality online learning and explains the evolution of services designed to support online student success. In the second half, one particular campus, SUNY Canton, is showcased. They intentionally leveraged Open SUNY's resources and expanded upon them to develop numerous practices to holistically support their online students. This chapter intends to give institutions of higher education mechanisms to create and assess student support services and to provide practices and strategies that will enhance student success and development.

OVERVIEW AND HISTORY OF SUNY ONLINE LEARNING

SUNY, the most comprehensive university system in the United States, comprises 64 campuses throughout New York State. It includes community colleges, technical colleges, comprehensive colleges, and doctoral-degree granting institutions. The SUNY System has a long history of innovation in online learning. In 1994, SUNY founded a system-wide asynchronous learning network, called The SUNY Learning Network (SLN), with generous support from the Alfred P. Sloan Foundation. A year later, they launched the first online multi-institutional learning management system (LMS) used by campuses within the SUNY System. During these early years, SLN identified a need for faculty development and support as well as online course design processes; they designed and implemented services to address those needs for SUNY faculty and instructional design staff who wanted to participate. Around the same time, SUNY developed a HelpDesk to provide centralized support directly to online students. As online education continued to grow within the SUNY System, and nationwide, SLN and the HelpDesk expanded and refined their offerings to SUNY campuses. However, online learning initiatives were primarily campus driven. Campuses could choose to utilize the SLN and HelpDesk resources and services, but there were no clear system-wide goals.

In 2013, Nancy Zimpher (SUNY Chancellor from 2009 to 2017), during her State of the University address, challenged the SUNY System to increase the number of online students to 100,000. At the time, most students who were taking online courses were blending online and face-to-face courses rather than enrolled in fully online degree programs. In fall 2012, there were about 66,000 students who took at least one course online that term (SUNY System Administration, 2020). Chancellor Zimpher wanted to expand access to higher education via online learning to reach traditionally underserved student populations throughout New York State. She revealed plans to develop a unit called Open SUNY, which, with input from stakeholders across the system, was formalized in 2014. SLN and the HelpDesk already promoted quality online teaching and learning at the course level, so Open SUNY brought them together and increased services to also support quality online education at the program and institution levels.

Parallel to the creation of Open SUNY, the SUNY System adopted SUNY Excels, a system-wide framework for measuring the performance, scale, and adoption of best practices across several initiatives pertaining to access, completion, success, inquiry, and engagement (https://www.suny.edu/excels/). This gave additional context and meaning to the development of Open SUNY's services. Two pivotal services that will be described in this chapter are the Open SUNY Institutional Readiness (IR) process and the Open SUNY+ program designation.

OPEN SUNY IR PROCESS

The Open SUNY IR process was designed to prepare SUNY campuses to expand online learning offerings (courses and programs) while ensuring quality. As a framework for the process, Open SUNY utilized the Online Learning Consortium's (OLC) *Quality Scorecard for the Administration of Online Programs*, a comprehensive rubric comprised of 75 standards necessary to ensure the effective delivery of online programs (https://onlinelearningconsortium.org/consult/olc-quality-scorecard-administration-online-programs/). The standards were organized into the following categories: institutional support, technology support, course development and instructional design, course structure, teaching and learning, social and student engagement, faculty support, student support, and evaluation and assessment (OLC, 2014). Campuses could opt-in to participate in the Open SUNY IR process, which consists of three facilitated meetings that bring together faculty, staff, and leaders from a variety of functional areas. Since this service began, 41 SUNY campuses have completed the process and 21 of those have submitted an implementation plan. Many campuses are currently engaged in the process.

The Open SUNY IR process begins by identifying key people across the campus who should be involved. During the first meeting, the process is explained and the OLC Quality Scorecard is shared and reviewed. Participants are asked to score each standard on the rubric individually and submit their scores. During the second meeting, the aggregate scores for each measure are discussed, and the group must come to a consensus to determine their campus scores. Scores of 0, 1, or 2 signal that there is room for improvement, while a score of 3 indicates that the campus has best practices in that area. During the third meeting, the group reviews the standards in need of improvement, identifies actions that can be taken to close those gaps, and starts to develop a written implementation plan.

Distance learning leaders from campuses that have completed the Open SUNY IR process have reported that it improved their understanding of online learning quality across the university, validated the good work they were already doing, and served as a catalyst for continuous improvement. One campus administrator explained,

> This was very eye opening. It clearly and vividly demonstrated that online programming requires infrastructure and resources. The process helped to bring everyone to the table and clarified what the issues were and action items needed to be. (Muller, 2017)

Open SUNY also benefits from the process because they gain insights into the strengths and gaps of the system, which have helped to inform the kinds of resources and services Open SUNY should provide to campuses.

Open SUNY+ Program Designation

Open SUNY also created a quality program designation, called Open SUNY+, to feature online programs that meet specific criteria, known as the Open SUNY+ Signature Elements. Through this initiative, campuses receive recognition for their best practices and have access to additional resources through Open SUNY. The programs eligible for the Open SUNY+ designation must meet standards in the following seven areas: personalized student services, engaging learning experiences, comprehensive faculty support, robust technology environment, institutional commitment to quality assurance, assessment of program effectiveness, and strategic commitment to growth. Campus distance learning leaders nominate their programs, which are then reviewed by the Open SUNY Leadership Team and a group of campus representatives. This process defined Open SUNY's expectations for quality online programs and provided an incentive for campuses to work toward meeting these standards.

EVOLUTION OF SIGNATURE ELEMENTS TO SUPPORT STUDENT SUCCESS

At the inception of Open SUNY, research on online education had yielded some disheartening results. Chief among them was a high attrition rate in online courses (Herbert, 2006). The most common reason SUNY students cited for dropping out is a feeling of isolation (Ali & Smith, 2015). Open SUNY recognized that online students needed additional resources and support to improve onboarding, retention, and persistence to graduation as they ran a risk of being entirely disenfranchised from the services afforded to their campus-based peers.

This assistance came in the form of Open SUNY+ Signature Elements – Personalized Student Services to minimize time to completion and enhance student academic experience (Scalzo, 2015). Each of the seven Open SUNY+ Signature Elements contains multiple criteria. These criteria follow recommendations made by the National Academic Advising Association (NACADA, 2010) for advising and supporting students in an online environment including but not limited to "responding to the unique needs of distance learning students, rather than expecting them to fit into the established organizational structure." This chapter focuses on the following five items within the "personalized student services" Signature

Elements: 24/7 support; concierge model, guide, and resources to support campus concierges; online student readiness website, including readiness assessment and tips for success; early alert monitoring and interventions; and online academic tutoring. These are aligned with the Access, Completion, and Success portions of the SUNY Excels framework, which became both a rationale and a context to the adoption of these best practices in student supports. These pillars comprised a seamless baseline of services intended to holistically support student success in the online modality. The belief was that human connections – dedicated relationships either with a group of individuals at the system level or at the campus level – could engender more consistent academic success for online students. The tacit expertise of the individuals in these roles acknowledged key frustrations for online students and essentially became advocates to help them locate and access needed resources – from navigating a confusing LMS to finding campus-based resources.

24/7 Support

The Open SUNY HelpDesk began in 1997. It initially focused on online student technical support for campuses requiring support beyond what they could locally provide. It was soon integrated into the Open SUNY suite of student services. The HelpDesk provides technical support for campus staff, faculty, and students using the learning management system, which is currently Blackboard Lean. Many faculty call regarding course design questions or issues with the grade center. Students may receive support accessing their course materials, such as viewing their grades or submitting a test or assignment. The HelpDesk is also the main point of contact for inquiries regarding the use of open-source, open educational materials. During peak times, such as the beginning of the semester, the HelpDesk receives an average of 250 calls per day.

In order to meet the Open SUNY+ Signature Elements criteria, campuses must provide "24/7" (24 hours a day, seven days a week) technical support to their online students. As it stands today, 24/7 does not mean that students have access to live-support at all hours of the day, but they do have access to live-support during most hours of the day (including nights and weekends), and they also have access to self-service supports and the ability to submit a ticket anytime. Campuses within the SUNY system are not required to utilize the Open SUNY HelpDesk, but over 35 SUNY campuses have chosen to take advantage of this cost-effective service with a total ticket number of 10,947 in 2019 (Open SUNY, 2019).

Concierge Model

The concierge is a "single point of contact" – the person or people to whom students can turn for information, support, and guidance. Depending on the campus culture, a concierge can also be called an "advisor" or a "mentor" or an "academic advisor." The concierge role varies depending on the determinations and needs of the campus. The overall intention is to assist online students along both operational and affective dimensions, including navigating various offices, policies, procedures, as well as encouraging and motivating academic success. Concierge services do not replace specialized academic advising. Instead, they were designed to assist students with the familiar and frustrating "office bounce" – transfer from one office to another – not to mention waiting for a call back. Concierges are familiar with general academic and degree requirements, basic financial aid, the availability of tutoring, and other educational supports and services.

Regardless of the terminology, the concierge role helps online students navigate their degree progress as well as encourage students to connect to campus resources such as tutoring or cocurricular opportunities. Research supports the importance of holistic student–advisor relationship as a key factor in retaining students in online programs (Gravel, 2012). Concierges understand a variety of topics appended to academic and social success and can associate students with supports to better acclimate them to college life. This model of a high-touch, single point of contact is supported by literature suggesting efficacy of "intrusive advising" – also called proactive advising (Giroir & Schwehm, 2014). Other universities have begun to identify the concierge model as a potential support solution to the many barriers facing students who do not precisely fit into a "traditional" profile. The Western Interstate Commission for Higher Education, for example, has emphasized the concierge model as a primary tactic to stimulate re-enrollment and retention (Michelau & Lane, 2010).

Online Student Readiness

One of the most crucial functions the Open SUNY concierges perform is level-setting student expectations about online learning. The online readiness assessment measures affective, behavioral, and cognitive domains to give a concierge or other campus personnel a snapshot of student preparedness. Campuses often assume that students will arrive with the resources, skills, and personal insight to create optimal conditions to complete their studies. Anecdotally, we know students often mistake asynchronous access with assumptions about the modality as easier than campus-based courses delivered face to face. The online student readiness tool is designed to give a window into the behaviors behind these hidden assumptions and expectations as well as highlight some of the more common barriers to academic success in the online modality. For example, our concierge community reports that efficiently managing time is one of the most vexing skills for online students to master. Students often have competing activities and obligations, and without a set time and place for their courses, they may forget to "go to class." Other students reveal that they are trying to complete entire courses on mobile devices. By highlighting domains such as time management and a need for consistent access to computers, the readiness scores provide a concierge with individualized knowledge to inform a student-centric success plan.

Early Alert Monitoring and Interventions

If a concierge is the single point of human contact, an early alert tool is a single point of customizable communication – an efficient, technology-driven solution conduit for monitoring and responding to student success and barriers. The use of early alerts is an attempt to centralize efforts around student support services. It is an early warning and student tracking system designed to identify and address roadblocks to student success. It focuses on creating a holistic approach to student academic and, eventually, cocurricular activity. Use of early alert tools show promise in terms of establishing strong relationships with online students; this is especially crucial to assist those potentially at risk for academic warning or failure as early and frequent reminders regarding course participation and the referrals to supportive campus resources and positive reinforcement to signal developmental and academic progress (Varney, 2009).

SUNY System Administration incentivized the adoption of early alerts by entering a system-wide contract with Starfish, a commercial student success product. SUNY committed to supporting a new shared service wherein 18 months of funding was provided for new instance campuses to implement a stepped integration of Starfish as well as begin to develop and analyze workflow. Early adopter campuses were also given funds to host meetings, attend professional development, and mentor new instance campuses as they began their own adoption.

Financial incentives were followed by the creation of a deliberative, coordinated *community of practice* – the group of campuses using the Starfish early alert tool. All campuses within this community of practice were asked to participate in monthly, themed meetings and presentations during which they detailed best practices, challenges, and proficiencies to both SUNY and national audiences. All campuses in the community of practice were asked to contribute to the development of SUNY-wide standards, guidelines, and recommendations for the integration and use of early alerts to improve retention, persistence, and academic success as aligned with the goals of SUNY Excels. Early alert tools engender student-centered practice, and use of this tool across campuses within the SUNY system encourages campus-wide commitments to student success.

Online Tutoring

Generally speaking, prior to development of the signature elements, campuses often directed online students to a campus-based tutoring service. This solution was contrary to the provision of services in the modality best suited for the average online student since coming to campus is a barrier to access. However, research into online tutoring shows it to be an effective mechanism to assist with specific course concerns as well as alleviate anxiety students may have before taking historically difficult courses like math or accounting (Varney, 2009). To solve this problem, Open SUNY contracted for a set number of hours with an outside vendor, NetTutor, a web-based, online tutoring service, to assist students when they were unable to access campus-based tutoring. As per research (Varney, 2009), one of the most popular foci for tutoring has been live math tutoring.

SUNY CANTON CASE STUDY ON ENGAGING ONLINE STUDENTS IN CAMPUS LIFE

SUNY Canton is a residential college that enrolls 3,200 students (a mix of on-campus, commuting, and online students) and offers a variety of online bachelor's degree programs in health care, finance, management, criminal justice, and nursing. All of its programs are designated as Open SUNY+ programs. Approximately one third of enrollments are online students (SUNY Canton IR, 2017). As the number of adult learners (post-traditional students) is expected to increase, and as more traditional students choose online programs to reduce college costs, the school seeks to improve the quality of its online offerings by elevating the student experience through targeted efforts to engage and connect online students to campus life.

SUNY Canton participated in the Open SUNY IR process and used the results of the process to launch its efforts to incorporate online students in all aspects of campus life. Canton decided to exceed the standards set in the Social & Student Engagement category of the OLC Quality Scorecard by supplementing course interactions with campus life experiences to create a comprehensive online student engagement model. To do this, the college received funding from the SUNY System Administration to recognize its "invisible" students and enhance their interactions with the college. The belief that online learners and campus-based students have similar socio-emotional needs (Kruger & Jarrat, 2018) provided the conceptual framework for the case study. The theoretical basis for the engagement model was the need to think differently about designing outside the classroom experiences for online students (Fontaine & Cook, 2014).

Assessing Student Interest in Campus Life

The following message was sent from an online student to a SUNY Canton administrator. It was responsible for initiating a campus conversation on ways to include online students into the life of the college:

> It would be nice if online students were included with campus (brick & mortar) students' events ... anything that shows we are just as important and equal to the brick & mortar ... activities to make me feel like a true student of SUNY Canton. (SUNY Canton online student)

As a result of the student's comment, the college began challenging its assumptions that online students were not interested in campus life activities (e.g., book clubs, student government meetings, etc.) and that campus life could not be replicated in an online environment. To explore these assumptions, and the feasibility of providing cocurricular and out-of-the-classroom experiences to online students, the college administered an electronic student interest survey to all online students ($n = 839$) in fall 2017. The response rate was 35%. The majority (67%) of students who responded were non-traditional (age 24 or older) and female (74%). The survey asked students if they believed that the college should invest time and resources in creating opportunities for online students to engage with campus life. It also asked students to identify activities of interest to them.

Findings

An overwhelming majority of students believed that the college should invest time and resources in creating opportunities for online students to engage with campus life. Activities of interest are displayed in Table 1.

Table 1. SUNY Canton Online Student Interests.

Answer Choices	Response (%)
Presentations and speakers that I could listen to live or recorded	20.1
Virtual career fairs	19.7
Career-focused lectures presented by alumni in my online courses	16.8
Virtual clubs and organizations	15.5
Traditional campus life activities as I would travel to campus	11.3
Streamed campus life activities that allowed me to participate in some way virtually	10.8
Student government meetings that I could listen to live or recorded	4.1
Other (please specify)	1.7
Total	100

Implementing the Online Student Engagement Framework

Canton used responses from the survey to design a model for engaging online students in campus life. The model used technology to connect students to the academic, social, and cocurricular aspects of campus life and to create the psychological experience of a community (Ferdman & Deane, 2014). Opportunities for online students to engage in campus life included:

Student Government, Social Communities, and Digital Badging Opportunities

The college's Student Government Association (SGA) included an Online Student Representative on their executive leadership board. SGA meetings were videostreamed and online students could participate in the live chat. Student clubs and organizations were encouraged to hold virtual club fairs to allow online students to familiarize themselves with the club offerings on campus and express their interest in joining. A Greek fraternity created an online chapter of their organization to offer fully online learners the opportunity to engage in Greek Life at SUNY Canton.

Campus events, speakers, presentations, and athletic events were recorded, streamed, and organized using an online engagement platform called RooSuccess. Students validated their involvement beyond the classroom, and in their local community, with digital badges. Digital badges document a student's participation in clubs/organizations, service learning, and philanthropy.

24/7 Online Student Listserv

The listserv, available via email at all times, was managed by the Student Life Coordinator for Online Students and provided a mechanism for sharing events of interest and collecting feedback from online students.

Welcome and Finals Stress Relief Care Packets

These packages helped online learners enjoy campus life's social and informal aspects. First-time online students were mailed a welcome kit from the campus that included a SUNY Canton t-shirt, keychain, and information about support services. This effort welcomed our online students to the campus community and connected them to the campus to students early in their academic careers. Stress-relief packages were mailed to online students during final examinations at the end of the semester. Packages included small snacks, a stress ball, and study tips. As one student stated, "I appreciate that you folks have been stepping up efforts to include online students. Keep up the great efforts" (personal communication, 2018).

Virtual Career Fairs
Career fairs give students opportunities to network, explore job opportunities, and practice professional behavior. As Fontaine and Cook (2014) observed, online learners value career-related activities that support their professional development. To give online learners access to this resource, SUNY Canton contracted with a virtual recruiting and career platform to host the fair. Revenue generated via the college's student placement fee sponsored the activity.

Virtual Clothing Fairs
Professional clothing can be expensive for new graduates and can influence their negotiating power during job interviews. Each year, SUNY Canton hosts a clothing fair on campus where the local community and campus donate professional clothing. Clothing is free for students. To serve the online cohort, the college moved the fair online and used an online retail host as a "storefront." Student-workers sorted donations, prepared descriptions, photographed, labeled, and shipped the clothing. The activity was well received, and over 300 students participated in the fair.

Virtual Study Abroad Fairs
Study abroad experiences have a positive impact on the development of twenty-first-century job skills, such as global competence (Farrugia & Sanger, 2017). The college used a technology platform and invited campuses across the system to participate in exploring study abroad opportunities in 72 countries. Online students accessed a "room" that allowed them to browse opportunities and interact with staff.

Virtual Student IDs
IDs provide online students with access to student discounts in their local community (e.g., at movies, sporting, and related events), giving online students access to the same benefits that campus-based students receive.

Virtual Book Clubs and Scavenger Hunts with Library and Tutoring Resources
These efforts help online students investigate and explore the academic support services available to them, establish connections with professional staff, and engage in an academic community.

Online Student Engagement Days

Online Student Engagement Days foster a sense of belonging and campus affinity. The campus devoted one day to its online students, video-streaming special events, and mailing each online student a package with campus swag.

Varsity Esports Teams

The Esports team (https://www.canton.edu/esports/), mirrored to look and feel like a varsity athletic team, engages students interested in competitive e-gaming and provides opportunities for non-traditional athletes to participate in campus life. Teams of 13–20 students competed in seven games (HearthStone, League of Legends, Overwatch, Fortnite, FIFA, Rocket League, and Super Smash Bros Ultimate). The majority of students on the Esports Teams are residential students, with approximately three online students participating each season.

Assessment

All of the online students ($n = 839$) were emailed a questionnaire at the end of the fall 2017 semester. Sixty-five online students responded. It is unknown how many other students participated in the events, yet choose not to return to the questionnaire. Virtual Career Fairs (12.2%) and Stress-Free Packages (6.8%) had the highest participation rates. When students were asked why they did not participate in some of these activities, 21.4% said they did not know that the event was happening, and 14.3% indicated that they were not interested in the activity. Fifty-three percentage cited other reasons for not engaging in campus life, and lack of time was often mentioned. The college used this feedback to improve their communication with online students and campus life engagement opportunities by emailing a weekly blog to the students and developing more career-related online activities.

In the comments section of the questionnaire, students indicated that they felt "just as important" as the face-to-face student when offered access to activities of value to them. Students stated they wanted an opportunity to be included in campus events, even if they choose not to participate. And they wanted their "online voices" represented at student meetings and in campus decisions.

Next Steps

Now that SUNY Canton has demonstrated that online students are interested in outside the classroom activities, and that a model that uses technology to connect them to the various dimensions of campus life is viable, further inquiry is needed to investigate the impact of such engagement efforts on student satisfaction and retention.

The college continues to seek feedback from its online students on how to involve them in campus life and to improve its online engagement efforts. New initiatives include creating partnerships across the SUNY System that leverage campus resources, such as the "food pantry" outreach that allows online students to access a food pantry by going to the closest SUNY institution. The overall goal of the outreach is in keeping with SUNY System's effort to reduce food insecurity for all its students, including those online.

Additionally, Canton will be launching an effort to connect online students with federal financial aid work-study opportunities by cultivating affiliation agreements with regional non-profit agencies to employ online students. Most importantly, the college seeks to share its model of online student engagement with all institutions of higher education to support the mission of serving the public good by developing all aspects of the student's experience.

BEST PRACTICES AND RECOMMENDATIONS

Institutions of higher education are challenged with providing online students with learning environments that contribute to their academic, personal, social, and professional growth. If higher education is to remain a valued vehicle for positive change and citizenship, it must develop the tools, systems, processes, and interventions that prepare online students for college and life success. The Open SUNY IR process provides a way for colleges to do this. The process gives schools a systematic approach to achieving and assessing the quality of their online programs and encourages campuses to use data and self-reflection to continuously improve the experience of their online students.

Open SUNY+ Signature Elements, focuses on the concept of individualized support that is technology based, not technology centered. Each point of contact is unique to the student and provides a mechanism for human-to-human interaction and connection to address individual issues. Personalized outreach informs each signature element and redirects student attention to efforts supporting student success.

As online education continues to grow and evolve, institutions of higher learning will need to adapt to its changes. Campuses that embrace best practices for student success and engagement, and seek to continuously improve them, position themselves well for the future of online learning (Faulconer, Geissler, Majewski, & Trifilo, 2013).

REFERENCES

Ali, A., & Smith, D. (2015). Comparing social isolation effects on students attrition in online versus face-to-face courses in computer literacy. *Issues in Informing Science and Information Technology, 12*, 11–20. Retrieved from http://iisit.org/Vol12/IISITv12p011020Ali1784.pdf

Farrugia, C., & Sanger, J. (2017). *Gaining an employment edge: The impact of study abroad on 21st century skills & career prospects in the United States*. Institute of International Education (IIE) Center for Academic Mobility Research and Impact. Retrieved from https://www.iie.org/Research-and-Insights/Publications/Gaining-an-employment-edge-The-Impact-of-Study-Abroad

Faulconer, J., Geissler, J., Majewski, D., & Trifilo, J. (2013). Adoption of an early-alert system to support university student success. *Delta Kappa Gamma Bulletin, 80*(2), 45–48.

Ferdman, B. M., & Deane, B. (2014). Diversity at work: The practice of inclusion. San Francisco, CA: Jossey-Bass.

Fontaine, S. J., & Cook, S. M. (2014). Co-curricular engagement for non-traditional online learners. *Online Journal of Distance Learning Administration, 17*(3), n3.

Ginder, S. A., Kelly-Reid, J. E., & Mann, F. B. (2018). *Enrollment and employees in postsecondary institutions, fall 2017; and financial statistics and academic libraries, fiscal year 2017: First look (provisional data) (NCES 2019-021rev)*. Washington, DC: National Center for Education Statistics. Retrieved from http://nces.ed.gov/pubsearch

Giroir, B., & Schwehm, J. (2014). Implementing intrusive advising principles for adult learners in online programs. *NACADA Clearinghouse Resource*. Retrieved from http://nacada.ksu.edu/tabid/3318/articleType/ArticleView/articleId/3033/article.aspx

Gravel, A. (2012). Student-advisor interaction in undergraduate online degree programs: A factor in student retention. *NACADA Journal, 32*(2), 56–67.

Herbert, M. (2006). Staying the course: A study in online student satisfaction and retention. Online Journal of Distance Learning Administration, *9*(4), 300–317.

Kruger, K., & Jarrat, D. (2018, December 16). Student affairs goes digital: Translating student support to the world of online learning. *Diverse: Issues in Higher Education*. Retrieved from https://diverseeducation.com/article/134371/

Lederman, D. (2018, November). Online education ascends. *Inside Higher Education*. Retrieved from https://www.insidehighered.com/digital-learning/article/2018/11/07/new-data-online-enrollments-grow-and-share-overall-enrollment

Michelau, D. K., & Lane, P. (2010). Bringing adults back to college: Designing and implementing a statewide concierge model. *Western Interstate Commission for Higher Education*. Retrieved from https://files.eric.ed.gov/fulltext/ED539563.pdf

Muller, K. (2017). Open SUNY institutional readiness impact study. Unpublished report.

NACADA. (2010). NACADA standards for advising distance learners. Retrieved from https://www.nacada.ksu.edu/portals/0/Commissions/C23/Documents/DistanceStandards_000.pdf

OLC. (2014). Criteria for excellence in the administration of online programs. Online Learning Consortium: Quality Scorecard 2014.

Open SUNY. (2019). Open SUNY annual impact report. Retrieved from https://drive.google.com/file/d/1stekR_B4G5kXhIP3K3gW1Sz50SQt-HL4/view

Scalzo, K. (2015, December 10). Quality and scalability: Key drivers to the success of Open SUNY. *The Evolllution*. Retrieved from https://evolllution.com/revenue-streams/distance_online_learning/quality-and-scalability-key-drivers-to-the-success-of-open-suny/

Seaman, J. E., Allen, I. E., & Seaman, J. (2018). Grade increase: Tracking distance education in the United States. *Babson Survey Research Group*. Retrieved from http://www.onlinelearningsurvey.com/highered.html

Steele, G. (2005). *Distance advising*. NACADA Clearinghouse, Academic Advising Resources. Retrieved from https://nacada.ksu.edu/Resources/Clearinghouse.aspx

SUNY Canton IR. (2017). Online only student demographic trends. Retrieved from https://www2.canton.edu/effectiveness/Demographic_Trends_Online.pdf

SUNY System Administration. (2020). SUNY data warehouse. Unpublished data source.

Varney, J. (2009). *Strategies for success in distance advising*. NACADA Clearinghouse, Academic Advising Resources. Retrieved from https://nacada.ksu.edu/Resources/Clearinghouse.aspx

BEYOND INSTRUCTION: SCALING SUPPORT FOR A LARGE ONLINE MASTER'S PROGRAM

David A. Joyner

ABSTRACT

In this chapter, we examine the program- and university-level infrastructure to support learners in a large online Master of Science in Computer Science program. The program is novel due to its cost and size: total tuition for the entire degree is around $7,000, and to date, it has enrolled over 25,000 total students with 11,000 enrolled in spring 2021. Prior research has largely focused on the program's administration of individual classes, but in this work, we examine the administration of the program at higher levels: at the program level, including its academic advisers, career counselors, and alumni relations, and at the university level where it integrates with on-campus infrastructure for academic integrity, student advocacy, and disability accommodations. We close by offering three guidelines for implementing similar programs at other schools, taking into consideration the full range of experience in building the program.

Keywords: Gender; underrepresented minorities; academic advising; career development; alumni relations; student employment; disability accommodations; learning management systems; computer science.

INTRODUCTION

In this chapter, we describe the program- and university-level constructs involved in running a large, online graduate program in computer science. Launched in 2014, the program has grown to 11,000 students as of spring 2021. The program is notable for a number of reasons: its tuition is very low at $7,000 for the entire degree; its accreditation is equivalent to the on-campus degree program and carries no "online" moniker on the diploma; and it is designed for asynchronous and remote interaction, with no on-campus component and no synchronous lecture attendance. It is the largest program of its kind in the world, and research has forecast that it independently can dramatically increase the total number of Master of Science in Computer Science (MSCS) graduates in the United States (Goodman, Melkers, & Pallais, 2019).

Prior research on the program has focused in large part on learning outcomes and in-class administration, but more recent research has noted the novel challenges associated with administering program-level elements of the degree as well as integrating the program with existing campus infrastructure.

This chapter delineates and articulates these two broad categories of support for online learners in the program. In doing so, we take both a historical and a prescriptive view, describing the historical development of these structures as well as our recommendations based on their current state.

First, we explore the structures put into place within the program itself to absorb the incoming student body. We cover four areas here: academic advising, career development, alumni relations, and student employment. In this exploration, we mix large-scale surveys with interviews with individuals involved in running the program. For example, our interviews regarding student employment have found that online students who express an interest in working as teaching assistants are motivated more intrinsically and altruistically than their on-campus counterparts. We also find that alumni from an online program self-identify more closely with the program itself than the university as a whole.

Important context to this analysis, however, is that students in this program are considered full, equal students within the university context and thus are entitled to many of the same support and resolution mechanisms promised to on-campus students. Thus, the second portion of this chapter explores those systems or organizations that must integrate or be offered by the university as a whole. These include disability accommodations, student advocacy, student conflict resolution, and student conduct processing. These have presented fascinating challenges on a number of fronts: the demographics of the student body lead to differential demand on these services, and many of these systems were designed with smaller audiences in mind. For example, we find online students are significantly more likely to have acceptable excuses to require assignment extensions (such as family emergencies), which joins with the larger student body to create enormous demand.

ABOUT THE PROGRAM

First, in order to understand the trends described in the remainder of this chapter, it is important to first have an understanding of the program itself. Some lessons or observations may be differently applicable depending on similarities between your program and the program under investigation here. For example, significant elements of this program are dictated by the positioning of the program as equivalent to the on-campus program, and the students as equivalent in standing to students attending in person. Differently accredited extension programs, thus, may find some generalizable lessons but also fewer requirements than those we have encountered herein.

Program Requirements

The online MSCS program shares most pertinent program-level criteria with the on-campus MSCS program. First, the admission standards are the same – applicants should have a four-year undergraduate degree in computer science, electrical engineering, mathematics, or another significantly similar field. International applicants must also achieve a prescribed minimum score on the Test of English as a Foreign Language (TOEFL) or the International English Language Testing System Academic test (IELTS-Academic).

Once admitted, students must fulfill the same requirements: 30 credit hours (10 classes, as all classes are 3 credit hours), a 3.0 or higher GPA, and fulfillment of the requirements of one specialization. Fulfilling a specialization commands 15–18 of the 30 credit hours, as each of the specializations has a number of core classes that must be taken and a number of classes that must be taken from curated lists (e.g., "Choose at least 2 of these 8 classes").

While enrolled in the program, students are bound by the same student code of conduct as on-campus students, including as it applies to academic integrity. Students must take at least one class every other semester to remain actively enrolled and must complete the program within six total years. Although the requirements are the same, there are notable differences in how online and on-campus students elect to fulfill the requirements; the vast majority of on-campus students complete the degree in 3–4 semesters taking 3–4 classes per semester, while the majority of online students complete the degree in 8–9 semesters taking one class, or occasionally two classes, per semester.

Program Demographics

Notably, while the online admission requirements are the same as on-campus, the application of those requirements varies significantly. As the on-campus program has a maximum capacity, admitted students typically far exceed the stated requirements. Online, there is no program capacity, and so anyone meeting the application standards may be admitted. This creates some interesting challenges: how do you classify a student with a four-year undergraduate degree in Biology who, through career transitions, has three years of professional data science experience? How do you classify a student with a weak GPA in a bachelor's degree they earned 30 years ago, but with impressive professional performance in the interim? These students would generally not be competitive for the limited capacity of the on-campus program anyway, and so these questions may generally go unanswered; online, however, where anyone meeting the minimum qualifications ought to be accepted, they become pertinent.

The alignment between this inclusivity, the program's flexibility, and the low cost of tuition has led to a significantly different student body compared to that found on campus. Online students are older, with a median age that has ranged from 34 to 39 over the lifespan of the program, compared to 23 years old in the on-campus program. Online students are also enormously more likely to be employed full-time, with one study finding 85% of online students are employed full-time compared to 5% of on-campus students. The online student body is also pronouncedly more likely to reside in the United States, to have a family with children at home, and to have more than five years of prior programming experience. Finally, the online student body is comprised of a greater proportion of underrepresented minorities but a lesser proportion of women; this latter statistic, however, is largely explained by the online program's greater fraction of American students, as other countries (especially India, from which many on-campus students arrive) have lowered gender disparities in computing (Yardi, Marathe, & Toyama, 2017).

A full explication of the demographics of the program may be found in prior research (Goel & Joyner, 2016; Goodman et al., 2019; Joyner, 2017; Joyner & Isbell, 2019). In the context of this chapter, the unsurprising but insidiously impactful takeaway is that part-time online students have significantly different demands on their time than traditional students.

Student Experience

Once enrolled in the program, the formal portions of the online student experience are largely the same as that for students on campus. Online students are bound by the same requirements, procedures, and tools for registering for classes, paying tuition, submitting assignments, receiving grades, applying for graduation, and so on. Both the online and on-campus programs heavily leverage Banner, Canvas, and Piazza. It is useful when considering the student experience in an online program to note how much of the in-person experience at many universities already happens online.

The deviation from the in-person experience largely concerns the synchronous meeting times. While some distance learning programs operate on synchronous tele-attendance, this one was designed with working professionals in mind who not only cannot take time during the workday to attend class, but who may also have competing family demands after hours. To truly represent their needs, the program needed to have no mandatory synchronous components whatsoever. As such, all lectures are prerecorded. Rather than just recording in-person lectures, however, the program opted to leverage the online medium as a design asset rather than merely a transmission mechanism; lectures were custom designed and recorded to take advantage of the online classroom with features like interspersed exercises, varied content modalities, and short videos (which support better video navigation and clearer course organization). Lecture videos are shared via a variety of mechanisms, some based on massive open online course (MOOC) platforms and others native to Canvas.

Discussions that might happen in a synchronous classroom are handled via a course forum tool, Piazza. While there are drawbacks to replacing a synchronous discussion activity with an asynchronous one, researchers have noted several benefits to the asynchronous environment as well. For example, students may self-select into discussions most fitting for their own interests and ability level rather than being required to participate in the same discussion as the rest of the class. A full distillation of the observed benefits of an asynchronous forum may be found in Joyner, Goel, and Isbell (2016).

Taken together, the online student experience can best be envisioned by beginning with the modern in-person experience (including its heavy reliance on online tools) and piecewise replacing those components reliant on in-person presence with online components, built to take advantage of the online environment. This, in fact, will be the second design guideline at the conclusion of this chapter.

PROGRAM-LEVEL STRUCTURES

In examining the administration of the program, we generally look at three levels. Most prior research on the program has focused on the class level, including tools developed specifically for individual classes (Goel & Polepeddi, 2018; Joyner, Isbell, Starner, & Goel, 2019; Kolhe, Littman, & Isbell, 2016) and how individual classes are run (Camacho & Goel, 2018; Goel, 2018; Goel & Joyner, 2016; Joyner, 2018; Ou, Joyner, & Goel, 2019). Some prior research has looked at the program level, including the policies and procedures used across classes (Joyner, 2017; Joyner & Isbell, 2019) and tools developed for usage in the program as a whole (Bilgrien et al., 2019; Graziano et al., 2019); there are, however, significantly more efforts to look at in this area. Very little prior research has looked at the university level, which is how the program integrates with the rest of the university. Here, we look at these latter two: first the program-level advising, career development, alumni relations, and student employment, and second the university-level accommodations, student advocacy, and conflict resolution.

Academic Advising

In our on-campus programs, a single adviser is often responsible for all students within a program; in larger programs, there may be a small team. Our in-person program, for instance, has two advisers, each responsible for approximately 250 students. Online, that ratio would be unsustainable with the lower cost of tuition. Online, the ratio is presently approximately 1,300 students per academic adviser, assigned in order based on last name.

Despite the lower ratio, this still leads to a larger-than-usual team, varying between five and seven advisers for most of the program's recent history. With these numbers, consistent messaging is a prominent concern, as students quickly become aware when advisers may give different answers to common questions. This is largely addressed in two ways: first, messaging is made publicly as often as possible, through emails to the entire student body and publicly available information. The scale of the program means that advice that usually would be individual is actually more often common to multiple students; an issue facing 1% of students would affect 5 on-campus students but 90 online students. Thus, there is sufficient demand to converge on standard, public answers to the large majority of questions rather than handle things as they come.

Second, the size of the online program has led to a vibrant and responsive student community. Students often find that while a response from an adviser would come on the next business day (or longer during peak times), student social communities on Google+, reddit, Slack, and other sites can often generate an accurate answer in minutes. This response time yields greater activity in these communities, which leads to greater participation, in a self-perpetuating feedback cycle. Although these communities can exist in residential programs, we observe they take on a greater significance online because (a) the raw size of the population yields greater responsiveness and (b) the student experience occurs online anyway, making students more likely to seek out these kinds of public communities. The nature of the online environment then makes it more feasible for a single student to have significant impact on and help out a large number of their classmates.

Career Development

The university offers career development support to students at varying levels: at the university level, the college level, and the level of individual programs. The program here presently employs a single career adviser for the entire student body. This is because of the dramatically different role 'that' career counseling plays in a program targeted at working professionals. On campus, a large portion of career advising focuses on helping students with the initial transition from college to career; in the online program, the vast majority of students are already employed in the field, and thus their interest is not in this initial transition. Researchers examining the motivations of students entering the program found only 35% reported career transition as a motivation; far more reported gaining additional knowledge in their present field (91%) and advancing in their current career (78%) as motivations.

Additionally, as in academic advising, the larger number of students means there are fewer niche or unique cases; as such, more information can be publicized to the program as a whole. For example, while a small fraction of students in the on-campus program might be interested in a career specifically in educational technology, the same percentage led to enough interest online to support a dedicated career seminar on the topic. Thus, we have observed online that the demands for career counseling in the online program are reduced, different and more general, all of which aid in scale.

Alumni Relations

A student's relationship to a university is not intended to be restricted solely to the duration of their enrollment; ideally, the relationship would be lifelong. This often takes the form of requests for donations, local networking events, and career connections.

Alumni relationships in an online program instantiate a unique challenge however; in the absence of a significant amount of time spent in residence at a school, what is the foundation on which a relationship to the alma mater is built? Five years into the online program's lifespan, we took our first alumni survey, with interesting results. While students overwhelmingly regarded the experience as worth the investment and worth recommending to friends (97% for each), they tended to self-associate more with the program than with the university. Given that alumni in this equally accredited program are every bit as included in the alumni community as on-campus graduates, this differing identity is suboptimal.

Thus, we have adopted three mechanisms for interacting with alumni, both with an eye toward building the community as more than just a fundraising opportunity and to help online graduates identify more as university alumni. First, we have constructed an increasingly inviting graduation experience for online students; for those able to attend campus, we offer a series of events (such as a tour) to build a personal connection between the graduates and their school. For those unable to come for graduation, we are constructing a "graduation in a box," giving students paraphernalia and photo opportunities usually available on campus. Second, in our communications with the alumni community, we regularly feature opportunities for graduates to return to the program, either to take newly launched elective classes or to join as Instructional Associates to help the program out; in the most recent semester, over a fourth of the instructional support staff (teaching assistants) were program alumni. Finally, alumni engagement is a positive effect of the program's previously mentioned heavy usage of social media; whereas access to official school channels typically ends upon graduation, the program's social channels are populated by alumni, current students, and prospective students all interacting together.

Student Employment

Prior research has noted the prominent role that online students play in administering the program through roles as teaching assistants and instructional associates (the job title assigned to alumni working as teaching assistants); these students are noted to be motivated more intrinsically and altruistically than on-campus students, who are primarily motivated by the stipend or tuition waiver (Joyner, 2017).

At the program level, however, the workflow involved in hiring these teaching assistants is an incredibly complex process. Not only are on-campus classes smaller, but they tend to have a known capacity in advance based on room capacity, and so teaching assistants can be hired even before students begin to register; online, hiring is dictated by enrollment, but capacity is dictated by hiring, presenting a causality problem. Secondly, teaching assistants fall into numerous categories (current part-time student, current full-time student, pre-qualifier PhD student, post-qualifier PhD student, program alumni), each with their own deadlines and pay structures (hourly vs. salaried), each potentially able to select their own number of hours of weekly availability (10, 15, or 20 hours), and each with their own preference for what class they will work on that are independent of those classes' needs.

Our workflow for addressing this complexity begins with a unified application phase where all types of applicants may apply. In this application, applicants provide a ranked preference list of the classes that would like to work with. These applications (900 in the most recent semester) are then pivoted to per-class lists that are shared with the instructors. Instructors rank the applicants, providing to the hiring director a long list of applicants, ideally enough to handle any level of enrollment demand. The hiring director then begins hiring teaching assistants, and for each teaching assistant hired, the capacity of the class is increased by 50 seats.

This workflow represents several years of refinement, but it still has numerous wrinkles adding to its complexity in practice. Returning teaching assistants are processed first, but there are always several cases of certain teaching assistants wanting to switch classes, certain instructors preferring not to retain certain teaching assistants (who might then be hired for other classes), and so on, all of which exist as one-off exceptions. Alumni must be hired by an earlier deadline and are automatically hired for a year rather than per term; current students must be deliberately rehired each term. The process of managing the team of student employees necessary to administer a program at scale is nothing short of the human resources department for a medium-sized company.

UNIVERSITY-LEVEL STRUCTURES

The above structures are managed at the program level; program funding in part supports hiring people within the program to hire teaching assistants, provide academic and career advice, and communicate with alumni. However, there are other procedures that by their nature must go through established campus channels; the demand this creates is not neatly tied into the program's budget and scale equations, but rather creates a demand felt by existing on-campus organizations.

Disability Accommodations

All students are entitled to the disability accommodations guaranteed under the Americans with Disabilities Act (ADA). Interestingly, for on-campus students, many of those accommodations concern constructs like dedicated note-takers, approval for disability-related absences, permission to record lecture material, and accessible classroom design – all constructs that do not apply online. As the material is prerecorded and captioned, note-takers and lecture recording are passively provided to all students. Rather than details of the classroom construction, ADA dictates accessible website design; most modern vendors, however, have robust support for ADA requirements. In the absence of a synchronous meeting time, disability-related absences are similarly largely absent.

In practice, only two disability accommodations are commonly needed by online students: extended time on timed tests (easily implemented as an override in the program's Canvas learning management system) and extended time to submit assignments. The latter presents an interesting conundrum, as many classes assign all assignments at the start of the term: extended time on one assignment thus inherently takes time away from the next one. In practice, this has manifested as permission to submit some assignments late, with few enough cases to not yet pose a significant challenge.

Online students are required to follow the same process for securing disability accommodations as on-campus students, but the limited applicability of these accommodations has led to a significantly lower prevalence in the online program. While numbers are not available for the total students in each program in need of accommodations, we anecdotally observe our on-campus classes often need ADA accommodations for up to 4%–5% of the students, while online, the number is rarely above 1%.

Student Advocacy

While disability accommodations tend to be less prevalent in the online student body, demands for student advocacy tend to be far higher. At the university level, students who encounter significant unexpected challenges (mostly health, family, and personal emergencies) may write to the Dean of Students for advocacy. Although the Dean cannot formally grant extensions for reasons outside a certain number of prescribed reasons (university-administered travel and religious holidays), the Dean does advocate to instructors on behalf of students (including an assurance that the excuse has been verified), and most instructors follow the Dean's recommendations.

The volume of such requests online is very large, both in terms of raw numbers and as a percentage of students. The challenge arises from the greater diversity of the online student body: as mid-career adults with families, online students are far more likely not only to have personal health issues, but issues affecting their spouses, children, or aging parents, all of which would place the student in the position of primary caretaker. While older students make up a relatively small percentage of the student body, the program size means these are nonetheless a significant number of students who themselves may be more likely to encounter significant health obstacles. Finally, the geographically distributed nature of the program means that any natural disaster anywhere in the world affects a non-trivial number of our students. Rather than closing campus as a whole in response to localized disasters in Atlanta, we must accommodate students in the path of every hurricane, wildfire, earthquake, and so on. Hurricanes Irma and Harvey accounted for an enormous number of extension requests to start fall 2017.

The volume of advocacy requests exceeds the volume the office is prepared to receive, and so the program has taken steps to limit the number of instances wherein faculty must actually direct students to the Dean of Students. First, during natural disasters, faculty are generally encouraged to be generally accommodating rather than validating students' circumstances case by case. Second, the program implemented a lightweight tool to track students' excuse-requesting behaviors across multiple classes; most instructors agree with a philosophy that they will take students at their word the first or second time they need an accommodation for a personal, health, or family issue; our concern is more about students taking advantage of this trust to repeatedly gain an unfair advantage across numerous classes. Thus, the tool allows instructors to see a student's excuse-requesting history; if they deem it to be excessive, they may ask the student to seek the Dean of Students' advocacy, which brings with it verification of the excuse.

Student Conflict Resolution

Finally, on the opposite side of the spectrum from student advocacy is student conflict resolution. This is primarily concerned with plagiarism and exam cheating. Students are entitled to the same resolution process as on-campus students, which includes (if the request it) having the evidence in their case ruled on by a third-party office aside from the class instructor themselves. The office is similarly responsible for ensuring that students who violate integrity policies across multiple classes receive escalating punishments.

Although our evidence shows that integrity cases happen no more often online than on campus (as a percentage of enrollment), the size of the online program generates significantly more actual cases, which command a linear time commitment to review. As a computer science program, the cases often require a level of content knowledge that surpasses that of a typical case reviewer. Finally, detecting such cases in the first place is non-trivial, requiring complex tools for comparing hundreds or thousands of assignments against one another to detect similarities in either plaintext or code.

To resolve all these issues, we have adopted a set of homegrown tools and workflows. First, we have developed original tools for detecting essay and code plagiarism, allowing for more customization of the workflow; we are not as dependent on the output generated by general tools, and although there is greater demand on us to maintain the tools, the added flexibility compensates. Second, we have standardized and streamlined evidence organization, email authoring, and case tracking. A major portion of this allows the process to be more fully shared across multiple individuals; although the core case ought to be between the student and the instructor (and the integrity officer, if the student chooses), this allows teaching assistants to detect violations, document evidence, and finalize reports. Third, we have put a major emphasis on attempting to resolve cases between students and the teaching team themselves; although students may request a ruling by the third party, most cases are now resolved internally between the student and instructor.

While the raw number of cases may be higher, there are elements of online cases that are easier to resolve than those in person and that thus are compatible with the workflow described above. Most significantly, because online activity is never live and synchronous, evidence is always documented and persistent. We do not have cases where "witnesses" are called to attest to cheating that happened during a synchronous exam; rather, the evidence is almost always either comparisons between work undoubtedly submitted by the student and existing sources or video evidence of exam misconduct. For this reason, more than half of cases are resolved quickly and between the instructor and student directly; the evidence is often so objective and clear that there is no denying that misconduct has occurred.

BEST PRACTICES AND GUIDELINES

The preceding sections provide short vignettes on the relationship between online learning, scale, and institutions above the level of administering individual classes. Many of the observations and experiences are unique to our university context. Thus, to close this chapter, we abstract out three guidelines to inform the development of programs in other contexts as well; specifically, these are derived to apply to online learning wherever it may occur but especially in at-scale environments.

Guideline 1: Explore the Implications of Novel Demographics

Our first guideline, first referenced under Program Demographics but invoked throughout this chapter, is to recognize the far-reaching impacts of the different demographics observed in an online program. That the demographics of online students are different is not new information, and this program launched with many of their needs in mind. For example, the original decision to have lectures prerecorded rather than delivered via synchronous tele-attendance was for the sake of working professionals.

However, the impact of these different demographics was much further-reaching than originally anticipated. At the outset, we did not anticipate the far greater demands on student advocacy that the program would create; it was only by experience that we began to observe the differing patterns in need for special accommodations, especially based on family emergencies or natural disasters.

Similarly, the interaction between the novel program requirements and student integrity presented unforeseen challenges. For example, in the online environment where tuition is low and students are not as rushed to complete the program (because they are not waiting to move and start a new job), we observe a greater likelihood to withdraw from classes simply to get a "better start" next time. In some cases, this intersects with academic integrity; students are observed more willing to engage in misconduct because they perceive less to lose. We find that we frequently invoke a rule that is largely irrelevant on campus, that students found to have engaged in misconduct may not withdraw from the class. The threat that an integrity violation may force a student to finish a class rather than withdraw has proven a greater deterrent than probation or other typical sanctions.

Thus, our first guideline is to investigate the broader implications of a program's non-traditional demographic makeup. This may be done by interviewing administrators of similar programs, performing needfinding exercises with prospective students, or beginning the program as flexibly as possible and preparing to formalize as time passes. This latter attempt has been our major process; we initially adopt flexible policies and only begin to establish workflows and procedures once we are aware of the patterns we are observing.

Guideline 2: Build from On-campus and Replace as Needed

As noted previously, a significant portion of the student experience is the same online and in-person. This derives partially from the heavy reliance that on-campus programs now have on online tools but also from this program's classification of online students as equivalent in standing to on-campus students. While it may be tempting to start from the ground up in designing an online program from scratch, doing so would sacrifice significant infrastructure investments that may be leveraged to the benefit of the online student body.

Thus, our second guideline is to start with the traditional on-campus program and make the necessary revisions to move students to entirely online environments. We found that the changes necessary to initially run the program in this fashion were relatively few: prerecorded lectures and a greater emphasis on forum interactions were sufficient to recreate the vast majority of the formal on-campus experience online. From then, we could branch out into questions like: how do you handle student conflict resolution, which typically comprises a face-to-face meeting between an instructor and a student? These can be replaced with teleconferences; but then, how do you do this at scale? These can be further systematized as highly organized asynchronous messages.

This guideline plays into the same flexibility as referenced in Guideline 1; we generally advocate for initially under-engineering rather than over-engineering, and only applying greater systematization and formalization once it presents itself as necessary. This approach helps avoid devoting significant resources to solving problems that are not fully understood or, worse, may not actually exist.

Guideline 3: Use Scale as an Asset, Not an Obstacle

The success of this program so far is derived in large part from its repeated ability to use the scale of the program as an asset rather than a liability or obstacle. As referenced above regarding academic advising, the academic advisers are each responsible for a much greater number of students; they are able to fulfill this because the large student community supplies much faster and comparably accurate responses to most common questions. Students only *need* to contact their adviser if they need a formal alteration made to their standing; informational questions can almost always be handled by the community.

Hiring teaching assistants is also an instance of scale at work to serve the broader program; the large size of the program affirms that sufficient applicants for teaching assistant positions will typically be available to allow classes to grow. Although the incentives are lower and a smaller percentage of online students may apply, enough applicants are reliably available. The same dynamic applied above to academic advising happens in individual classes as well, where teaching assistants can be less responsible for answering every single question because the forum-based environment allows students greater means to help one another.

Finally, scale creates an opportunity to systematize processes that have room, but not demand, for optimization. On campus, for example, the process of verifying student excuses for advocacy messages is time-consuming, but not so much that it may demand a radical reorganization for greater per-case efficiency; the cost of such a redesign would likely be greater than the time saved in the near term. Online, the large number of cases presents both an incentive and the resources to optimize that were previously absent.

CONCLUSION

This online MSCS program, entering its eighth year, has grown and thrived for a number of reasons; early on, it quickly iterated on delivering course instruction at scale, but once that challenge was met, attention turned toward the challenges of scale beyond instruction: administering the program as a whole and integrating the program with the university itself. Through that process, we have learned several lessons regarding the value and opportunity to streamline and systematize common processes and to leverage the incredible student body partnering with us on this journey.

Although numerous lessons have been learned, there are still many open challenges. Our most pressing obstacle at present is the mismatch between many pieces of university software and the demands of a large online program. Minor feature changes can have an enormous impact when administering classes to 11,000 students. It also remains to be seen how a relatively young program weathers changes overtime; as the program matures, students become less patient with perceived shortcomings as a greater expectation of sophistication sets in. Finally, there remain significant philosophical questions to address, such as what the success of the online program means for the value of the on-campus degree, and the extent to which centralization of instruction to a smaller number of larger programs may have unforeseen negative effects. To date, however, this program appears to be meeting a largely unmet audience, siphoning students from neither the university's on-campus program nor other universities but rather from the vast audience of students thirsty for further education but unable to make the sacrifices presently necessary to pursue it.

REFERENCES

Bilgrien, N., Finkelberg, R., Tailor, C., Murali, G., Mangal, A., Gustafsson, N., ... Arriaga, R. (2019, June). PARQR: Augmenting the Piazza online forum to better support degree seeking online masters students. In *Proceedings of the Sixth (2019) Annual ACM Conference on Learning @ Scale*, London (p. 48).

Camacho, I., & Goel, A. (2018, June). Longitudinal trends in sentiment polarity and readability of an Online Masters of Computer Science course. In *Proceedings of the Fifth Annual ACM Conference on Learning at Scale*, London (p. 21).

Goel, A. (2018). Preliminary evidence for the benefits of online education and blended learning in a large artificial intelligence class. In *Blended learning in practice: A guide for practitioners and researchers*. Cambridge, MA: MIT Press.

Goel, A., & Joyner, D. A. (2016). An experiment in teaching cognitive systems online. *International Journal for Scholarship of Technology-Enhanced Learning, 1*(1), 3–23.

Goel, A. K., & Polepeddi, L. (2018). Jill Watson. In C. Dede, B. Saxberg, & J. Richards (Eds.), *Learning engineering for online education: Theoretical contexts and design-based examples*. New York, NY: Routledge.

Goodman, J., Melkers, J., & Pallais, A. (2019). Can online delivery increase access to education? *Journal of Labor Economics, 37*(1), 1–34.

Graziano, R., Benton, D., Wahal, S., Xue, Q., Miller, P. T., Larsen, N., Vacanti, D., Miller, P., Mahajan, K., Srikanth, D., & Starner, T. (2019, June). Jack Watson: Addressing contract cheating at scale in online computer science education. In *Proceedings of the Sixth (2019) Annual ACM Conference on Learning @ Scale*, London (p. 52).

Joyner, D. A. (2017). Scaling expert feedback: Two case studies. In *Proceedings of the Fourth (2017) Annual ACM Conference on Learning @ Scale*, Cambridge, MA.

Joyner, D. A. (2018). Squeezing the limeade: Policies and workflows for scalable online degrees. In *Proceedings of the Fifth (2018) Annual ACM Conference on Learning @ Scale*, London.

Joyner, D. A., Goel, A., & Isbell, C. (2016). The unexpected pedagogical benefits of making higher education accessible. In *Proceedings of the Third (2016) Annual ACM Conference on Learning @ Scale*, Edinburgh.

Joyner, D. A., & Isbell, C. (2019). Master's at scale: Five years in a scalable online graduate degree. In *Proceedings of the Sixth (2019) Annual ACM Conference on Learning @ Scale*, Chicago, IL.

Joyner, D. A., Isbell, C., Starner, T., & Goel, A. (2019, May). Five Years of Graduate CS Education Online and at Scale. In /Proceedings of the ACM Conference on Global Computing Education/ (pp. 16–22), Chengdu, China.

Joyner, D. A., Isbell, C., Starner, T., & Goel, A. (2019). Five years of graduate CS education online and at scale. In *Proceedings of the ACM global computing education conference (CompEd)*, Chengdu.

Kolhe, P., Littman, M. L., & Isbell, C. L. (2016, April). Peer reviewing short answers using comparative judgement. In *Proceedings of the Third (2016) Annual ACM Conference on Learning @ Scale*, Edinburgh (pp. 241–244).

Ou, C., Joyner, D. A., & Goel, A. K. (2019). Designing and developing video lessons for online learning: A seven-principle model. *Online Learning, 23*(2), 82–104.

Yardi, P., Marathe, M., & Toyama, K. (2017). Differences in stem gender disparity between India and the United States. *Human–Computer Interaction Across Borders, 1146*.

PART II

INNOVATIVE APPROACHES

CONNECTING WITH ONLINE LEARNERS: CASE STUDIES FROM A SCOTTISH UNIVERSITY

Lorraine Syme-Smith, Louise Campbell and Lynn Boyle

ABSTRACT

In this chapter, we consider some of the key ideas that impact on the creation of online learning environments. By exploring some aspects of theory, namely connectivism and its relation to wider ideas of community-building, heutagogy, and motivation, we articulate some of the factors that have influenced the authors' practice in creating online learning. We illustrate these influences by outlining examples of three courses which we have been party to creating, so that interlinked theory and practice are in evidence. By looking at a teacher education program, a childhood practice program, and a short access course, we provide examples of some of the ways in which we have scaffolded the development of learning communities, encouraged students to have autonomy over the direction of their learning, and engaged students to maintain their motivation for learning. At times, these three dimensions are interpenetrating, and in two of our case studies, longevity and ongoing improvements have enabled the authors to have confidence in the quality and value of these courses, while the third focuses on a newly created course.

Keywords: Access course; autonomy; blog; case study; childhood practice; collective activities; community-building; connectivism; distributed knowledge; professional learning

INTRODUCTION: OUTLINING THE CHALLENGE OF CONNECTING WITH ONLINE LEARNERS

The provision of a learning environment in which all students feel valued, have a sense of belonging, and are able to be successful learners is not a challenge particular to online learning. However, there are a range of challenges in providing these online. This chapter explores how students are supported to feel a sense of connection with, and are welcomed to, the university within an online environment, alongside consideration of what constitutes effective practice via a review of relevant literature.

It is important that the online learning environment (and pedagogical practice relating to it) gives all learners the opportunity to feel welcome, included, and to own their learning experience. In this chapter, we explore three case studies from a Scottish university to demonstrate how online distance program development can achieve connectivism and relatedness and hence provide a successful learning environment. These case studies demonstrate how virtual learning environments (VLEs), social media, webinars, and blogs are utilized to provide a sense of belonging and a welcoming online learning environment in which learners are motivated and can determine their own learning path. The intention here is to share the authors' practice and to offer suggestions, based on our professional experience, of how to meet students' needs. Our case studies are necessarily brief. We intend these to be illustrations of our thinking and practice.

When considering the challenges facing those developing online learning programs within the context of tertiary education, three areas offer particular insights to the case studies shared within this chapter.

These areas are:

- the process of creating online communities, where the difficulties of temporal and geographical isolation can lead to learners working and thinking alone, if this is not addressed as a primary goal of online learning environment design;
- the increasing need to facilitate the independence and autonomy of the learner and designing structured support that allows learners to follow their individual learning pathway while being offered guidance and feedback relevant and relative to their individual needs; and
- the idea of motivating and engaging learners, particularly through recognition of their need for a social context within which to develop a critical evaluative stance in relation to progression in their learning.

However, it should be noted that although these three areas have been identified as separate ideas, in practice, they are intertwined in fundamental ways. Each has the capacity to enhance the online learner's experience if well planned, or to undermine it if not thought through. Learner attrition is a significant concern for those preparing and running online courses (Mcmahon, 2013) but one which can be reduced with appropriate consideration of these issues.

LITERATURE REVIEW AND THEORETICAL FRAMEWORK

This section discusses the ideas and theories that overarch our work in developing online learning. These have helped us to frame our approach to design and analysis of the case study courses. The idea of connectivism (Siemens & Conole 2011), where knowledge acquisition is focused by human connections in the online learning environment, and ideas about the sense of relatedness that learners need from their learning in order to remain motivated (Hartnett, 2015, 2016), is one that is integrated into our thinking about developing designs for online courses, but it is multifaceted and bears some depth of discussion.

Connectivism has been of interest to those developing online learning since the work of Siemens (2004, 2005) and Downes (2008, 2012), who argue for the interpretative character of knowledge and promote the value of connections made by learning online. They see this as a progression from earlier learning theories of behaviorism and constructivism (Bell, 2009). Although some authors (Goldie, 2016; Kop & Hill, 2008) question connectivism being a learning theory, there is broad acceptance of its value as a lens for the design of online learning, as the discussion that follows will suggest.

Siemens (2004, 2005) was the first to use the term *connectivism* in relation to online learning and identified several principles for connected learning. He described connected learning as being provided by a network where learners and teachers build connections in an environment made up of learning resources and physical machinery. This learning is self-determined as learners negotiate their own paths depending upon their own interests and needs. As the learners learn, they build larger networks making connections with new people and resources and expanding their own knowledge and understanding through engaging with this network. The identifying feature of connectivism in this environment is not the learning of fact but the building of personal connections to resolve individual needs and interests. Connectivism advocates for learning and forms of knowledge that are distributive rather than centrally located and can be accessed via the interactions that develop across digital spaces and the people and organizations that inhabit them (Goldie, 2016). This characteristic of distributed knowledge is one that is pervasive in higher education online learning environments and therefore something that must be accounted for in the design and development of these.

There are many facets to connectivism. Downes (2012) identifies a host of characteristics including the importance of recognizing types of knowledge, awareness of theories of interpretation, associationism, and the development of shared meaning and social knowledge. Downes (2012) goes on to identify four key components of connectivism, these being (i) *autonomy* (where individuals are empowered to make their decisions with regard to goals and objectives); (ii) *diversity* (where consideration of the individuals in the network and the extent to which they are similarly different is taken into account); (iii) *openness* (where attention is paid to whether/how people are able to communicate with each other and take part in activities); and (iv) *interactivity* (where people in the network communicate with each other and knowledge emerges as a result of this). These four core elements overlap in terms of their relationships to the structure of online learning environments and the content provided through these. While each of these four components could be seen as primarily relating to the online learning designer's awareness of learners' needs, it is arguable that these might also be seen as characteristics that are largely learner dependent insofar as learners' self-perception will guide their engagement in these areas.

Connectivism sees the learning environment as much broader than the classroom, and hence, education is not bound by the classroom perimeters. Educators who aspire to connectivist principles aim for learners to both build and use their own networks. As autonomous agents, learners are therefore expanding the network and hence contributing to expanding the learning environment in which they are operating. As they do this, they are also building social capital as they become sources of information for others. This presents a situation where there is a move away from a "do it on your own" attitude, prevalent in non-networked education, to one of collaboration and learning within a knowledge economy (Kivunja, 2014). This form of learning is organic in its pattern of growth and dependent on engaged, participatory learners to come to fruition.

BUILDING LEARNING COMMUNITIES

There are different contexts in which connectivism can take place. Groups or classes are often a closed learning environment with the learners in the group known to each other and a teacher or lecturer providing the lead (Anderson, 2010; Dron & Anderson, 2014). In these groups, the learners proceed through a known set of activities which may be both independent and collaborative. As the learners undertake the activities, they support each other and build trust which allows learners to engage with and critique each other. In groups, the means and methods of learning are preassembled (Dron & Anderson, 2014), with learners working within set parameters. This kind of context is suited to introductory or provisional learning, where learners are somewhat supported but also somewhat constrained by the structured nature of learning.

Moving beyond groups into networks, there are two aggregations. First, *networked learning activities* allow learners to engage with other learners through the learning environment. Second, there are *collective activities* which can take place over the broader internet, accessing search software such as Google (Anderson, 2010). Networks are made up of connections rather than formal or informal processes (Dron & Anderson, 2014). There are, in networked learning design, no limits placed on sources of learning or on the possible connections that may be made along the exploratory learning journey.

HEUTAGOGY

Working within this network of connections, learners are encouraged to be self-determined and prepare themselves for future careers, with the technology being used to support them build their skills. This is in keeping with a heutagogical approach, which identifies the learners as being in control and deciding upon their own path (Blaschke, 2012). Effectively done, this allows the learners to build their efficacy and independence helping them to prepare for employment and lifelong learning. The role that educators need to take in providing an environment that promotes connectivism is one that should prioritize learner autonomy and encourage creativity and independence among learners (Lee & Yang, 2019) in order to build capacity for learners' self-determination in their own education.

However, in spite of the many positive potentials that are offered by networked online learning, there are some areas of critique that need to be taken into account. While skills for utilizing online searches and engaging with online resources are largely intuitive for many users, the more complex skills of critical evaluation of sources and interpretation of the materials found online offer a more complex challenge. Equally, online discussants and data shared online can be unreliable, raising questions about the quality and validity of such sources. Online learners' ability to discern what constitutes a valuable and trustworthy source is variable (Kop & Hill, 2008). It may also be problematic for them to discern what is of primary interest and what is secondary or extraneous without guidance. Similarly, the motivations of those individuals and organizations encountered online can be called into question, as can the organizational structures that may contribute to learning by offering biased views or inhibit learning by demarcating perceived boundaries. These issues lead to questions about the role of the teacher/tutor and whether some direction for learners is still required in online learning environments, rather than the educator simply taking the role of facilitator.

MOTIVATION

Another important issue, alongside the extent to which learning pathways need to be designed for learners, is the question of how best to enhance their motivations for engagement with learning through online course design. Students' expectations are often that online learning experiences should mirror or parallel those of on-campus learners, with peer and tutor engagement as a core part of the learning process (Holzweiss, Joyner, Fuller, Henderson, & Young, 2014), but the differences in these two forms of learning environment mean that, of necessity, the cognitive processes at work in the individual participating in online learning are not the same as those at work in face-to-face contexts.

Building on theories of self-determination in learning (Hartnett, 2016; Ryan & Deci, 2000; Scottish Social Services Council, 2019), the role of relatedness in online learning settings is argued to be integral to distance learning students' development of motivation for participation in, and engagement with, learning in tertiary online education contexts. A sense of belonging is key. Relatedness is one of three pillars of motivation that enables successful online learning, the others being autonomy and competence. While these are three distinct concepts, they are interpenetrating. Autonomy is associated with the sense of having a choice in one's actions, competence is associated with perceptions of one's own capacity to be effective in taking such actions, and relatedness is associated with the social context within which judgments about choice and effectiveness are formed (Hartnett, 2015). Where learners perceive a sense of belonging, that is, a shared positive social context, autonomous motivation and feelings of competence can blossom.

Consequently, it has been suggested that one of the priority areas of concern for those designing online learning lies with the recognition of the need to support motivation for learning through development of a social learning context. It has been shown that there is a relationship between motivation and how much boredom or enjoyment learners experience in the course of their online studies, with a positive correlation demonstrated between a sense of relatedness and enjoying and valuing the course of study (Buhr, Daniels, & Goegan, 2019). Therefore, to engage online learners fully and maximize their motivation for learning, creating opportunities for community-building is essential. Supportive peer relationships and tutor engagement are key to this (Holzweiss et al., 2014).

However, online learning courses are often created with the intention of providing widened access to learning via contexts that are asynchronous and therefore divorced from the strictures of both space and time. While access may increase, opportunities for synchronous engagement with others diminish, and relatedness can be the price that is paid for this. It has been argued that asynchronous online learning courses have characteristics that may initially appear to be "the antithesis of community" (Kruger, 2000). Yet it is arguable that alternative forms of social engagement, which do not prioritize immediacy, are more readily accessible through asynchronous learning environments. For example, students have the time to process ideas and reflect on their thinking in asynchronous online discussions, providing richer, more considered responses than are usually possible in synchronous environments (Kruger, 2000). While the social context within which interactions take place may not benefit from spontaneity, it has significant capacity for depth. If they are well designed, providing a range of opportunities for learning engagement, asynchronous online courses can support the creation of effective learning communities and offer opportunities to build the sense of relatedness so vital to motivation for learning.

As we have shown in the discussion above, three areas provide a theoretical framework for our thinking about the case studies that follow. Broadly speaking, these areas are (1) community-building, (2) heutagogy, and (3) motivation.

RATIONALE FOR THE CHOICE OF CASE STUDIES

The three case studies chosen for inclusion here represent a range of online course types that are offered at the authors' higher education institution. In each case, one of the authors has had close engagement with the design and development of the course in question and has been privy to the discussions and concerns that are related to the design of these. Case Study 1 centers on an online course designed to support practicing Further Education lecturers to achieve a teaching qualification, with close attention paid to individuals' experiences of practice and their own professional context. This is ordinarily a one-year course that is completed while students are working in-service. Case Study 2 focuses on an undergraduate degree course for people working in the Early Years education sector. As with Case Study 1, it is designed for students who are working full time and studying part-time. Case Study 3 looks at a short online access course that has been designed to bridge a qualification gap for graduate candidates wishing to access our Professional Graduate Diploma in Education.

Case Study 1: A Teacher Education Program

The Teaching Qualification in Further Education (TQFE) is an in-service program for the college sector centered on the Professional Standards for College Lecturers (College Development Network, 2018). The students on the program are lecturers employed in colleges or other educational establishments. There are two versions of the program, one for UK-based students and one for international students. The former of these is by far the larger in terms of participant numbers. Within the UK program, the students are spread geographically from Dumfries and Galloway in the South of Scotland to Shetland in the North. Due to the distance learning, part-time nature of the TQFE program, with students being both in employment and studying at a distance, both connectivity and relatedness have had to be considered in the design of the program. The development of connectivity is important to save participants from feeling isolated and ensuring that there are opportunities for them to discuss their practice and relate with other participants. The diversity of the participants also needs to be considered within a learning environment that motivates students and allows them the opportunity to self-determine their learning paths.

The learning environment provided to students centers around a VLE housed on a Blackboard platform, with a program blog (Wordpress) and e-mail (Microsoft Outlook). Both the learning materials on the VLE and the program reading list have been designed to be accessible by online learners at a distance. Learners are able to determine their own way through these resources to match with their own interests and professional setting, thus matching with our aim to support a heutagogical approach.

The teaching team work collectively as TQFE-Tutor to provide seamless communication to students. There is one e-mail address and blog identity supported by members of academic staff for which there is a rota of cover. This means that students always have quick and consistent communication available assuring connectivity between the student and the university team.

The learning experience is designed to allow students to be members of a learning community from the point at which they enter the program and start the induction. This has been designed to help students become familiar with navigating around the VLE and to use and engage with posts from fellow students and program staff on the program blog. With the blog being transparent to all, through the induction phase of the course, participants are encouraged to start reflecting upon their own practice and to identify with how others are reflecting upon and developing theirs. This low-risk environment provides the new students with online activities, which are constructively aligned with the underlying learning outcomes and encourage interaction with other students and the program team. As students become more competent and confident in viewing the work of others, this helps them to develop their own practice, as well as enabling them to become active members of a community of practice and of learning. The links between the activities and professional practice motivate the students to reflect upon their own personal development as educators.

During the rest of the program, students are encouraged to time the progression of their studies through the use of "Keep on track" messages sent by e-mail and with reference to a shared timeline. These connections motivate students to proceed with the program activities mindful of deadlines like assignment submissions and to maintain communications with the program team through either the blog or through e-mail.

Webinars are offered to students to aid with key parts of the program. These primarily center around assessments, enabling students to ask questions about assignment tasks. Webinars give the advantage of being accessible by multiple students and participants can feel reassured by hearing the questions that others have asked and by the answers given. As self-determined learners, the students are able to engage with the webinars as they choose and self-select which aspects of learning are important to them.

The blog remains available to the students throughout the program to communicate and discuss ideas and as a source of connectivity. There are two main sections designed for ongoing use which help the learners develop a feeling of community. The first of these provides an opportunity to ask questions which are then answered by the program team or by fellow students. The second is a student-only discussion area which allows the learners to discuss anything related to the course among themselves. Looking at usage of these sections for session 2019–2020, there has been regular, limited usage of the ability to ask questions (on average two questions per week) but little usage of the student discussion section.

Communications from students after the induction phase tend to center on assignment progress, either in the interpretation of the assignment requirements or in the timing of submissions, and these questions tend to be made directly to the program team through e-mail rather than openly through the blog. This ability to communicate with other students has been seen as important since early versions of the online program, with message boards and Twitter both having been unsuccessfully used. The blog has been the most successful of these, but encouraging relatedness among students is something on which the program team continue to work.

Motivation for engagement and progression on the TQFE course is largely a matter of necessity, since students are usually funded by their employing institution. A key factor that motivates learners is the authenticity of the activities and assessments, which enables the students to identify the worth of undertaking the tasks (Dron & Anderson, 2014). Assessments are based on the students' own practice, and examples in the learning materials are authentic having come from previous students. As well as the support given by the tutor team, within each student's institution a supporter is nominated to monitor progress and offer additional advice to students.

Case Study 2: A Childhood Practice Program

The BA Childhood Practice (BACP) online program is a compulsory professional qualification for Early Years practitioners to enable them to register with the Scottish Social Service Council (2019) to manage a childcare setting in Scotland. The learners all study part-time while working full time in a childcare setting from every region in Scotland. Traditionally, this group of students has entered the program using recognition of prior certificated learning and experiences, which, for many learners, can mean there is an escalation in academic expectation in contrast with previous learning experiences. With this escalation comes student doubt in efficacy and feelings of inadequacy (Meehan & Howells, 2018).

Students working together with peers and being able to ask questions, to get reassurances on understandings of set assignments and teaching, has been part of the previously experienced face-to-face education cycle for this group of learners. Instructions can be explicit with learning intentions and the criteria against which the learners will be assessed, aligned, and visible to the learners. Yet most learners still need peer-to-peer reassurance and discussion, particularly in those areas where subjective perceptions are at the forefront. Universities hope to have a student alumnus who will be able to work creatively, think analytically, and be able to transfer theory to practice. The goal of the independent and autonomous learner who will take the skills of study and transfer these, alongside new knowledge, into the workplace is in every university's set of institutional aims. Therefore, while ensuring there is curricular alignment, clear learning materials, libraries with accessible online reading, and clear formative and summative feedback, the online learner alongside their on-campus counterparts needs the opportunity to communicate with their peers and to feel they can trust and find support in one another (Goodchild, 2017). With the support of peers, the learners feel a community connection to and with the university.

The BACP online program has reflected and recognized this need for community over several years and, within that time, opportunities for enabling peer-to-peer connections have been built into the program. This need for connection has been facilitated through online tools such as e-mail, interactive portfolios, wikis, blogs, and webinars. With the increase in social media platforms, however, the program has experienced a shift in the ways learners now prefer to communicate with one another beyond the gaze of the teaching team (Aleksandrova & Parusheva, 2019). The explosion of technologies in the "real world" means that, even with the best intentions, education platforms cannot upgrade and replicate the ease and freedom of choice and design which is available beyond the VLE.

The BACP learners have a closed, student-led Facebook group, which is beyond the closed environment of the VLE. There is also a tutor-led Twitter page, where the lecturers provide the lead to useful connections. What has evolved is the increasing number of course-focused communications between learners through small group chat platforms such as WhatsApp, where social capital and the sharing of information can be honed to a specific topic. Students can return to an output model for information via a whole program e-mail system and a student peer/tutor discussion area now embedded into modules through Blackboard Ultra. It is also essential that the tutors can facilitate whole program systems but not dominate or even participate in small organic peer-to-peer connections.

It has been argued that online learners cannot be "managed through some sort of motivating process" (Downes, 2012, p. 91) but rather the motivation is organic and collective. Commonly, BACP learners perceive they are the only one feeling lost, isolated, or to have poor self-efficacy, and the role of the program team has shifted to focus on prioritizing course design which can enable peer-to-peer connections. This aligns with Downes' (2008) idea of interactivity and the educator being the conduit to enable learners to connect with one another, often without the gaze of the educators themselves (Holzweiss et al., 2014). This motivation to connect easily, and by using familiar social media platforms, negates the less contemporary notion of the "isolated learner." This is exemplary of Kruger's (2000) richer forms of engagement where the platform, in this case WhatsApp, can be either synchronous or not, depending on the needs of the learner. Learner motivation becomes collective, through safe and supportive environments, which mirror the face-to-face interactions of on-campus students, where discussions enjoy the security of being peer to peer.

Case Study 3: An Access Course in English

In contrast with the two previous courses explored in this chapter, Access English for Professional Graduate Diploma in Education (PGDE) is a short course (nominally up to 160 hours of study) aimed at candidates who wish to be considered for the PGDE in initial teacher education. Successful completion of the Access course is a condition of acceptance for candidates who have not obtained the Scottish Qualifications Authority's Higher English qualification but have been offered a place to undertake the PGDE teaching qualification at the authors' Higher Education institution. Higher English is the Scottish secondary school qualification in communication and literacy that is required as a minimum competency for those aiming to be secondary school teachers, along with a number of other stipulations including an undergraduate degree in a subject relevant to the teaching qualification sought. The requirement to have passed Higher English or an accepted alternative is set out by the General Teaching Council for Scotland (GTCS, 2013). The GTCS is the body that regulates and monitors teachers' professional standards in Scotland.

The authors' institution undertakes initial teacher education in a number of secondary subjects, with a particular focus on sciences and mathematics. These are areas for which there is, at the time of writing, a teacher shortage. One of the possible reasons hypothesized for this is the GTCS' requirement for potential teachers to have passed Higher English, which some learners choosing sciences or mathematics as the focus of their undergraduate degree may not have undertaken or may not have passed. As a means of offering potential PGDE candidates the opportunity of filling this qualification gap, with a view to increasing recruitment, the authors' institution developed an alternative to Higher English, targeting reading and writing skills at level 6 of the Scottish Credit and Qualification Framework (2012).

As the learners who undertake the course are doing so as a condition of acceptance to initial teacher education, are not yet enrolled or matriculated as learners of the university and so are not able to use the university's library facilities or other resources and support normally available to the main body of our students. This meant that we needed to think carefully about how we structured the course, as well as what kinds of textual resources and learning materials would be appropriate. We decided to utilize universally available texts and resources through newspapers, magazines, video clips, and other materials that are free to view online. By creating hyperlinks to the relevant online resources, this helped to create a seamless interface, where learners could move easily from the course platform (Campus Press) to the texts prescribed for study.

Another consideration that impacted on the design of the course was the varied profiles of the learners who would be studying. While these learners would share the experience of prior undergraduate study, their knowledge, interests, age, and experience would be widely divergent. Therefore, it was important to build in scope for learners to study in more or less depth according to their interests and needs. We did not want the course to be treated dismissively by those whose skills and confidence were high. We also did not want to overwhelm those whose skills and confidence needed more support. One of the currently unresolved challenges of this course, which is an ongoing area for development, was how to create a sense of community, when the nature of the course necessitated that students would undertake it at different times and work at their own pace.

Humanizing the online learning environment, in order to create a sense of relational engagement between learners and tutors, was an important consideration. Given the very limited time allocated to student/tutor interaction on this course, it was important to consider other ways in which to create a sense of relatedness, to build the sense of belonging and intrinsic motivation that is theorized as being so significant for learners learning online (Hartnett, 2016). One such method involved developing a conversational but unambiguous tone in the course materials. By utilizing a combination of the passive form in the description of language effects and other learning content, and direct address in the outlining of learning tasks, we sought to depersonalize content and to simulate a more personal interaction in the sharing of instructions. In addition, voice recordings (podcasts) welcoming learners to the course and introducing tutors was seen as a way of adding a more human touch to the course online learning environment, helping learners to gain some sense of the individuals who had created the course and would be assessing their work.

It was important that all tasks and materials empowered learners to take individual perspectives on their study. We aimed to enable this by developing learning tasks that offered scope for individual interpretation and autonomous action (Blaschke, 2012). For example, in the Reading unit, learners are offered the opportunity to refresh their memories or learn for the first time about a range of features of language. As one of the formative learning tasks that follows, learners are asked to identify a non-fiction source of their own, and to annotate it with their understandings, analyses, and evaluations in relation to the use of language techniques identified and explored in the unit. The intention here is to allow learners the opportunity to engage their own interests through their chosen text, and to demonstrate their learning positively, by noticing and annotating whatever techniques appear most salient to them. The heutagogical dimensions of this approach were intended to overcome any disparities that might exist between learners in terms of their knowledge and needs.

At the time of writing, this is a very new course and one which will be the recipient of further evaluation and development on an ongoing basis, in the light of experiences of participating students and tutors.

CONCLUSIONS

These case studies demonstrate how, in the design of learning environments, steps can be taken to allow learners to feel connected and part of a community, either of practice or of learning, sometimes both. Further, in each of the case studies outlined here, provision has been made for learners to have the opportunity, at least in part, to self-determine their path through learning.

In these case studies, the learner is able to establish a good learning relationship with the teaching team and, for the larger programs, with their fellow learners. The case studies show different degrees of success in establishing communities among the learners, with the social media use in the childcare program having proved successful but the blog usage on the teacher education program showing fewer engagements once the learners do not need to participate. This lack of engagement may be regarded as not entirely negative, as it shows students' self-determination. They may choose not to engage with those parts of the program with which they do not identify an interest.

In our experience of each of the case study courses, the tutor takes the role of facilitator with students having some opportunity to determine their own path through the learning environment. Each of these instances shows some degree of leading the learner by identifying the steps required to negotiate the course and signposting possible routes to completion. This is a motivational tool, as well as a practical one, helping students to build their own sense of purpose and autonomy in relation to their learning.

Our purpose in sharing these case studies is to illustrate how connectivist thinking has been applied in a range of contexts within the authors' organization, particularly in relation to community-building, heutagogy, and motivation. These are illustrations of practice that the authors have found effective in their work with online learners, and while each case is appreciably different to the others, these three considerations have guided our thinking in developing our respective courses. What we hope is clear from the cases we have shared here is that there are diverse ways to structure online learning to aid engagement and motivation.

REFERENCES

Aleksandrova, Y., & Parusheva, S. (2019). Social media usage patterns in higher education institutions – An empirical study. *International Journal of Emerging Technologies in Learning, 14*(5), 108–121.

Anderson, T. (2010). Theories for learning with emerging technologies. In G. Veletsianos (Ed.), *Emerging technologies in distance education* (pp. 23–39). Edmonton: Athabasca University.

Bell, F. (2009). Connectivism: a network theory for teaching and learning in a connected world. *Educational Developments, The Magazine of the Staff and Educational Development Association, 10*(3).

Blaschke, L. (2012). Heutagogy and lifelong learning: A review of heutagogical practice and self-determined learning. *International Review of Research in Open and Distance Learning, 13*(1), 56–71.

Buhr, E. E., Daniels, L. M., & Goegan, L. D. (2019). Cognitive appraisals mediate relationships between two basic psychological needs and emotions in a massive open online course. *Computers in Human Behavior, 96*, 85–94.

College Development Network. (2018). Professional standards for lecturers in Scotland's colleges. Retrieved from https://www.cdn.ac.uk/professional-standards/

Downes, S. (2008). An introduction to connective knowledge. In T. Hug (Ed.), *Media, knowledge and education: Exploring new spaces, relations and dynamics in digital media ecologies* (pp. 77–102). Innsbruck: Innsbruck University Press.

Downes, S. (2012). Connectivism and connective knowledge. Essays on meaning and learning networks. Ottawa, ON: National Research Council Canada.

Dron, J., & Anderson, T. (2014). On the design of social media for learning. *Social Sciences, 3*(3), 378–393.

Goldie, J. G. S. (2016). Connectivism: A knowledge learning theory for the digital age? *Medical Teacher, 38*(10), 1064–1069.

Goodchild, A. (2017). Part-time students in transition: Supporting a successful start to higher education. *Journal of Further and Higher Education, 43*(1), 1–14.

Hartnett, M. (2015). Influences that undermine learners' perceptions of autonomy, competence and relatedness in an online context. *Australasian Journal of Educational Technology, 31*(1), 86–99.

Hartnett, M. (2016). Motivation in online education. Singapore: Springer.

Holzweiss, P. C., Joyner, S. A., Fuller, M. B., Henderson, S., & Young, R. (2014). Online graduate students' perceptions of best learning experiences. *Distance Education, 35*(3), 311–323.

Kivunja, C. (2014). Do you want your students to be job-ready with 21st century skills? Change pedagogies: A pedagogical paradigm shift from Vygotskyian social constructivism to critical thinking, problem solving and Siemens' digital connectivism. *International Journal of Higher Education, 3*(3), 81–91.

Kop, R., & Hill, A. (2008). Connectivism: Learning theory of the future or vestige of the past? *International Review of Research in Open and Distance Learning, 9*(3), 1–13.

Kruger, K. (2000). Using information technology to create communities of learners. *New Directions for Higher Education, 2000*(109), 59–70.

Lee, J. J., & Yang, S. C. (2019). Professional socialisation of nursing students in a collectivist culture: A qualitative study. *BMC Medical Education, 19*(1), 1–8.

Mcmahon, M. (2013). A study of the causes of attrition among adult on a fully online training course. *Irish Journal of Academic Practice, 2*(1), 1–26.

Meehan, C., & Howells, K. (2018). In search of the feeling of 'belonging' in higher education: Undergraduate students transition into higher education. *Journal of Further and Higher Education, 43*(10), 1376–1390.

Ryan, R. M., & Deci, E. L. (2000). Intrinsic and extrinsic motivations: Classic definitions and new directions. *Contemporary Educational Psychology, 25*(1), 54–67.

Scottish Credit and Qualification Framework. (2012). SCQF level descriptors. Retrieved from https://scqf.org.uk/

Scottish Social Services Council. (2019). The children's services workforce 2017. Retrieved from https://data.sssc.uk.com/data-publications/194-the-childrens-services-workforce-2017

Siemens, G. (2004). Connectivism: A learning theory for the digital age. Retrieved from https://www.learningnetwork.ac.nz/shared/professionalReading/TRCONN2011.pdf

Siemens, G. (2005). Connectivism: Learning as network-creation. Retrieved from http://masters.donntu.org/2010/fknt/lozovoi/library/article4.htm

Siemens, G., & Conole, G. (2011). Special issue – Connectivism: Design and delivery of social networked learning. *International Review of Research in Open and Distance Learning, 12*(3), i–iv.

The General Teaching Council for Scotland. (2013). Memorandum on entry requirements to programmes of initial teacher education in Scotland. Retrieved from http://www.gtcs.org.uk/web/FILES/about-gtcs/memorandum-on-entry-requirements-to-programmes-of-ite-in-scotland-0413.pdf

FACILITATING CO-CURRICULAR CONNECTIONS AMONG MILLENNIAL AND GENERATION Z STUDENTS IN DIGITAL ENVIRONMENTS

Shelley Price-Williams and Pietro A. Sasso

ABSTRACT

Developing student engagement in the online classroom and within co-curricular digital spaces is about relationship building more than technology or class structure. Where the learning management system is used effectively, online learning can equal or exceed the engagement levels of face-to-face classrooms particularly with Millennial and Generation Z students. Beyond technology is the need to create a higher value aspect of learning by developing models closely aligned with "communities of practice" (Wenger, 2000) or "communities of inquiry" (Garrison, 2007). This chapter will examine how to engage Millennial and Generation Z traditional undergraduate students through distance learning approaches in ways that support student learning and development.

Keywords: Advising; student development; asynchronous advising; academic advising; technology; Millennials; Gen Z; digital native; digital engagement; sense of belonging

As Millennials born between 1984 and 1994 exited college campuses in the United States and moved to graduate or continuing education student status, a new "echo" generation of traditional undergraduate students emerged on college campuses beginning in 2013 often referred to as Generation Z (Gen Z; Sasso & DeVitis, 2015). The current student generation refers to those born from 1995 to 2010 (Seemiller & Grace, 2016). Gen Z now comprises most traditional age undergraduate students (18–24) on college campuses today as defined by Seemiller and Grace (2016).

With each new student generation comes new characteristics, attitudes, and beliefs (Howe & Straus, 1991) as they are born into a distinctive era (Seemiller & Grace, 2016). However, engaging these students requires new approaches and additional consideration in being intentional with each generation's characteristics. Just as higher education lacks a thorough understanding of supporting new and emerging populations of students (Frederick, Sasso, & Maldonado, 2018), higher education lacks a complete understanding of each new generation of undergraduate students (Seemiller & Grace, 2016). Higher education administrators need to consider how to engage their programs with these students to promote this sense of belonging. In particular, it is important to consider how to connect students with both their institution and peers to promote this sense of belonging. The most efficacious way, in consideration of generational traits, is through digital engagements by creating virtual spaces (Frederick et al., 2018; Sasso, Dayton, & Rosseter, 2015).

William Glasser (1988) and his theory of sense of belonging conceptualizes the notion that institutions of higher education have been highly responsive to meeting the basic safety needs of students and meeting cognitive development needs in many ways. However, they seem to have fallen short of meeting the needs of connectedness and affective growth, especially with co-curricular (out-of-class) programs that can be used to engage students. Tinto (2012) found the more engaged with faculty, staff, and peers, the more likely the college student will succeed. Tinto (2012) identified out-of-class contact as an independent factor of student learning and growth and found a link between learning and persistence toward graduation which he maintained was a result of involvement and quality (not quantity) of expended effort. Institutions can influence this notion of quality with their capacity to connect students with faculty, staff, and student peers through co-curricular programs.

This concept of belonging is important to connecting Millennial and Gen Z students who have difficulty in socializing due to the social isolation caused by technology (Seemiller & Grace, 2016; Twenge, 2006). This social isolation often correlates with mental health, according to Tinto's theory of student departure (2012). However, rethinking how technology is used within co-curricular programs can actually connect students, rather than isolate or silo them.

This chapter will explore the challenges related to creating digital environments through co-curricular programing to better connect together to promote a sense of belonging. This will be problematized through the use of the theory of student engagement by Kuh, Schuh, Whitt, and Associates (1991). This theory will be defined as a construct, and implications for practice will be provided as consideration for approaches to engaging Millennial and Gen Z students. These two distinctive student generations will also be profiled as the target audience for these student engagement approaches.

Differences in these generations will be explored using generational theory by Howe and Strauss (1991, 2000) to demonstrate distinction between Millennials and Gen Z. This chapter analyzes common descriptors for both Millennials and Gen Z to facilitate best practices and recommendations regarding their proclivity for co-curricular engagement with technology.

GENERATIONAL THEORY

The work of Neil Howe and William Strauss (1991, 2000) provides the theory of student generations, which underpins the framework to further explore the profile of Gen Z and Millennial students and their asynchronous engagement on college campuses. Howe and Strauss (1991) introduced their framework of generational theory in the book *Generations: The History of America's Future, 1584 to 2069*. They suggested that generations evolve in cycles. With each new generation come different beliefs, attitudes, and perceptions to college campuses. Howe and Strauss (1991) defined a generation as, "a cohort-group whose length approximates the span of life and whose bound by peer personality" (p. 60).

They purported that the length of time is important regarding when a new generation begins and ends and determined this time by *life cycles*. Each life cycle lasted approximately 21 years and then a new generation should begin based on peer personality. Howe and Strauss (1991) defined peer personality as "a generational persona recognized and determined by (1) common age location, (2) common beliefs and behavior, and (3) perceived membership in a common generation" (p. 64). There is no set length or time frame for each generation, rather they are bound by a defining historical event or common personality traits.

Howe and Strauss (1991) used the two components of the generation definition to create the four-part cycle. This cycle shows that at any given time, there are four living generations at different phases of their lives: elders, midlife adults, rising adults, and youth. Each generation plays an important role in the cycle. When a generation cycles out of youth, a new generation enters the cycle. For example, Rickes (2016) characterized Gen Z as multitaskers and achievement orientated and predicts Gen Z will be another sandwich generation caught between the very large cohort of Millennials and an unnamed future generation the author purports will mirror the Baby Boomers generation. With each new generation comes a new set of beliefs and behaviors. Howe and Strauss (1991) suggested that new generations bring different beliefs, attitudes, and perceptions, to their socially constructed world. The last generation they examined was the Millennial generation, where they identified characteristics that made this generation different from the generations before them. This chapter is informed by the application of generational theory based on the framework created by Howe and Strauss (1991), given the focus on Gen Z entering college campuses and what makes them different from their Millennial peers.

Generational formation is influenced by historical events, parental ideology, and cultural influences. Rickes (2016) maintained each generation differentiates itself apart and establishes itself differently. Each new generation also corrects for the woes of the preceding generation. The G.I. Generation (1901–1924) is known as the "greatest generation" and is dwindling (Rickes, 2016). They flooded higher education after the war and impacted higher education structural development. The Silent Generation (1925–1942) was the sandwich generation between the war heroes and the children of the Boomer Generation. The Silent Generation played by the rules and committed to family, career, and friends (Rickes, 2016). The Baby Boomers (1943–1966) were the largest generation until outnumbered by the Millennials (Fry, 2015; Seemiller & Grace, 2016). They are optimists, confident in themselves, distrustful of authority, and question the relevance of social structures (Rickes, 2016). They were risk takers. Rickes (2016) noted that Boomers led to the campus building boom with quick construction we now deem inferior. They are also very present in higher education as Boomers occupy 40% of faculty and staff (Rickes, 2016).

Gen X (1961–1981) is known as the cynical and disconnected generation (aka latchkey kids) (Rickes, 2016). Due to the lack of a collective identity, this generation never received a nickname like that of Boomers, the G.I. Generation, or Millennials (Seemiller & Grace, 2016). A decline in birth during this era is one influential factor on higher education that led to admission of more women and minorities. Gen X comprises 25% of faculty and staff in higher education of today (Rickes, 2016). More importantly, Gen X plays a pivotal role as parents to Gen Z (Seemiller & Grace, 2016).

Millennials (1982–2004) are children of the Baby Boomers and are digital natives who grew up with access to technological advances. For these individuals, the cell phone is the third screen along with the television and computer. They motivated the amenities war and originate from overprotective parents called *helicopter parents* (Seemiller & Grace, 2016). They are the largest cohort in the US workforce (Rickes, 2016). Gen Xers occupy a large territory of graduate schools with Millennials encroaching (Walker, Martin, White, Norwood, & Haynie, 2006). There is some debate of the age cutoff for Gen Z and when they will occupy in totality higher education (Williams, 2015). Seemiller and Grace (2016) purport this group is in college now, while others maintain this generation will arrive a few more years.

STUDENT GENERATIONS

Millennial Students

Howe and Strauss (2000) specifically explored the Millennial Generation in *Millennials Rising: The Next Great Generation*. With this, they introduced seven key characteristics that define Millennial college students. Millennials are those who were born from 1980s to early 1990s. This generation is also referred to a Generation Y (Seemiller & Grace, 2016).

The Millennial generation was born with technological luxuries like cell phones and more than one color television per household (Howe & Strauss, 2000). Their global shaping moments include Columbine, terrorist attack on 9/11, and the Virginia Tech shooting. Technology and the ability to connect would also place an influence force on the Millennial generation. Researchers built off the work of Howe and Strauss (2000), showing a different perception of the Millennial generation. Twenge (2006) highlighted some negative characteristics and characterized them as the "Me" generation. Millennial students are part of a trend against conformity and have showed lower levels of a need for social approval. Millennials' behaviors are not influenced by the need to obtain approval but are influenced to obtain recognition from others. They strive to present themselves in a favorable manner when interacting with others.

While there is a new majority generation on college campuses today as aforementioned, Millennials were the majority generation on campus and were a popular research topic. Millennials marked contrast to their prior student generation counterparts. Howe and Strauss (2000) found there to be seven key characteristics to define the Millennial college student. First, Millennial students come from smaller families and had fewer siblings. From this, the "helicopter parents" emerged by providing their children with constant support and attention (Howe & Strauss, 2000). With parents providing Millennial students with increased hovering and attention, they felt unique and special even when compared to their peers. Second, Millennial students' use of technology allowed their parents to keep them within an ear's distance and closer to home (Howe & Strauss, 2000). This kept Millennial students sheltered from the realities of the world outside their home. Third, Millennial students had constant praise and support from adult involvement providing an inflated sense of self-worth. This allowed Millennial students to build a high level of confidence (Howe & Strauss, 2000).

Fourth, diversity increased with every prior American generation. Millennials were the most diverse generation at one time (Howe & Strauss, 2000). They were raised to become civically engaged and less individually focused. They even experienced team-oriented and group environments at younger ages than the generations before them. Fifth, Millennials focus on immediate and threatening issues (Howe & Strauss, 2000). This has been used to explain why they are so conscious about the environment. Sixth, Millennials were overscheduled and mentored to succeed among their peers (Howe & Strauss, 2000). This was with the goal of attending college to provide for a successful life. Seventh, Millennials were predicted to be future oriented and planners with focus on long-term success (Howe & Strauss, 2000).

These seven common characteristics as found by Howe and Strauss (2000) provide for a better understanding of Millennials. These characteristics are similar to those of the next and current student generation, Gen Z. These students are perceived as they are the "echo generation." An echo generation is one that is smaller than previous and is comprised of similar traits but further refines and advances those of its predecessor (Sasso et al., 2015).

Therefore, these characteristics serve as the foundation that Gen Z evolves from as they become college age. Rickes (2016) predicted Gen Z to be another sandwich generation due to their position between Millennials and those that follow, and like the Boomers who are risk averse and conforming. Among traditional aged students (18–23), Millennials are being replaced on college campuses by Gen Z (Hope, 2016).

Gen Z Students

Little research has been conducted on the newest generation on college campuses in the United States – *Generation Z*. Seemiller and Grace (2016) released the first book, *Generation Z Goes to College*, introducing how this new generation will change college campuses. The internet shapes the world of Gen Z. Some researchers are still agreeing on a name for this generation and they are sometimes referred to as Net Generation or iGeneration (Seemiller & Grace, 2016). Twenge (2017) characterized them "iGen," and those born during or after 1995 grew up with cell phones and do not remember a time before the internet.

Gen Z is the most used term to refer to this group of birth years from 1995 to 2010. They are often referred to as *device dependent* (Seemiller & Grace, 2016), because their world has been shaped by access to the internet (Brown, 2016). Gen Z makes up a quarter of the US population and will be one third of the population come 2020. The US Census Bureau's release of race and age statistics (2017) showed that Gen Z is comprised of 48% non-Caucasian. They are said to be the most racially diverse generation to date (Seemiller & Grace, 2016). With technology advancements, such as tablets, smart televisions, and the smartphone, Gen Z is accustomed to having a world that is always connected.

According to Seemiller and Grace (2016), Gen Z students do not know a time without being able to carry the internet in their pocket (via smart phones and tablets). Seemiller and Grace (2016) add:

> where their predecessors had a special device for video games, another for playing music, another for making phone calls, and a paper calendar, Generation Z can do all of that with one device that fits in their pocket. (p. 6)

They are used to having access to any information they want, wherever they want around the clock. Unlike their Millennial peers, Gen Z grew up in an economic recession and are skeptical of the cost and value of a higher education. Understanding their mindset is important to supporting their college success (Seemiller & Grace, 2016). Many of them are just beginning to earn degrees, but not much research has been conducted on Gen Z retention and graduation rates. The oldest group belonging to Gen Z just recently graduated in 2016, and more of their Gen Z peers are entering college and continuing to challenge the current paradigm of higher education (Seemiller & Grace, 2016).

Gen Z names education, employment, and racial quality as their greatest concerns (Seemiller & Grace, 2016). Loveland (2017) found that 81% of Gen Z students believe a crucial part of starting a career involves earning a college degree. According to Loveland (2017), Gen Z students and their parents are more concerned about the cost of a college education than ever before. Gen Z is the first generation born into a world where every aspect, objects, people, and places, has a digital equivalent (Stillman & Stillman, 2017).

Gen Z is predicted to be the "most racially and ethnically diverse generation in US history" (Rickes, 2016, p. 16), with higher numbers of biracial and multi-racial members in the population are growing fast (American Academy of Child and Adolescent Psychiatry, 2011). More of Gen Z youth originate from urban areas, allowing for exposure to a mixture of cultural perspectives, compared to the generations before them (Tacoli, 2012). The secrecy with sexual orientation previous generations experienced is not the case with Gen Z, and the LGBTQ community continues to grow.

Stillman and Stillman (2017) identified seven key traits of Gen Z. First is the concept of *Phigital* where they are born into a world where every physical aspect has a digital equivalent (Stillman & Stillman, 2017). For Gen Z, the real world and the virtual world overlap naturally. Second is the concept of *Hyper-Custom* as Gen Z desires to customize their own brand for the world to be known. They want to be able to customize job titles and career paths (Stillman & Stillman, 2017). Third is the concept of *Realistic* as they grew up in the aftermath of 9/11 and the knowledge of terrorism in everyday life, as well as living though the recession (Stillman & Stillman, 2017). Gen Z has a realistic view of the world they live in. The fourth concept is *Weconomist* as they have only known a world with a shared economy (Stillman & Stillman, 2017). With companies like Uber and Airbnb, they will continue to challenge the structure of the market. The fifth concept is *FOMO* as Gen Z will suffer from the fear of missing out (Stillman & Stillman, 2017). They have access to what their friends are doing at all times with social media. The sixth concept is *DIY* as Gen Z is the do-it-yourself generation (Stillman & Stillman, 2017). They have grown up with YouTube – a source they use to access, entertainment, music, information, and *how to* instructions (Seemiller & Grace, 2016). The seventh concept is *Driven* as they will be more competitive and private than any of the generations before them (Stillman & Stillman, 2017). For example, Stillman and Stillman (2017) found 72% of Gen Z stated they are competitive with people performing the same job as them.

The Intersection of Millennials and Gen Z

Both Millennials and Gen Z comprise higher education, hold many characteristics in common, and yet are quite different in other respects. Both are confident, value diversity, and maximize technology for learning (Debard, 2004; Rickes, 2016; Seemiller & Grace, 2016); however, the latter relies on YouTube for on-demand learning (Seemiller & Grace, 2016) that is immediate and timely versus scheduled learning preferred by Millennials (Rickes, 2016). Moreover, Millennials are often referred to as the "Me Generation" (Seemiller & Grace, 2016) assumedly focused on themselves and personal benefit, while the up and coming Gen Z students embody a collective identity of what is good for all as the "We Generation" (Seemiller & Grace, 2016). Relatedly, an orientation to service is valued by both generations, but Gen Z place higher value on service that facilitates social change (Seemiller & Grace, 2016).

Unlike Millennials and regardless of their reliance on the mobile phone as the "only screen," Gen Z strives for a slower and simplified being than that of their predecessors. Rickes (2016) pointed to the admiration for board games, vinyl records, and other forms of what once was evidence of a more simplified existence. The focus of Gen Z is upon curriculum, technological skills, and clear pathways to meaningful careers rather than college campus amenities and recognition of achievement likened to Millennials. These characteristics influence the shape and structure of curriculum delivery and academic support.

The aforementioned intersections of Gen Z and Millennials result in consideration of how the intersection of both generations in higher education might warrant expansion or change in practice for supporting and engaging college students, especially within digital environments. Gen Z, like the Millennials before them, are challenging the established student engagement approaches that were used. This challenging of current practices suggests that the current status quo of engagement approaches needs additional reconsideration. There are some direct implications for practice that can be gleaned in response from this challenge from Gen Z. However, it is first important to understand how students engage in college and how universities are defining this concept.

STUDENT ENGAGEMENT IN COLLEGE

Kuh's Theory of Student Engagement (Kuh et al., 1991) emphasized the importance of out-of-class experiences where a great deal of learning occurs. In relation, Kuh et al. (1991) remarked that "all aspects of the institution's environment contribute to student learning and personal development" (p. 374). The campus environment can be experienced along a continuum from confusing and alienating to coherent and supportive (Kuh et al., 1991). Four reasons were identified to support the relevance of out-of-class activities (Kuh et al., 1991). First, college students spend most of their time out of class, and second, how they spend their time is influenced by their peers. Students acquire valuable skills not often presented through their academic curriculum. Finally, involvement in out-of-class activities enables the student to experience a sense of community. Kuh, Schuh, Whitt, and Associates (2005) identified two components of engagement: the time and effort of students to engage and the way in which the institution frames resources and opportunities. The authors maintained resulting student effort would yield greater critical thinking, problem-solving, effective communication, and responsible citizenship.

Student interaction with faculty has a "salutary effect on student satisfaction and feelings of belonging" (Kuh et al., 1991, p. 257). In their work, Kuh et al. (1991) presented a historical shift in faculty involvement with students outside of the classroom wherein the commitment to the welfare of students experienced shrinkage due to changing faculty roles and institutional expectations. At involving colleges, Kuh et al. (1991) found students developed meaningful relationships with other institutional members, such as upper-class students with junior and senior status, coaches, and staff members. When engagement is contingent upon the educational environment and institutional size, "institutional agents" (Kuh et al., 1991, p. 259) challenge students to take risks and engage in developmental learning processes, while providing support and encouragement.

Kuh et al. (1991) emphasized the importance of the campus environment and considered students' behavior to be reflective of interactions with its various subenvironments. Subcultures of involving colleges, such as student organizations, fraternity and sorority life, and learning communities, provided a sense of community and belonging. Kuh et al. (1991) maintained high-quality out-of-class experiences exist in environments where the mission, faculty priorities, and student affairs' objectives work are interwoven and complementary. All members of the educational community are vital to the student experience. However, Kuh et al. (2005) stressed the importance of a dense network of efforts and found most effective institutions utilized paraprofessionals, or peer students, which improved the climate for learning.

The confluence of support from institutional agents and peers enables the student to grow and develop and acknowledges the student as a valuable member of the educational community (Kuh et al., 1991). However, support and encouragement must reflect the needs, culture, and differences of the student themselves. For example, Kuh et al. (1991) threw caution to student overinvolvement and highlighted the importance of institutional agents in modeling and teaching skills needed for balance. In addition, reflection and processing of experiences (tending to affective states) must exceed beyond planning and management of the student's engagement (Kuh et al., 2005). The overall goal of student engagement is to facilitate a stronger sense of belonging as defined by Glasser (1988) for students as an outcome. Sense of belonging as an outcome can be challenging in the context of online engagement.

Therefore, facilitating community to create a sense of belonging is essential to student learning and persistence toward graduation. There is a myriad of approaches that can combine hybrid technology approaches for Gen Z and Millennial students as distance learners to better promote sense of belonging.

IMPLICATIONS FOR PRACTICE

Kozinsky (2017) described contemporary college students and suggested that traditional undergraduates are invested in a learner-centric environment where students will become the directors of their own futures driven by the innovation of new learning tools, teaching styles, and unlimited access to digital resources. This presents challenges for student engagement as current student support models such as academic advising are restructured and resituated to accommodate for Gen Z students. This recalibration impacts academic support structures and programing, which are suggested in the next section.

Academic Advisors

Online students desired for advisors to initiate contact proactively, as they preferred a sense of connection with their advisor and program (Cross, 2018; Gravel, 2012; Schroeder & Terras, 2015). Seemiller and Grace (2016) characterized interpersonal interactions as extremely important to Gen Z. Transparency is also important to this Gen Z as they are problem solvers. Distance learners also desire timeliness of response (Schroeder & Terras, 2015). In their study, Schroeder and Terras found online learners relied heavily on their advisor for understanding programatic and institutional policies. Finally, Cross (2018) found learners prefer their advisor is knowledgeable and demonstrates positive support through an ethic of care, advocacy, and accessibility. Beyond faculty mentors, it is important in supporting distance learners to create an academic advising system where students have one-on-one access to a generalist expert who can support them in areas not necessarily related to the content of the course. These are often referred to as "performance coaches" to provide students with connections to coaching in writing, project management, leadership, research, presentation delivery, or even career advice.

At some institutions, distance education students should be aware that their tuition pays for the same resources as on-ground students. At other institutions, there might be a differential tuition between on-ground students and that of distance learners. Often, distance education students may need support in navigating their access to the library, online databases, or discount tickets to arts and entertainment events. Helping them feel a part of a physical campus community strengthens motivation and sense of belonging. Gravel (2012) emphasized the importance of developmental academic support that employs both synchronous and asynchronous communication.

Optimizing Technology for Student Engagement

Both Millennials and Gen Z student populations require academic learning and support as well as professors to be agile and adaptable in adaptation of course curriculum (Mazer & Hess, 2016). Mazer and Hess (2016) recommended curriculum be meaningful, wherein students contribute knowledge from an array of nontraditional online sources in expansion beyond course materials. Considering the unique traits of both Millennial and Gen Z college students, one must consider the most effective methods for engaging both in the virtual classroom. A lecture without images or hands-on learning will fall short in connecting with this contemporary college student. Professors must optimize technology and evolve innovatively to engage students in collaborative work.

Rickes (2016) also identified visual literacy as well as practical and hands-on learning as imperative to the meaningful experiences Gen Z desires. Because the cell phone is the only screen upon which this population relies, the optimization of technology is void of user barriers and easy to deploy in physical or virtual classrooms.

Both Millennials and Gen Z hold experience in electronic gaming. Virtual academic gaming, such as that provided by Jeopardy or Kahoot, prove useful as a tool for mastering or reviewing content and in engaging students in the virtual classroom (Cameron & Pagnattaro, 2017). Last, apps and blogs within learning management systems serve as a substitute for physical journaling in harvesting reflection and mindfulness. Lastly, alignment of learning with industry is key to engaging the career-minded Gen Z (Seemiller & Grace, 2016). This generation values initiatives for social change and expects social consciousness to be a component of curriculum (Seemiller & Grace, 2016).

Collaborative Learning Formats

Specifically, faculty in virtual classrooms can create assignments that are co-curricular experiential learning experiences (Frederick et al., 2018). This can be in the format of community-based learning in which randomly assigned student groups have "clients" or interact with organizations that utilize the student expertise. This forces students to work with organizations and produce materials that will actually be used in real time (Frederick et al., 2018). This approach as client-based, community-based learning work requires personal interaction and produces positive pressure, which both influences motivation to learn. Beyond requiring that students work with a client in a group collaborative format, students should repeat the learning experience with a different group and client. With any client-based, community-based learning, students should establish team roles, assigning one as a different leader for each of the two client projects. Overall, this type of learning experience may have the following outcomes: (1) students work with two different clients in one semester which connects with professionals; (2) reinforces learning as they engage in the same work twice with different conditions, but with peer collaboration in which they engage in reciprocal learning from one another; (3) builds critical leadership and teamwork skills identified as important to Millennials and Gen Z students; and (4) teaches soft skills of time management and motivation as students are accountable to each other for both learning and production of the client-based projects.

In-person Residency

Hybrid education formats that require an in-person residency two to three times per year should bring students to the physical campus (Frederick et al., 2018). This will allow them to interact and network with each other, faculty, and other relevant college staff members. This facilitates a sense of belonging, which enhances motivation, retention, and student success (Tinto, 2012). Often students who live out of state or the geographic region of the program will fly in for these residencies.

Faculty/Staff Site Visits

For those programs that have clinical placements or experiential learning experiences such as internships, program faculty and staff should facilitate site visits to connect with their students (Frederick et al., 2018). This is especially meaningful to students if they do not live in the same state or geographic area as the academic program. Additionally, for ease of administration, the burden of responsibility can be placed on the student in which they are required to set up their own visits. Site visits can also assume the format of students visiting key locations or professionals in their fields of study (Frederick et al., 2018). For example, if the program is an online public relations or marketing program, the students can be required to visit a sports branding agency or complete a walk-through of a large-scale printing press.

Consistent and Substantive Interaction

Student affairs professionals and faculty in facilitating online learning spaces can readily facilitate substantive interaction using distance technology (Frederick et al., 2018). These can include visual formats beyond phone calls or students who live near campus meeting with you in person. The concept of "substantive" interaction is more than just written feedback on assignments. It should include interpersonal communication where conversations can be elaborated and insights can be deepened. Therefore, experiences such as using Zoom or other concurrent synchronous video chat platforms can humanize the student experiences for events such as speakers or other class discussions. Other experiences can be facilitated through a variety of other accessible free technologies that facilitate interaction. These may include Slack for project management; Google Hangouts, Zoom, or Skype for video conferencing; or WeChat which is social media that allows file sharing. This allows students to engage in regular conversation with faculty or staff such as their academic advisor. Higher education should move beyond their common learning management system and email (Frederick et al., 2018). Higher education should also communicate the way Gen Z and Millennials communicate in real life as social isolation should rarely happen in confluent online programs.

Course Travel or Immersion Experience

Many institutions through their division of student affairs offer events such as a service-learning experience alternative spring break or a winter ski trip (Frederick et al., 2018). Other academic programs may offer large-scale international trips to the Cape of Good Hope or to the straits of Gibraltar. It is the opinion of the authors that often distance education students are forgotten as they are invisible to traditional undergraduate student affairs engagement programs.

These co-curricular engagement opportunities might seem unrealistic for some institutions, programs, faculty, and student (Sasso & DeVitis, 2015). However, a short-term faculty-led experience such as for in-state, regional, or national trips may also be considered where students travel as a group, network, and establish relationships. It is highly encouraged that such experiences should be "flat rate" and is integrated as part of tuition. This encourages students to attend and to not back out based on financial limitations. Gen Z and Millennials are very price-point conscious due to the burden of cost to attend higher education (Seemiller & Grace, 2016). The learning experience should include some sort of project to connect to their programatic learning, which then becomes more tangible and valuable. Students make long-lasting professional relationships from these experiences and connect it to their professional identity (Sasso & DeVitis, 2015).

CONCLUSION

This chapter highlighted the complexities involved when considering the intersection of Millennial and Gen Z students in college. Student engagement theory provides an understanding of the importance of engagement, connection, and support, especially that of distance learners. While both generations are digitally bound, the reliance of Gen Z on technology with a desire for interpersonal connection warrants strategic innovation in higher education. This expands beyond the virtual learning environment to academic support and other respective out-of-class experiences.

For Gen Z distance students, every element of their virtual classroom experience needs co-curricular experiences to facilitate a sense of belonging that allows students connection with classmates. Millennials already have the comfort level with technology and willingness to make relationships at a distance. By infusing any online class with discussions, live sessions, collaborative projects, small group work, faculty can be the conduit by which students find the affiliation and belonging. Concurrently, student affairs professionals and academic advisors should remember to facilitate connections to available co-curricular experiences and academic supports that are accessible to them as these students are not invisible.

REFERENCES

American Academy of Child and Adolescent Psychiatry. (2011). Facts for families: Multiracial children. Retrieved from http://www.aacap.org/App_Themes/AACAP/docs/facts_for_families/71_multiracial_children.pdf

Brown, P. G. (2016). College students, social media, digital identities, and the digitized self (Doctoral dissertation). Retrieved from ProQuest Dissertations and Theses. (Accession Order No. 1776598125).

Cameron, E. A., & Pagnattaro, M. A. (2017). Beyond millennials: Engaging Generation Z in business law classes. *Journal of Legal Studies Education, 34*(2), 317–324.

Cross, L. K. (2018). Graduate student perceptions of online advising. *NACADA Journal, 38*(2), 72–80.

DeBard, R. (2004). Millennials coming to college. In M. D. Coomes & R. DeBard (Eds.), Serving the Millennial generation (pp. 33–45). New Directions for Student Services, No. 106. San Francisco, CA: Jossey-Bass.

Frederick, M., Sasso, P. A., & Maldonado, J. (2018). The dynamic student development meta-theory: A new model for student success. New York, NY: Peter Lang Publishing.

Fry, R. (2015). This year, Millennials will overtake Baby Boomers. Retrieved from http://www.pewresearch.org/fact-tank/2015/01/16/this-year-millennials-will-overtake-baby-boomers/

Garrison, D.R. (2007) Online community of inquiry review: Social, cognitive, and teaching presence issues. *Journal of Asynchronous Learning Networks, 11*, 61–72.

Glasser, W. (1998). *Choice theory: A new psychology of personal freedom*. New York, NY: HarperCollins.

Gravel, C. A. (2012). Student-advisor interaction in undergraduate online degree programs: A factor in student retention. *NACADA Journal, 32*(2), 56–67.

Hope, J. (2016). Get your campus ready for Generation Z. Dean & Provost, 17(8), 1–7.4.

Howe, N., & Strauss, W. (1991). Generations: The history of America's future, 1584–2069. New York, NY: William Morrow and Company.

Howe, N., & Strauss, W. (2000). Millennials rising: The next great generation. New York, NY: Vintage Books.

Kozinsky, S. (2017, July 24). How Generation Z is shaping the change in education. *Forbs*. Retrieved from https://www.forbes.com/sites/sievakozinsky/2017/07/24/how-generation-z-is-shaping-the-change-in-education/?sh=5f587ec66520

Kuh, G. D., Schuh, J. H., Whitt, E. J., & Associates. (1991). Involving colleges. San Francisco, CA: Jossey-Bass.

Kuh, G. D., Schuh, J. H., Whitt, E. J., & Associates. (2005). Student success in college: Creating conditions that matter. San Francisco, CA: Jossey-Bass.

Loveland, E. (2017). Instant generation. *Journal of College Admission, 234*, 34–38.

Mazer, J. P., & Hess, J. A. (2016). Forum: Instructional communication and Millennial students. *Communication Education, 65*(3), 356–376.

Rickes, P. C. (2016). How Gen Z will continue to transform higher education space. *Planning for Higher Education Journal, 44*(4), 1–25.

Sasso, P. A., & DeVitis, J. L. (2015). *Today's college student: A reader.* New York, NY: Peter Lang Publishing.

Sasso, P. A., Dayton, B., & Rosseter, S. (2015). A generation divided: An in-depth view of millennial students. In P. A. Sasso, & J. L. DeVitis (Eds), *Today's college student.* New York, NY: Peter Lang Publishing.

Schroeder, S. M., & Terras, K. L. (2015). Advising experiences and needs of online, cohort, and classroom adult graduate learners. *NACADA Journal, 35*(1), 42–55.

Seemiller, C., & Grace, M. (2016). Generation Z goes to college. San Francisco, CA: Jossey-Bass.

Stillman, D., & Stillman, J. (2017). *Generation Z @ work: How the next generation is transforming the workplace.* New York, NY: Happer Collins.

Tacoli, C. (2012). Urbanization, gender, and urban poverty: Paid work and unpaid care work in the city. Retrieved from http://www.unfpa.org/webdav/site/global/shared/documents/publications/2012/UEPI%207%20acoli%20Mar%202012.pdf

Tinto, V. (2012). *Completing college: Rethinking institutional action.* University of Chicago Press.

Twenge, J. M. (2006). *Generation me: Why today's young Americans are more confident, assertive, entitled – and more miserable than ever before.* New York, NY: Simon & Schuster.

Twenge, J. M. (2017). *iGen: Why today's super-connected kids are growing up less rebellious, more tolerant, less happy – and completely unprepared for adulthood – and what that means for the rest of us.* New York, NY: Atria Books.

U.S. Census Bureau (2017). *Births, deaths, and migration transform communities.* Retrieved from https://www.census.gov/library/stories/2017/08/changing-nation-demographic-trends.html

Walker, J. T., Martin, T., White, J., Norwood, A., & Haynie, L. (2006). Generational age differences impact on the college classroom. *Journal of the Mississippi Academic of Sciences, 51*(4), 215–219.

Wenger, E. (2000). Communities of practice and social learning systems. *Organization, 7*, 225–246.

Williams, A. (2015, September 18). Move over, Millennials: Here come Generation Z. *New York Times.* Retrieved from https://www.nytimes.com/2015/09/20/fashion/move-over-millennials-here-comes-generation-z.html

PROMOTING STUDENT ENGAGEMENT WITH DATA-DRIVEN PRACTICES*

Jeremy Anderson, Heather Bushey, Maura Devlin and Amanda J. Gould

ABSTRACT

Online learning can present challenges and barriers for students, especially when it comes to self-motivation and discipline. Non-traditional learners and those who may be underprepared are often the students most likely to seek virtual learning options. As a result, methods of supporting online learners must be intentional and robust to stay attentive to students' needs. The American Women's College (TAWC) at Bay Path University designed its Social Online Universal Learning (SOUL) model to promote degree completion through a constellation of evidence-based practices that cultivate student engagement in a personalized online learning environment. SOUL employs an innovative adaptive technology approach with Universal Design for Learning (UDL) principles to promote accessibility and affordability. Foundational to these frameworks is a commitment to leveraging technology to gather data that drives action-oriented analytics, triggering interventions by faculty and staff and generating predictive models to inform wrap-around support. SOUL's high-tech, high-touch attributes give students agency over their unique learning paths and provide instructors and administrators the meaningful insights needed to target efforts in a personalized yet scalable way, to promote and

---

*This chapter is derived in part from an article published in *Change: The Magazine of Higher Learning* in November/December 2019. Retrieved from https://www.tandfonline.com/doi/full/10.1080/00091383.2019.1674096

positively impact student success. Lessons learned in the process of developing data-driven "high-tech, high-touch" practices are presented.

Keywords: Adaptive; advising; analytics; coach; data-driven; engagement; online; personalized; predictive; technology.

As a private, non-profit, regionally accredited institution, Bay Path University has had a long history of innovating to provide practical, career-oriented programs to its region since 1897. In the 1990s, the university recognized a challenge that needed to be addressed: Adult learners in the United States were enrolling in part-time, semester-long classes, pursuing studies at night, taking years to accumulate sufficient credit, and finding the path to degree completion prohibitively long and winding. The prevailing traditional model did not serve well nontraditional students who were older than 24, working full-time, raising children (many single-handedly) while pursuing education.

Bay Path University responded in 1999 by adding the One-Day-a-Week Saturday Program to its women's only undergraduate offerings to provide the opportunity to pursue education around the myriad other responsibilities competing for adult women's time. The One-Day model disrupted the traditional academic calendar with accelerated six-week, face-to-face sessions offered six times over an academic year, each of which could be an entry point. For the first-time, prospective adult women students were able to enroll full-time and to complete bachelor's degrees in as little as three and a half years.

As part of this model, Bay Path cultivated a number of support services that enhanced the promise of degree success for these women, many of whom had experienced little encouragement or attention from traditional programs. With a goal of making higher education more accessible and affordable, and in response to shifting demographics, learner preferences, and advancements in technology, Bay Path University introduced The American Women's College (TAWC) in 2013 as a way to further expand access provided by the One-Day model. TAWC offered a low-cost, fully online, accelerated baccalaureate degree and was the first entirely online program exclusively for women in the nation. Early in its history, TAWC received federal funding through the Department of Education's Fund for the Improvement of Postsecondary Education (FIPSE) to develop a revolutionary model called Social Online Universal Learning (SOUL), to deliver high-quality and socially connected learning experiences to underserved students who depend on affordable but effective distance education opportunities.

ELEMENTS OF THE SOUL MODEL

TAWC developed SOUL after initially writing a strategic white paper that drew from educational research and literature to identify elements necessary to support adult women undergraduates in remote learning environments. The white paper explored pedagogical frameworks and adult learning theory (Akbulut & Cardak, 2012; Aslanian & Clinefelter, 2012; Brusilovsky & Peylo, 2003), motivational sources of support among women (Bond, 2008; Cragg, Andrusyszyn, & Fraser, 2005; Dweck, 1986; Furst-Bowe & Dittmann, 2001; Owens, Hardcastle, & Richardson, 2009), and variables that enhance online retention (Allen & Seaman, 2013; Dupin-Bryant, 2004; Moody, 2004). The result of this research was the thoughtful incorporation of six major aspects that comprise the SOUL approach, each of which contains initiatives, structured workflows, and opportunities to collect evidence of student achievement (see Fig. 1).

This ecosystem capitalizes on consistent practices in teaching and advising that promote systematic data collection. Well-structured data, in turn, generates business intelligence that prescribes proactive approaches for impacting student success. Collectively, the constellation of pedagogical innovations, student-centered supports and coaching, virtual opportunities to engage socially, and faculty professional development facilitate student persistence at TAWC at average rates consistent with first-time full-time, traditional face-to-face learning environments and more than double those of fully online education providers serving non-traditional populations (US Department of Education, National Center for Education Statistics, 2016).

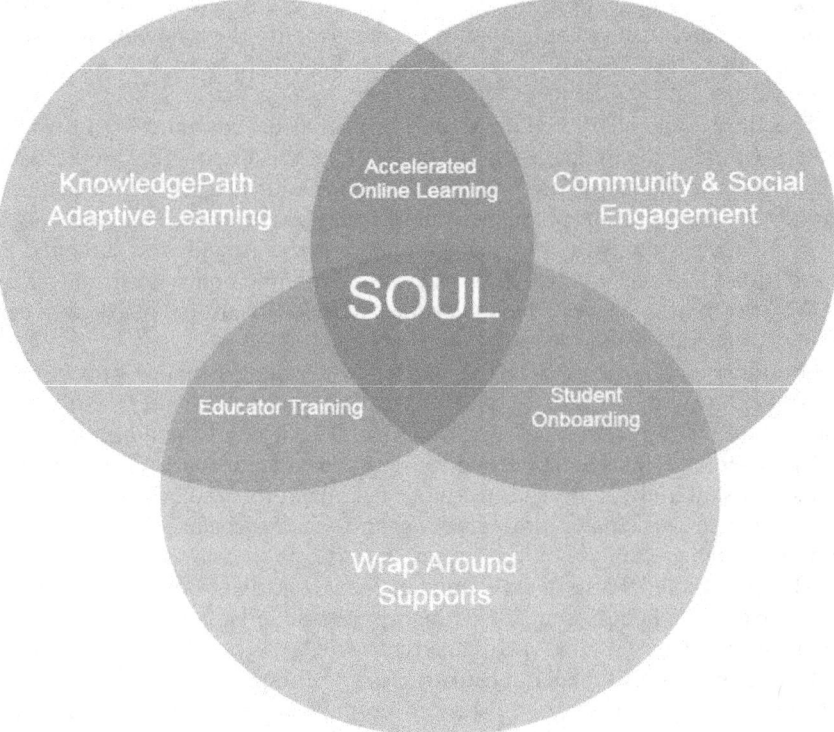

Fig. 1. Social Online Universal Learning model

A primary aspect of SOUL is the accelerated nature of the coursework that facilitates students' immersion and momentum in only one or two courses at a time. This enhances course completion rates, which tend to be around 90%, for all attempted credits; this compares to 78% for online courses in other institutional contexts (Poulin, 2013). The six-week, session-based model also can lessen the time to degree completion. For the majority of non-traditional learners who enroll with transfer credits or who earn credits for demonstrating mastery of course competencies through TAWC's Prior Learning Assessment process, a customized in-house process that requires completing a three-credit course on adult learning theory, knowledge acquisition, and understanding of competency in order to develop course equivalency-based portfolios of evidence, the time to degree at TAWC has an average duration of two and a half years.

Next, SOUL incorporates an intentional on-boarding process (SOUL Connect) for all new students, including a mandatory orientation course. The goals of this element are to familiarize students with the virtual classroom and to assess college readiness habits and dispositions. This fosters immediate opportunities to connect with a dedicated professional academic advisor to talk about coursework, academic success skills such as time management, and the college's support services, such as tutoring, disability accommodations, experiential learning opportunities, peer mentors, and career programs. Through early, low-risk introductions to advising staff and peers, new students also begin to develop relationships that enhance persistence into the following semester, a rate that like course completion rates is consistently around 90% for entering students.

The third element of SOUL is the intentional on-boarding for instructors (SOUL Connect for Educators). Two goals guide this orientation. First, faculty are introduced to pedagogical practices for online adult learners. One orientation module, for example, promotes the skill of leveraging learning analytics in data-rich virtual classrooms to optimize personalized engagement with students. The orientation course also prepares faculty to navigate the online environment and TAWC's learning tools. As a result, by the end of on-boarding, instructors demonstrate an ability to blend theory and practice.

Another key aspect is SOUL Communities, which includes opportunities for students to engage socially and academically with their peers, with career coaches, and with professional mentors. Virtual Learning Communities (VLCs), discipline-specific hubs for accessing content and career resources specific to students' fields of study, is one such example. Peer mentors, who engage one-on-one with students, participate in orientations, and manage social media groups, are another vital means of promoting community in our virtual environment.

The SOUL model also directly impacts the virtual classroom. Approximately one quarter of all courses at TAWC incorporate adaptive assignments using an adaptive learning system (ALS) called KnowledgePath. The ALS provides a method that allows students and instructors to follow granular learning maps that link concepts into pre-, post-, and co-requisite relationships. Data gathered through students' interactions in course assignments enable instructors to scale personalized instruction and learning opportunities to each student and provide just-in-time remediation when needed. Adaptive courses thus engender "high-tech, high-touch" practices to personalize teaching.

SOUL's final element, and the one discussed in most detail in this chapter, is wrap-around supports, a variety of interventions and proactive outreach by faculty and support staff, powered by data on student activity or generated with predictive analytics models. This element also includes the use of social media platforms and mentors in intentional intervention strategies. A case management model facilitates the planful bridging of communication among those engaging with students within and outside the virtual classroom to capture all touchpoints in the student life cycle.

Over the past five years, Bay Path has invested substantial resources, both financial and human, to fine-tune the development and delivery of SOUL. This has included clearly defining staff and faculty roles and responsibilities, providing training and development, and incorporating key vendor partners to efficiently and cost-effectively manage and scale its academic operations as enrollment has grown. TAWC's success in supporting online students is evident in its metrics: Overall satisfaction rates from graduating students in May 2019 were 93% and completion rates were 64%, a rate more than 20 percentage points higher than the national average for adult learners (Shapiro et al., 2019).

INFRASTRUCTURE SUPPORTING THE SOUL MODEL

A suite of integrated technologies provides the infrastructure that undergirds the model. Advisors and support staff work within a customer relationship management (CRM) system to guide students through their educational journey. The learning management system (LMS) and social media platforms provide an avenue for the virtual community of peers to inspire and motivate one another. Sitting at the center of these tools is a data warehouse that serves to aggregate various data streams pertaining to student engagement and success. Included in the feeds are sources such as the student information system (SIS), CRM, LMS, ALS, financial aid system, and tutoring platform, which are often housed in siloed systems at higher education institutions. When combined, they provide a holistic picture of the student experience that otherwise would be elusive. Data analytics and business intelligence tools then ride atop the warehouse to facilitate interventions and to visualize each student's path and potential roadblocks to degree completion (see Fig. 2). Students who are considered "at risk" for various reasons, such as low levels of interaction or poor course performance, are identified via analytics and provided with appropriate outreach to promote academic engagement and successful course completion.

To achieve the supports embedded in SOUL, TAWC populates courses in the LMS through a centralized development model, wherein all sections of a course begin with the same core content and assessments. Consistent business rules govern the functioning of courses, including expectations for feedback on

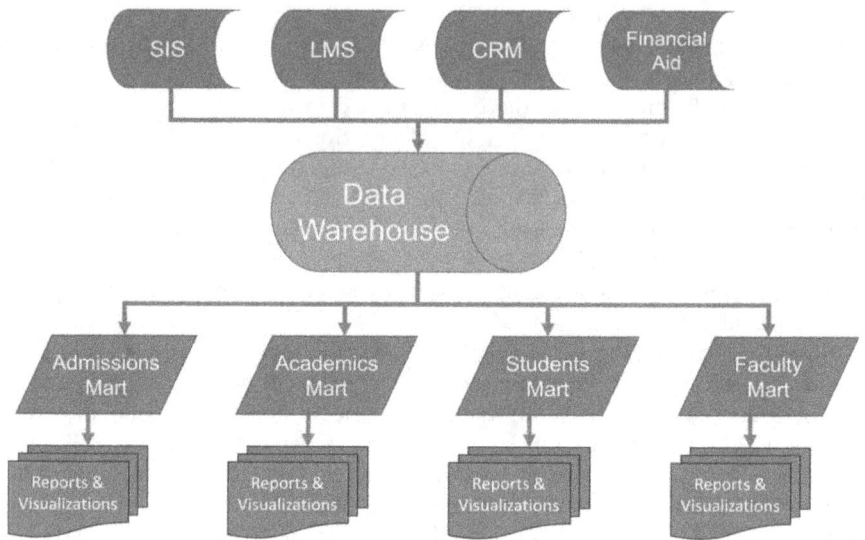

Fig. 2. Sources of student data integrate into a data warehouse

assignments, faculty and student interaction, and faculty interventions. Because student performance data in the warehouse can be consistently identified and retrieved at the assignment level, these attributes allow academic leaders to ensure high levels of quality in course design, instruction, and assessment, fostering student success. Together, the technology tools and business practices combine to drive day-to-day interactions with students and strategic decision-making.

WRAP-AROUND SUPPORT FRAMEWORK FOR STUDENT ENGAGEMENT

To capitalize on data to inform wrap-around support practices that leverage technology to proactively provide students with advising and support services throughout the student life cycle, SOUL employs a predictive analytics framework (Ice et al., 2012). Dedicated professional advisors, called educator coaches, play the most visible role in the student life cycle, outside of the online classroom, by acting upon each student status and enacting the appropriate high-impact practices from a toolbox of intervention strategies. These "high-tech, high-touch" interventions, multiple human interactions for each student facilitated by data and technology, are the supports that wrap-around a student's learning experience in each of her courses. Using technology, data and social networks, TAWC thus promotes constructive, active engagement, which, when combined with learners' agency augmented through curricular incorporation of the ALS and Universal Design for Learning (UDL) principles, positively impacts online students' success.

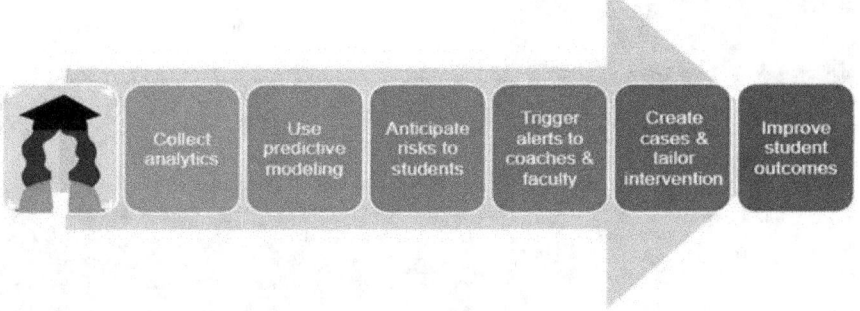

Fig. 3. Predictive analytics workflow that ensures that data are used consistently. *Source*: Devlin & Bushey, 2019, p. 22.

Predictive Analytics

Data facilitate the construction of student profiles that lead to better understanding of each student's full experience. Similar to the personalization afforded by adaptive learning, the creation of a network of support that adapts to meet each student's unique needs is central to the model. TAWC's student-centered, wrap-around support model uses data-driven intervention strategies and predictive triggers to be as attentive as possible to distance learners.

Qualitative and quantitative data brought together via the data warehouse from the LMS, the ALS, the SIS, as well as other technology tools such as an online tutoring service, provide a complete view of each student's experience and profile in order to support students with varying levels of academic preparedness and differing educational experiences. TAWC's CRM software, Salesforce, allows educator coaches to convert predictive analytics data into actionable and trackable cases. By marrying the technology of the CRM and data from the warehouse, predictive analytics grant educator coaches the ability to "explore and analyze factors affecting student retention, progression and completion" (Ice et al., 2012, p. 65) and tailor interventions accordingly.

Insights into students' behaviors can be nuanced. In the case of participation, for example, a student can be compared against two profiles. First, since each student tends to be one of hundreds enrolled across multiple sections of the same course, trends in each week's online discussion board can be used as a basis to compare a student to average participation. Second, each student has her own profile of engagement in discussion boards that has been built across her time at the institution. While the course instructor focuses on the quality of students' discussion posts and whether competencies are demonstrated, quantitative deviations from both the course mean and the student's past performance serve as warning flags incorporated in the predictive analytics model that drive automated and manual interventions. Outreaches to students based on predictive analytics are aimed at guiding students toward beneficial behaviors that engender success.

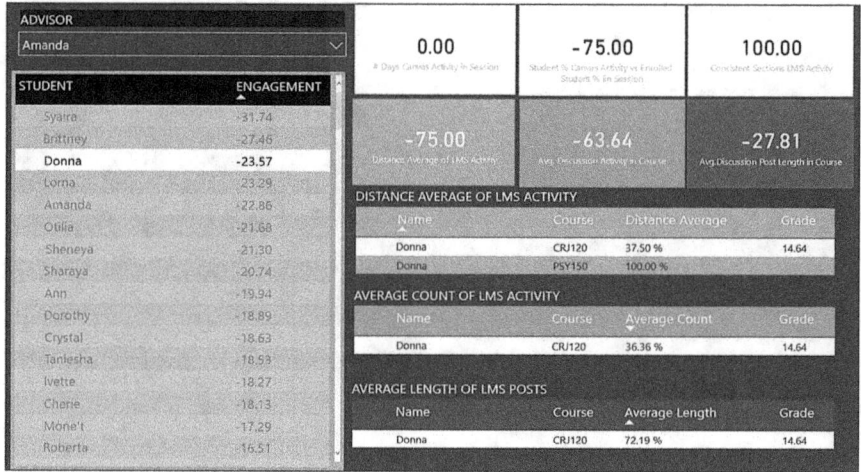

Fig. 4. Student engagement dashboards display data for advisors
Source: Devlin & Bushey, 2019, p. 24.

Data-informed Interventions

The consistent application of business rules paired with systematic approaches enable TAWC to identify meaningful data-informed intervention opportunities to target students at risk of not persisting. Specifically, TAWC's data inform proactive outreach by educator coaches to students who are not participating in the LMS, to those with low scores on assignments, and to those who miss assignments altogether. Timely outreach, especially in six-week sessions, is imperative to keep students on track.

TAWC's intervention strategies derive from predictive analytics and from literature and research on academic success. For example, adult students without previous experience in higher education or with low grade point averages (GPAs) are known to be at academic risk in online classes (Bernard, Brauer, Abrami, & Surkes, 2004; Packham, Jones, Miller, & Brychan, 2004). TAWC educator coaches therefore utilize data to identify incoming students who fall into this risk category and pair them with more academically experienced peer mentors. Pairing new online students, who potentially have low levels of academic self-efficacy, with peer mentors who have accumulated academic capital but who also share similar life experiences increases the likelihood of their success.

Building Community

Social media platforms connect learners and educators in the online environment by allowing a designated space for social, academic, and advising interactions, a form of virtual community that mitigates the effects of isolated learning. At TAWC, this is accomplished through a private advising Facebook group, a tool for interaction and support that is popular among online learners (Dougherty &

Andercheck, 2014; Hurt et al., 2012). Nearly 50% of TAWC's online students are members of the private Facebook group, and in a recent 12-month span (September 2018–September 2019), Facebook analytics data indicated that over 1,940 posts were created, soliciting nearly 45,000 comments or reactions by group members (TAWC Advising Community, n.d.). Activity in the private group ranges from messages of support, to venting concerns, to seeking input from more experienced peers. Facebook analytics also provide insight into the most active days and hours among group members. TAWC uses these data to inform other areas of support for online learners such as tutoring and library services.

Technology also makes it possible to create opportunities for collaborative and interactive learning experiences within the virtual classroom. All courses at TAWC utilize some form of collaborative assignments, such as group projects, peer review assignments, and discussion prompts that require multiple peer responses. Students demonstrate mastery of learning through the use of video responses to discussion board prompts, presentations, or group project work. Embedded in the process are relevant technology tools, such as a live meeting collaborative document platform, which are intended to foster connectedness in an online learning environment. By providing social and academic experiences to online students, collaborative learning occurs naturally, and learner satisfaction is increased (Rovai, 2003; Tinto, 1993).

Membership in a learning community can help diminish feelings of isolation and cause an upsurge in student satisfaction among online learners (Rovai, 2001). "The central purpose of a virtual learning community (VLC) is to bring people together to provide support, exchange knowledge, and facilitate interactions and connections among members" (Blanchard & Cook, 2012, p. 86). TAWC uses VLCs in its LMS, not only to promote a sense of community and collaboration but also to assist students in making clear connections between education and chosen career fields to ensure more consequential student learning experiences (Knowles, 1984).

Discipline-specific, career-focused VLCs provide students with a venue for exploring job postings, inquiring about their desired field of study, keeping current on trends in the field, and connecting with professionals. VLCs connect students, faculty, staff, and community members who have interests in similar fields, providing them with space outside virtual classrooms where they can network (Blanchard & Cook, 2012). Engaging students in a VLC is a way of addressing the lack of engagement in online learning that can lead to attrition (Omar, Hassan, & Atan, 2011) and promoting "individualized goal setting and career plan development" (Brinthaupt, 2010, p. 58). Linking education to employment and professional pathways also promotes students' motivation and pursuit of goals (Bandura, 1993; Dweck, 1986; Elliott & Dweck, 1988; Knowles, 1984; Zimmerman, 2000). Student interaction with each of these virtual communities is a sign of engagement and, when collected and tracked, can be predictive of student success.

Faculty Early Alert

Proactive faculty support is a far more effective strategy aimed at student retention than waiting to intervene only if a student initiates outreach (Simpson, 2004). Faculty members are uniquely positioned to anticipate student needs given their practice of the art of teaching. Their qualitative insights, informed by innumerable interactions with students, are a perfect complement to the quantitative nature of data analytics, and consistent communication between faculty and student support team members is a strong and necessary pillar of wrap-around support.

Faculty feedback is particularly helpful in identifying students who are disengaged from a course. Leveraging technology to make this as easy as possible increases the likelihood that faculty will pass this information along, especially "if a distance learning student hasn't been responding the first few weeks of the course, the instructor can pass on the student's name through this automated system" (Faculty Focus, 2009, p. 4). Data communicated through the faculty alert form are also stored in the data warehouse, in conjunction with the CRM, creating an automated case that is actionable by educator coaches. Aggregations over time of early alerts at the level of the individual student also create an overall profile of how a student engages and performs in courses. Both views of the data – just-in-time and longitudinal – allow all constituents to assess student classroom behavior in order to play an active role in promoting student success.

Fostering Relationships in the Online Classroom

At the intersection of advanced technology and traditional teaching techniques, there is a unique teaching methodology in more traditional classroom settings that is not exactly replicable in virtual learning environments (Rowntree, 1995). TAWC's online course pedagogy involves an interactive teaching role that requires faculty to utilize technology to personalize the learning experience. For online students, having the ability to form trusting and supportive relationships with faculty members is vital to their ability to feel a meaningful connection to their education and the institution.

To combat the challenges of building a positive rapport when teaching and learning activities are performed remotely, faculty use video announcements and brief recorded lectures so that students can connect a name and written feedback with a face and a voice. Online instructors are required to post weekly videos on the topic of their choice but often include mini-lectures, clarification on assignments, and supplemental learning resources. Videos not only promote inclusion in online classrooms, but they can also positively impact completion rates of online courses (Geri, 2012). Connections facilitated through video create a more personalized and meaningful learning experience and make it possible for faculty members to add a personal touch to their teaching methods.

There are several additional ways for online instructors to engage students in the online classroom. Quality and detailed feedback on assignments, interactive discussion board requirements, and group work are other useful ways instructors facilitate engagement in the LMS (Geri, 2012). When social interaction and collaboration are encouraged in the online classroom and modeled by the instructor, students become more invested in their own success and the success of their classmates (Abrami & Bures, 1996) and learn how to reciprocate engagement and social interaction.

Through all of the methods described above, TAWC employs data collection methods to understand students' engagement in a variety of virtual interfaces, in addition to course learning experiences, to assess holistically ways to provide intentional support. The predictive analytics framework facilitates meaningful retrieval of formerly siloed data from the warehouse in order to identify student needs and provide purposeful, proactive interventions, deployed early and often, to students most at risk. Consistent application of data elements and consistent capitalization of data-informed strategies thus facilitate wrap-around supports that foster online adult learners' persistence and degree completion.

LESSONS LEARNED

Having spent the last five years constructing, assessing, and improving aspects of the SOUL model, our experiences yielded many lessons learned. There is no easy mechanism to manage the multifaceted aspects of delivering learning experiences and supporting students in a higher education environment. Each student has unique needs given her life circumstances, each faculty member has different strengths and talents, and the journey to degree completion has many intersection points and possible barriers. There is no question, however, that attentiveness helps students stay on track to complete their educational pursuits. This is achievable when technology facilitates opportunities for instructors to have clear indicators of student progress and for support staff to be alerted when student engagement or performance trends signal the potential for a meaningful touchpoint. Here are some of our key takeaways as we have implemented our strategies to promote online student engagement.

Lesson 1: Data Consistency

Promote an appreciation for data-driven action. Lack of consistency in applying data rules undermines the integrity of a data-driven intervention model.

Interventions like those described throughout this chapter depend on the collection of consistent data. Accurate and thorough data collection depends on the willing application of standardized data definitions, systematic approaches to data collection, and the enforcement of business rules that are centered in student success. Online organizations that use an LMS have the opportunity to collect valuable student data points that can allow for more holistic interventions. These include attendance, participation, engagement, grades, and additional measures of the student learning experience. Although the first reaction to systematic approaches and consistent business rules is often fear of administrative burdens for educators, with some basic framework, the administrative aspects should ultimately lead to less manual work and more valuable insights that help support students.

In an environment where all touchpoints and transactions are intertwined, an appreciation for a data-driven culture is imperative. Buy-in is only achievable if an appreciation exists for how staff and faculty decisions and actions impact one another and combine into a holistic support framework with the student at the center. This is done through constant communication and reinforcement of collaboration. The same is true for other intervention strategies, such as the need for logging cases into the CRM with consistent coding conventions so that work across a multiperson team of coaches can be assessed for impact, especially if these intervention strategies require funding or the redistribution of resources. As with all effect analyses, n-counts matter, and the trends in aggregate are sometimes as important as those collected at the student level. Additionally, if predictive models are employed to help identify the top predictors of student persistence, the accuracy of the source data can make or break the model.

Data collection in higher education is often done solely to meet accreditation, compliance, and federal reporting requirements. However, data collected to drive action is a true asset to an organization. Time invested in defining terms, building coding conventions, and establishing processes and procedures is well spent when it not only informs organizations of important patterns or trends but can shift courses or help make an improvement. Such is the case, for example, when data are collected on student engagement in the LMS and an academic program director learns that a seemingly clear and concise learning activity ends up taking students a significant amount of time to achieve mastery. A data point indicating that a single student is struggling is of value – it could lead to a recommendation for a much-needed tutoring session, for example. If the majority of the class has similar behavior patterns, however, it may lead the academic program director or instructional designer to revisit the activity, rewrite the instructions, provide new examples, or frame the question in a different way.

These continuous improvement strategies are only achievable when all contributing members of the organization see value, invest time, and are rewarded for applying a data-driven culture in their respective roles. This also requires a willingness to be vulnerable and to accept that continuous improvement is an ongoing and eternal loop, not an attainable state. Data collection and systematic approaches have allowed our organization to scale high-touch practices for non-traditional, high-risk students in a virtual environment with significant student outcomes.

Lesson 2: Collaborate

Be willing to collaborate. Students interact with many departments, instructors, and staff in and outside of the virtual classroom. To be effective, consideration must be given to the collective experience.

Many interactions with students in higher education institutions happen in isolation of one another, yet to the student, all interactions are felt in the aggregate. The touchpoints that a student may have with a variety of offices across campus can and should inform one another. Whether touchpoints are clear and tangible or more ancillary, they compound in the world of our students. Systematic solutions for collecting interactions help keep frontline staff well informed about all aspects of students' experiences.

Beyond the consolidation of information is the more important aspect of collaboration – genuinely partnering to improve the journey for the students. When putting the student experience at the center, there may be obvious ways that departments can come together. For consideration, if a variety of different offices need to collect important student information and do so with multiple isolated forms that have overlapping data points, the onus is on the student to manually populate, manage, and return completed forms to a variety of offices. This leads to wasted time and energy and ultimately frustration. For adult students who juggle school with the demands of work and family, this is especially disappointing. Yet when offices are willing to collaborate, they may quickly notice overlaps in student recruitment, on-boarding, and registration processes that, when eliminated, would save students time and reduce confusing administrative barriers. Business practices such as routing electronic forms, centralizing databases, and pre-populating fields for self-service can benefit students tremendously.

Similarly, when communication is cultivated among instructors and staff who see the value in others' contributions toward student success, students benefit. As students, and perhaps most notably first-generation students, migrate from course to course, faculty member to faculty member, and among administrative offices, they weave together a tapestry of perceptions about your organization. Your tapestry can represent beautiful patterns if you invest in communication streams and a culture of respect that fosters student development. All contributors have valuable roles to play.

Lesson 3: Focus Actions

Focus on where you can make an impact. You only know if you are making an impact if you are constantly measuring and assessing in order to continuously improve or redirect efforts as needed.

The most important aspect of this work is committing to action. There is inevitably more to do than can be done. To maximize impact, focus your energy and resources toward actions that will reach the most students or the students who you suspect will be most responsive to interventions. For example, a review of predictive analytics may suggest that the highest performing students transfer out of your organization. Are there steps you can take to make those students feel valued and challenged, such as developing special recognition, awards, honors programs, or apprenticeships with faculty to help them see the benefit of completing at your institution?

We often assume that students requiring interventions are the lowest performing students. Another lesson learned is that sometimes middle performers get the least attention and may fall through the cracks. When running a predictive model that was hypothesized to highlight poor mid-term grades as an indicator for students at risk, we discovered that those students often persisted. Rather, the students who were close to the threshold but did not get the outreach from the instructor or an intervention from an advisor ended up doing most poorly. This is a reminder that sometimes a data point is a proxy for another indicator of student success. Careful attention to which data points generate activity helps when assessing impact.

Another example includes the investment of resources to develop our adaptive learning experiences. A substantial amount of time, money, and energy is involved in designing adaptive learning activities, yet the value to student mastery of competencies via adaptive learning activities may be limited to objective rather than subjective or reflective course content. As a result, additional development and redesign of adaptive courses in the SOUL model are based on careful review of data collected on student engagement and performance, course activity performance, and student and instructor feedback from course evaluations. Now that we have an abundance of data, to proceed in our course development efforts without evaluation of these inputs would be neglectful and careless.

Creating an environment where all actions generate data and all data further inform actions has empowered us to operate in a cycle of attentiveness and continuous improvement. It is incumbent upon us, and all institutions of higher education, to align effort and resources in this way to honor students' substantial investments of time and tuition dollars in their educations.

Lesson 4: Engage Networks and Partners

Don't reinvent the wheel. The days of having to recreate every service at every higher education institution have been disrupted by technological advances. Take advantage of networking and partnering to scale services in ways that allow you to increase efficiencies and affordability.

There is a paradoxical and dependent intersection between personalized and standardized in teaching and learning practices. The empirical need for business rules and normalized environments where the outliers are evident allows for personalized interventions or pathway variations. TAWC's frameworks for course structure, due dates, deadlines, and processes allow us to accommodate high-touch practices that make our work meaningful. Although the effort that goes into building this type of architecture for learning and support may feel daunting, once established, it lends itself to scaling to additional students and future enrollments. When automation can simplify the work of a team who then can focus on the most meaningful aspects of engagement, everybody wins.

Technology also allows an organization to tap into services and resources, such as tutoring or career readiness platforms, and professional networks, such as online course sharing platforms, outside the confines of its region or company. Gaining access to expertise that can scale up and down during peak times or with unexpected volume keeps an organization nimble and responsive. Tutoring is an example of a service where we have benefited from responsive resources, while also maintaining the holistic data approach by defining integration of tutor session data extracts as a requirement to our partnership. Having limited dedicated internal resources who could serve at all hours, for all subjects, with constant turnover in subjects needed, meant that we could not sustain tutoring on our own. Turning to a service provider who had mastered its service model, built a team that serves a network of organizations, covers a broader spectrum of subject matters, and provides availability during off-hours (when our adult students are actually working on their coursework), allowed us to provide more comprehensive services to our students.

The same logic can be applied to our learning environments. As universities have come to accept the concept that a Psychology 101 course, for example, can be transferred between most institutions of learning, there is some belief that learning should be interchangeable across organizations. However, we have not done an adequate job in being transparent about the learning. We have remained convinced that we need to do it our own way, with our own experts, with the belief that we have figured out the secret for doing it better than our peers. This is counterproductive for students who ultimately pay the cost for perpetual duplicative efforts that add minimal value and differentiation.

CONCLUSION

Inevitably, the higher education ecosystem of the future will increasingly depend on digitally connected environments for learning, virtual collaboration, and social networking. Students are already moving toward a self-service realm to obtain "just-in-time" information and training whenever needed through personal devices outside classroom walls. As a result, they will need to be better equipped with skills such as cognitive load management and computational thinking in order to decipher the knowledge and skills that are vital at certain points in time and obtainable from credible sources. In response, higher education will need to be increasingly focused on preparing students to make meaning of their learning in relation to work and career by incorporating long-standing pedagogical theories with modern technology-enriched environments and methodologies. By embracing the intersection of technology and data with learning and student support in higher education, we are more equipped to be proactive and attentive facilitators and guides. The key strategies described here are intended to provide such an example.

TAWC's SOUL model was designed to promote degree completion through a constellation of evidence-based practices and wrap-around supports that cultivate student engagement in a personalized online learning environment. Bay Path University is committed, as demonstrated through SOUL, to leveraging technology to gather data to drive action-oriented analytics, which trigger interventions by faculty and staff. The wrap-around support framework embeds "high-tech, high-touch" attributes that allow for the intentional targeting of resources that improve online student success.

There are three things that an organization can do to get started with this approach. First, establish cross-divisional data teams that include staff and faculty who interface with student data at different points across the student life cycle. Let them share with one another about their practices, key data definitions, and primary goals for gathering and acting on student information. Second, commit to data warehousing, both the approach and the tool. Consolidating information from a variety of sources generates a much more holistic picture. Finally, invest in a CRM-type solution to conduct the intervention strategies in a scalable way, made possible by joining data from across the organization. This methodology inevitably takes collaboration and requires departments to appreciate how they intersect in serving students. Ultimately, these efforts for establishing data-driven practices raise the level of attentiveness that faculty and staff are able to offer each individual student, leading to more personalized attention to promote student engagement.

REFERENCES

Abrami, P. C., & Bures, E. M. (1996). Computer-supported collaborative learning and distance education. *American Journal of Distance Education, 10*(2), 37–42.

Akbulut, Y., & Cardak, C. S. (2012). Adaptive educational hypermedia accommodating learning styles: A content analysis of publications from 2000 to 2011. *Computers & Education, 58*(2), 835–842.

Allen, I. E., & Seaman, J. (2013). Changing course: Ten years of tracking online education in the United States. *Babson Survey Research Group and Quahog Research Group, LLC.* Retrieved from https://files.eric.ed.gov/fulltext/ED541571.pdf

Aslanian, C., & Clinefelter, D. (2012). Online college students 2012. *The Learning House, Inc. and EducationDynamics.* Retrieved from https://www.learninghouse.com/wp-content/uploads/2017/09/Online-College-Students-2012.pdf

Bandura, A. (1993). Perceived self-efficacy in cognitive development and functioning. Educational Psychologist, *28*(2), 117–148.

Bernard, R. M., Brauer, A., Abrami, P. C., & Surkes, M. (2004). The development of a questionnaire for predicting online learning achievement. *Distance Education, 25*(1), 31–47.

Blanchard, A., & Cook, J. (2012). Virtual learning communities centered within a discipline: Future directions. *New Directions for Teaching and Learning, 132*, 84–97.

Bond, L. T. (2008). *Women negotiating collaborative learning: An exploratory study of undergraduate students in a select university study.* Ph.D. thesis, Texas A&M University. Retrieved from https://oaktrust.library.tamu.edu/bitstream/handle/1969.1/85927/Bond.pdf?sequence=1&is Allowed=y

Brinthaupt, T. M. (2010). Development and implementation of an online careers seminar in psychology. *Teaching of Psychology, 37*, 58–62.

Brusilovsky, P., & Peylo, C. (2003). Adaptive and intelligent web-based educational systems. International Journal of Artificial Intelligence in Education, *13*(2–4), 159–172.

Bushey, H. (2017). *Social engagement of undergraduate, online learners.* Unpublished Ph.D. thesis, Northeastern University, Boston, MA.

Cragg, C. E., Andrusyszyn, M. A., & Fraser, J. (2005). Sources of support for women taking professional programs by distance education. *Journal of Distance Education, 20*(1), 21–38.

Devlin, M. & Bushey, H. (2019). Using Data Holistically to Create a Student Success Safety Net. *Change: The Magazine of Higher Learning, 51*(6), 17–25.

Dougherty, K. D., & Andercheck, B. (2014). Using Facebook to engage learners in a large introductory course. *Teaching Sociology, 42*(2), 95–104. https://doi.org/10.1177/0092055x14521022

Dupin-Bryant, P. A. (2004). Pre-entry variables related to retention in online distance education. *The American Journal of Distance Education, 18*(4), 199–206. https://doi.org/10.1207/s15389286ajde1804_2

Dweck, C. S. (1986). Motivational processes affecting learning. *American Psychologist, 41*(10), 1040–1048. https://doi.org//10.1037//0003-066x.41.10.1040

Elliott, E. S., & Dweck, C. S. (1988). Goals: An approach to motivation and achievement. Journal of Personality and Social Psychology, *54*(1), 5–12. https://doi.org//10.1037//0022-3514.54.1.5

Faculty Focus. (2009). Strategies for increasing online student retention and satisfaction. Retrieved from http://mnabe-distancelearning.org/sites/default/files/strategies-for-increasing-online-student-retention.pdf

Furst-Bowe, J., & Dittmann, W. (2001). Identifying the needs of adult women in distance learning programs. *International Journal of Instructional Media, 28*(4), 405–413.

Geri, N. (2012). The resonance factor: Probing the impact of video on student retention in distance learning. *Interdisciplinary Journal of E-Learning & Learning Objects, 8*, 1–13. https://doi.org/10.28945/1629

Hurt, N. E., Moss, G. S., Bradley, C. L., Larson, L. R., Lovelace, M. D., Prevost, L. B., & Camus, M. S. (2012). The 'Facebook' effect: College students' perceptions of online discussions in the age of social networking. *International Journal for the Scholarship of Teaching and Learning, 6*(2), 1–24. Retrieved from http://academics.georgiasouthern.edu/ijsotl/v6n2.html

Ice, P., Diaz, S., Swan, K., Burgess, M., Sharkey, M., Sherrill, J., ... Okimoto, H. (2012). The PAR framework proof of concept: Initial findings from a multi-institutional analysis of federated postsecondary data. *Journal of Asynchronous Learning Networks, 16*(3), 63–86. https://doi.org/10.24059/olj.v16i3.277

Knowles, M. (1984). *Andragogy in action*. San Francisco, CA: Jossey-Bass.

Moody, J. (2004). Distance education: Why are the attrition rates so high? *The Quarterly Review of Distance Education, 5*(3), 205–210.

Omar, N. D., Hassan, H., & Atan, H. (2011). Student engagement in online learning: Learners' attitude toward e-mentoring. *Procedia – Social and Behavioral Sciences, 67*, 464–475. https://doi.org/10.1016/j.sbspro.2012.11.351

Owens, J., Hardcastle, L., & Richardson, B. (2009). Learning from a distance: The experience of remote students. *Journal of Distance Education, 23*(3), 53–74.

Packham, G., Jones, P., Miller, C., & Brychan, T. (2004). E-learning and retention: Key factors influencing student withdrawal. *Education & Training, 46*(6/7), 335–342.

Poulin, R. (2013). Managing online education 2013: Practices in ensuring equity. *WICHE Collaborative for Education Technologies*. Retrieved from https://wcet.wiche.edu/sites/default/files/2013ManagingOnlineEducationSurveyExecutiveSummary.pdf

Rovai, A. P. (2001). Building classroom community at a distance: A case study. *Educational Technology, Research and Development, 49*(4), 33. https://doi.org/10.1007/bf02504946

Rovai, A. P. (2003). In search of higher persistence rates in distance education online programs. *The Internet and Higher Education, 6*(1), 1–16. http://dx.doi.org.ezproxy.neu.edu/10.1016/S1096-7516(02)00158-6

Rowntree, D. (1995). Teaching and learning online: A correspondence education for the 21st century? *British Journal of Educational Technology, 26*(3), 205–215. https://doi.org/10.1111/j.1467-8535.1995.tb00342.x

Shapiro, D., Dundar, A., Huie, F., Wakhungu, P., Bhimdiwala, A., & Wilson, S. (2019, February). Completing college: A state-level view of student completion rates (signature report no. 16a). Herndon, VA: National Student Clearinghouse Research Center. Retrieved from https://nscresearchcenter.org/signature-report-16-state-supplement-completing-college-a-state-level-view-of-student-completion-rates/

Simpson, O. (2004). The impact on retention of interventions to support distance learning students. *Open Learning, 19*(1), 79–95. https://doi.org/10.1080/0268051042000177763

TAWC Advising Community. (n.d.). In Facebook [Private Group]. Retrieved from https://www.facebook.com/groups/823071691073095/?ref=group_header

Tinto, V. (1993). *Leaving college: Rethinking the causes and cures of student attrition* (2nd ed.). Chicago, IL: University of Chicago.

US Department of Education, National Center for Education Statistics. (2016). Digest of education statistics. Retrieved from https://nscresearchcenter.org/signaturereport14/

Zimmerman, B. J. (2000). Self-efficacy: An essential motive to learn. *Contemporary Educational Psychology, 25*(1), 82–91. https://doi.org/10.1006/ceps.1999.1016

ONE UNIVERSITY: AN INTERDEPARTMENTAL COLLABORATION MODEL TO ENHANCE ONLINE STUDENT ENGAGEMENT

Roland Nuñez

ABSTRACT

As higher education institutions see the increased enrollment of online students, the services they provide must adapt to meet their needs. This chapter presents an in-depth case study of the steps that one private American university took, following Kezar's model (2005), to improve online student engagement. The first phase involved buy-in from leadership and creating a valid justification for the collaboration efforts. The second phase involved taking the first steps to create a culture of collaboration across the institution. The third phase involved the development of programs that continued collaboration efforts through various campuses and departments to create tangible products promoting student success. The institution focused more on the process of collaboration than the results in an effort to create a foundation that could outlast staff changes and restructuring of departments. Early results indicate a potential for other universities to examine their processes used for collaboration between colleges and departments.

Keywords: Kezar; case study; collaboration; communication; process; online students; online learning; commitment; engagement; private university.

Online university programs are on the rise, with a third of all students taking at least one online course, and one in six students enrolled exclusively in online programs (Clinefelter, Aslanian, & Magda, 2019). Despite this, engaging these students, both inside and outside the classroom, becomes more challenging than traditional students due to the lack of face-to-face interaction. Higher education institutions must adapt to meet the needs of this increasing population. This chapter provides an overview and case study analysis of an American private university's three-phase collaboration initiative to serve its online student population. This chapter begins with an overview of data on online students, including some relevant statistics to provide context for this chapter. Then, a brief overview is provided of the university and its own online student population. Next, the theoretical framework for the case study will be introduced, including its application to three university initiatives aimed at increasing online student engagement. This chapter will end with a discussion of the successes and challenges of these initiatives.

ONLINE STUDENT CHALLENGES

As of 2016, 31% of all students in the United States were enrolled in at least one online course (Clinefelter et al., 2019). Of those students, 16% took multiple online courses and 14% were fully enrolled online (Clinefelter et al., 2019). The number of fully online students increased by 13% between 2012 and 2017 (Newton, 2019). The demographics of these students are different from those of traditional college students. More than half (51%) of undergraduate students and 70% of graduate students are employed full-time while taking college classes (Paterson, 2019). Despite a growing interest in online learning, one may be surprised to learn that the students enrolling in an online program still selected a college within 50 miles from home (Clinefelter et al., 2019).

A quick analysis of these statistics reveals a few things. The nature of online instruction provides a flexibility that is increasingly popular for students with full-time jobs and otherwise limited time. The attractiveness of online education comes from the ability to study at one's own time, something that a traditional classroom setting does not allow. Despite this, students still choose to enroll in online programs at institutions that are relatively close to their home. Local colleges typically have more visibility with local employers, which online students often see as a benefit of enrolling in a nearby college (Clinefelter et al., 2019).

At the time of writing, the author served as the campus director for two campuses within a private university system that consists of more than 130 campuses around the world. Two of the campuses are traditional, residential campuses. The rest are satellite branch campuses that serve primarily online students. The university has offered distance education since 1970, ranked as a top five institution in undergraduate online education for the last seven years, according to US News and Report 2020. At the time of this writing, 71% of the students who attend the two campuses are fully online. The rest of the students enroll in either a hybrid course experience that combines some online learning with some in-person instruction or fully in-person instruction at the satellite locations. The majority of the students, both undergraduate and graduate, hold full-time jobs while attending classes. They either work on their own time from home or they attend evening classes at campus locations. While a few of the students are located in distant parts of the world, the majority live within 50 miles of either of the two campuses. Roughly half of the students at the campuses managed by the author occasionally stop by a local campus for advisement or events. The rest communicate primarily through email or phone call.

The author's experience at this institution involved working with students facing a variety of challenges when enrolling in online education. Older students often struggled to navigate the numerous learning systems used for coursework and advisement. Power outages and interruptions in internet service have caused challenges in taking tests and submitting assignments, resulting in working with students and instructors to make up or retake interrupted tests. The flexibility of asynchronous discussions and assignments required that the students be disciplined and exhibit strong time management skills. This was often difficult for new students who are not accustomed to the online learning format. Despite these challenges, the students continued to persist, with year-over-year growth in the student persistent rate of students at both campuses managed by the author for three consecutive years.

Recently, the institution took steps to improve online student engagement in a systematic and holistic way. To illustrate the development and implementation of this engagement initiative, this chapter will provide a case study analysis of three initiatives implemented by the institution. The theoretical framework used to guide the case study is Kezar's (2005) Collaboration Model, which provides the foundation for the three initiatives. The next section will provide a brief overview of the model and its components.

KEZAR'S COLLABORATION MODEL

The core of the engagement strategy used at the institution, and the initiatives that followed, was based on university-wide collaboration. The process began with a change in university leadership. The new, incoming president set the stage for a collaborative strategy that would improve the way the university supported its online students, following the collection of feedback from relevant stakeholders. For this case study, the most appropriate theoretical framework was Kezar's (2005) Collaboration Model. Although many other collaboration models exist and could have been used, they focused primarily on corporate organizations. Adrianna Kezar had experience working in both Student Affairs and Academic Affairs. After noticing a divide between the departments at her institution, she sought models on collaboration to help her understand the relationships between different departments. The lack of models focusing on higher education institutions and its unique characteristics resulted in the development of this new model. The foundations of the collaboration model were developed out of George Kuh's (1996) seamless change model. This model focused on intentionally initiating change at all levels of leadership, and that the success of the change could be evaluated by both leadership's actions and the responses to leadership's actions. Kezar's model and Kuh's model were similar in that they both required a proactive plan to lead change, rather than reacting to unexpected external pressures. However, Kuh focused on changing core values as a way to initiate change. Kezar focused on changing processes and evaluating the change of those processes. Unlike other collaboration models that focus on a specific project or initiative, Kezar's model focuses on the process of collaboration itself, and the variables required to create a culture of collaboration within an organization. It takes Kuh's model of seamless change and applies it more directly to collaboration efforts. This process involves three phases that must occur for interdepartmental collaborations to be successful: building commitment, commitment to collaboration, and sustaining commitment. The following sections will describe each phase and how they applied to the institution's emerging engagement strategy.

Building Commitment

The first stage, building commitment, requires an institution to build a story. The institution first must acknowledge that there needs to be collaboration and be able to explain *why* the need exists. This usually begins with external pressure. In the case of this university, the external pressure came from two sources. The first source came from a changing student demographic. Traditionally, the students were primarily older adults who worked full-time and veterans looking to transition to civilian life. In the last few years, however, there has been increasing interest from recent high school graduates who want to pursue online education full-time. Some of the reasons for this interest include cost, flexibility, and ability to live at home while attending college. As a result, these students (and their parents) have asked for additional programs and resources that students have typically come to expect from residential colleges. University officials quickly realized that they were not doing enough to serve this population. The second external pressure came from other institutions. As the number of online learners increase, more institutions are creating online programs to serve the need. As competition increases, institutions must create programs that differentiate them from the competition. Internal pressures also led to the need for a more collaborative approach. Staff at the satellite campuses often felt disconnected from both the residential campuses and other satellite campuses. At university town hall meetings, the most common feedback from staff at all campuses was a need for increased communication between campuses and departments within each campus.

The need for collaboration often develops when an institution creates or reevaluates its values (Kezar, 2001). In the case of this institution, the new leadership created a five-part strategic plan to improve the university in areas such as student success, alumni engagement, and global presence. The strategic plan came as a result of both the external and internal pressures mentioned above, following formal and informal feedback from relevant stakeholders. As the strategic plan was developed, it became increasingly apparent that the university had to improve its collaborative efforts between the different campuses and the departments within each. Historically, the university operated in silos with little communication between campuses, resulting in inefficient use of resources and duplication of efforts.

Kezar (2005) suggests that learning and the ability to identify the need for collaboration at all levels are necessary steps in phase one of her collaboration model. As the strategic plan was developed, it was important to be able to communicate the importance of collaboration to all related parties, namely the internal stakeholders of the institution. Institutional leaders emphasized that the upcoming changes were as a response to feedback from students, faculty, and staff. University leadership initiated the learning phase through announcements and town halls explaining the need for the new collaboration initiative.

The last variable associated with building commitment is the development of campus networks. This variable is prominent in all three phases, as it is arguably the most important variable and should continue to be developed throughout the process. This involves the creation of cross-departmental relationships. The key to success in these relationships is that they should not be tied to a particular program or initiative. At this phase, the building of relationships should be organic and not solely done for a specific purpose. During the phases, it was important for campus networks to be established within all these divisions to improve collaboration.

Commitment to Collaboration

Once the foundation has been set for collaboration, the institution must secure its commitment to collaboration. To achieve this, the institutional leaders must lead by example. They must demonstrate a visible sense of commitment to the strategy to instill a sense of confidence within the institutional community. In the first phase, leadership is tasked with communicating the need for collaboration. In the second phase, leadership must take action to lead the change. Failure to do this will cause any collaboration efforts to stall.

Another important aspect of the second phase is defining a clear mission. The values created in the first phase must be demonstrated through a clear mission statement and the steps necessary to act on that mission. This was demonstrated at the institution through the creation and publication of the five-part strategic plan that would be enacted over the next several years.

Last, university departments at all levels must continue to strengthen campus networks. The focus should not be on any particular program or initiative but to eliminate the communication barriers that have previously existed in order to facilitate interaction with different departments.

Sustaining Commitment

In the third and final phase, sustaining commitment, the institution has the responsibility to keep the fire lit. Now that some initiatives have been developed, the structure must be put into place to support the initiatives through completion. This requires institutional leaders to provide the resources necessary to support collaborative efforts. This can include reorganization of departments, hiring of new staff, and providing funding for critical programs. At the institution, new committees were created to provide the foundation for collaboration. This will be discussed further in the next section.

Another aspect important to this phase is having a reward system. There should be incentives to encourage and celebrate successful collaboration. These rewards could range from monetary incentives to positive words of affirmation in the day-to-day management of departments. This variable is crucial to the continued sustainment of collaboration beyond any individual project or initiative.

Finally, campus networks must continue to be strengthened. Departments must be given opportunities to interact with each other in both formal and informal settings, outside of specific projects or programs. Combined with rewards and structural support, this would ensure that a culture of collaboration is maintained through changes in employees and leadership.

ANALYSIS OF INITIATIVES USING COLLABORATION MODEL

Using Kezar's Collaboration Model as the theoretical foundation, the author conducted a case study analysis on three initiatives led by the university in support of increased collaboration.

It is important to note that the focus of Kezar's Collaboration Model is not primarily on the results of any particular program or initiative. The focus is on the structural process of collaboration itself. It is a study of how the collaboration was formed and maintained throughout the process. In this sense, it is possible to have a program that failed in its primary educational purpose but could still be successful in the collaboration that took place to create it. This section analyzes several institutional initiatives under the lens of Kezar's Collaboration Model. The initiatives will be described based on which phase of the model they took place.

Building Commitment: Unified University Vision

The university is comprised of over 130 campuses around the world. The university system is separated into three main divisions, the two residential campuses and the worldwide campus. The worldwide campus is then further divided into three subdivisions: US satellite campuses, international satellite campuses, and the online campus. Although the campuses may differ slightly in their program offerings, they generally fall under the same overarching university umbrella. Despite this, the campuses have traditionally operated in silos. Everything from course scheduling to marketing to enrollment management was separated by campus. This would sometimes result in duplication of efforts and staffing where recruiters from different campuses would end up at the same college fair, unaware of the other's presence. In addition, the diplomas for the two residential campuses looked different from the satellite campuses, further amplifying the divide. The nature of this disconnect, compounded by the geographical distance between campuses, made it difficult for collaboration to take place.

To begin the implementation of the new collaboration process, university leadership embraced a new, "one university" philosophy. This basic principle of the vision was that all campuses were part of one university. Every campus, whether residential or online, whether US-based or international, was an extension of one overall university vision. This meant that all the campuses would start marketing themselves in one unified way. The initiative was inspired by faculty, staff, and student feedback that was provided during institution-wide town hall meetings and targeted focus groups. A consistent theme among the comments was the conflict of one campus being "lesser than" other campuses. These comments were most visible on institution-affiliated social media pages, where students joked about the perceived elitism in some of the campuses over others. The details of the initiative were first introduced at a university-wide virtual town hall meeting and then further elaborated over the next few months through announcements. The largest initiative related to this strategy was the development of a new strategic plan developed over 10 months through a collaboration of students, faculty, staff, and community stakeholders. The plan would be executed over a six-year period.

The first concrete step taken by institution leaders was the unification of the institutional diploma and transcripts among all campuses. This change, which had been requested by staff through informal channels for several years, was made relatively quickly in an effort for leadership to show they were serious about this new vision. This gesture, though largely symbolic in nature, was necessary to show the institution's initial commitment to creating a collaborative atmosphere. This would allow an online military student attending the university overseas to receive the same diploma as a traditional student attending one of the residential campuses.

As part of the first phase of Kezar's (2005) model, the institution needs to build the story of collaboration and commitment to collaboration. This story must have the *why*, *what*, and *how* of collaboration. Why is collaboration necessary? What would this collaboration look like? How will the institution get there? Some important elements were present that allowed this phase to occur. The external pressures of an increasingly diverse student population and more competition from other online programs were present. University leadership understood the importance of unifying the institution and created a set of values that highlighted this unification strategy through a strategic plan. The need and plan for collaboration was communicated to employees at all levels of the institution, getting input from all relevant parties. Departments were encouraged to increase their communication. The initial first step of unifying the institutional diploma across all the campuses was meant to illustrate the urgency of the new vision and a way to get the campuses on board with the idea of a unified campus. The idea was planted that the institution was about to embark on a journey of change and everyone had their part to play.

Implementing Commitment: Standardizing Campus Processes

Once the foundation was set during the building phase, the institution had to create a sense of urgency and communicate this urgency to all employees. To do this, a number of university summits were created that would take place at different university campuses, where key representatives from other campuses would be invited. The goal of these summits was to learn about the unique attributes of each campus, the programs offered, and the personnel who worked there. The summits included a variety of workshops, presentations, and team-building activities over the course of a few days. Each summit was led and organized by faculty and staff from that respective campus, from all levels of the institutional hierarchy.

The purpose of these campus summits was to provide employees an opportunity to get to know employees who lived and worked hundreds, or even thousands, of miles away. The summits, attended by the author, consisted of a mixture of formal and informal programming over the course of three to five days. The formal programming involved presentations by faculty and staff about each campus' academic programs, processes and procedures, statistics about student population, and local features and attractions. Informal programming involved opportunities for team bonding such as hiking trips, dinners, picnics, canoe rides, and shopping. These efforts served to break barriers of communication by allowing staff and faculty to interact and become comfortable with the idea of collaboration through different settings. After the summits, communication between staff at different campuses improved. In the author's campuses, there was a notable increase in calls to and from other campuses to share best practices, to ask questions about unclear processes, and to assist students moving from one campus to another. The summits, and resulting communication afterward, illustrate Kezar's (2005) second phase of implementing commitment by removing barriers to collaboration and strengthening campus networks.

In addition to being knowledgeable about all the university campuses, another important initiative was to maintain a consistent message coming out of the university. Traditionally, online students would be contacted for specific reasons, such as registration, balance owed, or due to risk factors such as poor grades. However, this left a segment of the student population generally unattended. Students who registered themselves for class, paid for their classes on time, and made decent grades had little reason to be contacted. As a result, the student would likely not be noticed until something adverse happened, such as a job loss resulting in lack of payment or health issue resulting in withdrawing from a class. An important goal for increasing online student engagement was to create a systematic process for communicating with students.

This resulted in the creation of a standardized communication plan that would be shared across the campuses. The communication plan was a master shared document that would contain timelines for when to contact students and for what reason. It was created using Microsoft Excel and various macros that linked up with university databases. The timeline included typical traditional student communication touch points regarding financial aid, registration, and tuition payment reminders. However, the communication plan also allowed for additional methods of communication. This created a timeline for reaching out to students who had a birthday, students who had not taken a class for a while, and students who had made the Dean's List. Every campus would have the same timeline and would contact the students the same way. The communication plan was used to download queries containing lists of students with anticipated contact times. It also included email templates and sample scripts that could be personalized to the specific campus. More importantly, every campus had access to every other campus' notes within that communication plan through the shared document in an online server. This made it easier to assist a student regardless of which campus the student called. For example, if an online student who lived in California moved to Florida, the California advisor would be able to switch the student over to the Florida advisor through a seamless transition. The Florida advisor would instantly be able to see all the communication with the student up until that point and be able to personalize their communication with the student using that information.

The communication plan, created jointly by three campus staff members at three separate satellite campuses, was implemented in phases, with a few pilot campuses trained to use it first. The plan was then broadened to include more campuses until every campus had the training and access to interact with students in this formalized manner. The plan was embraced by leadership as a continuation of implementing commitment to collaboration. However, not everyone embraced the communication plan during implementation. While some directors and advisors appreciated the added structure and streamlining of communication processes, others saw the plan as a way to limit their campus autonomy. At a few task force meetings, staff would share their concerns about the rigidity of the plan and their struggle to keep to the timelines that the plan recommended. Over time, as more campuses became accustomed to the plan, some of those who questioned the communication plan saw its value and supported the endeavor. This was evident throughout the continued town halls and task force meetings where staff were able to share their thoughts on an ongoing basis.

The communication plan was a result of the foundation work that was done to create better communication between campus staff. The summits served as a valuable first step to break down barriers of communication between campuses, who often operated in silos and had processes that vastly differed from one another. As communication strengthened between directors, admissions counselors, advisors, and administrative assistants, staff were able to see an opportunity for working together in a more systematic way. A key distinction in Kezar's model versus other collaboration models is the process used to improve collaboration. The communication plan, as helpful as it was, is merely a product, not a process. Kezar's model acknowledges the focus on the communication plan's creation. The plan was created through an initiative that was started by staff members at three satellite campuses and worked its way up to campus leadership, rather than a top-down approach where leadership brought the plan to the satellite campuses (at least initially). Phase one of the plan allowed individual campuses the flexibility, freedom, and motivation to find solutions to increase collaboration in phase two.

Sustaining Commitment: Formal Collaborative Programs

The success of the initiatives during the first two phases allowed the institution to move forward with more formalized collaboration programs. These programs required more time and resources to implement than the previous initiatives. Two programs that were formed during phase three were the ambassador program and the Pathways to Success program. Each program was created to increase collaborations between key departments to improve student engagement across the campuses. The ambassador program was a collaboration between Enrollment Management, Marketing, and Campus Operations to create a stronger system for communicating with university prospects. Under the old system, each campus would initiate its own recruitment strategies, which would sometimes cause confusion as the messaging was different depending on the campus. Campuses would compete with each other for students and for resources. The purpose of the ambassador program was to create a unified message that would go out to prospects and pair the prospect with the correct campus based on their degree interests, financial situation, and learning modality preferences. The students who would benefit more from online education would be referred to the more online-friendly campuses and the students wanting a more hands-on experience would be referred to the residential campuses. Unlike previous recruitment efforts where admissions recruiters would highlight a specific campus they represented, university ambassadors, which consisted of different staff members (not just recruiters), represented all the campuses as one university system. As relationships were formed with prospects and their parents, the ambassador would then suggest a campus that best met the prospect's needs and interests. Another responsibility of university ambassadors involved outreach to the local community and introducing them to the university system. As an ambassador, the author attended various community events to build brand awareness for the university. Trained with the knowledge of the different campuses, the author was able to speak confidently about the various programs and learning experiences available throughout the university system.

The implementation of the ambassador program was only possible through the efforts completed in the first two phases of the collaboration model. Prior to the phases, recruitment would be solely the jobs of the recruiters in the enrollment management division. It was unusual for someone other than a recruiter to be out in the community speaking to prospects and their families. By having support from every level of university leadership, as well as the increased communication between campuses to build trust, it became easier to establish a cross-campus recruitment strategy. It allowed recruiters to trust faculty and advisors to give accurate information about the university at college fairs and community events. It also allowed campus staff to trust that recruiters from other campuses would represent them properly. This trust developed over time but still has a way to go. There have been incidents where different campuses would still compete over which college fairs they would attend, since this new initiative meant that only one campus would attend a particular fair. Having two campuses holding booths from the same university would be redundant and go against the spirit of collaboration. This sometimes caused conflict since individual staff members had a difficult time trusting that a different campus would send students over to them and not keep them for themselves. One strategy for minimizing this conflict was to have one representative from each campus attend the same fair using the same booth. This would allow further strengthening of campus networks and further building trust as the staff members worked together.

The second program is the Pathways to Success program. This is an initiative aimed at supporting current students. This was a collaboration between Academics, Advising and Operations, Registrar, Scheduling, and Enrollment Management. Its purpose was to create a set of experiences that would help improve student engagement and retention. One of the first initiatives to be implemented from this program was a series of online student success webinars. Academic advisors worked together with faculty to create a list of topics that would be presented to students in an online workshop. These topics included financial literacy, personal branding, APA skills, and math skills. The faculty used the same teleconferencing software that they used in their online classes and students could join from all around the world. The staff at the advising offices marketed the workshops to the students and hosted local viewing parties at select campuses for online students who lived within the area. As the Pathways to Success program continues to be developed, additional collaborative initiatives are being implemented.

The process for developing this program was supported by the previous phases of the model. The author had previously collaborated with faculty at the multiple summits attended earlier in the year. The relationships built with these faculty members made it much easier to collaborate on the Pathways to Success program. Prior to these initiatives, it was rare for campus staff to interact with the faculty. Most faculty teach fully online and do not live near the campuses where they teach. As such, communication with faculty was limited to targeted communication about an at-risk student. The increased communication throughout the three phases allowed for more faculty–staff interaction, which developed into several programs such as the Pathways to Success program.

Both programs described above involved the collaboration between multiple departments and multiple campuses to create tangible products that no individual department or campus could do alone. Phase three of Kezar's model is typically where many collaborative projects begin. The "product" phase is the most visible of the three phases and often produces the most tangible results, such as the marketing materials developed in the ambassador program or the webinars in the Pathways program. As mentioned in this section, the third phase on its own may not be effective without the foundation laid in the first two phases. Even if the collaboration results in a successful program, there is no guarantee that the next program will also be successful. Department restructuring or personnel changes can disrupt an ongoing collaboration. For example, if two departments collaborate well because two employees from the departments get along, such collaboration could end if one of the employees resigns. The first two phases of collaboration are necessary to create a culture of collaboration that transcends any one individual person, department, or campus. It allows for systemic collaboration that can persist through structural changes, budget cuts, and unexpected external pressures. This was illustrated at the institution as a university ambassador resigned from her position shortly after the designation. Despite this, her replacement was quickly assigned the ambassador status and embraced the collaborative nature with support from colleagues at other campuses. This was due, in part, to the culture of collaboration that had been created, which allows collaboration efforts to survive personnel changes.

DISCUSSION

The initiatives described above are a result of intentional structural changes that took place at the university at all levels. It started with the need for collaboration, emphasized by external pressures from changing student demographics and internal pressures from personnel wanting better communication between campuses. University leadership took steps to create a story by creating a strategic plan with faculty, staff, student, and community input. This was followed by campus-led summits where representatives from the campuses could learn about the differences and similarities between programs and get to know each other through team-building activities. Leadership further supported collaboration by promoting grassroots efforts and ideas, which resulted in a communication plan developed by staff at three different campuses. Further collaborations between faculty and staff created additional programming opportunities that were previously absent from the institution. University leaders further supported these efforts through incentives such as providing the necessary resources to help these programs take shape.

While it is still too early to quantify or analyze the results of these new processes, Kezar's model does not focus on the results, as other collaboration models often do. The focus is on how well the structural changes were implemented and how they could be improved in the future. As with any large-scale change, conflict was inevitable. Some staff and faculty members were more resistant to the rapid changes, often citing their lack of autonomy as a primary reason for their resistance. One major factor in the implementation of these changes was the open channel of communication available throughout. Regular town hall meetings were open to every staff and faculty member. Task force groups were created by leadership that had representatives from each campus to meet monthly and report on feedback from personnel about changes. In addition, the university president held frequent virtual meetings where anyone could set up an appointment and discuss what was on their mind. These channels of communication helped to bring concerns out into the open and address issues as they were presented. The key to these changes required participation from everyone. It was not simply a top-down decision, although leadership was crucial in assessing the changes and providing much-needed support throughout to increase collaboration opportunities.

Institutional collaboration has allowed the university to better serve its online students in a variety of ways. First, by having more knowledgeable staff, they are better prepared to provide exceptional customer service to students regardless of location. Through the standardized communication plan, students can be confident knowing that staff can assist them no matter where they are in the world. They can call any campus and be able to receive the same level of service they have come to expect. The new interdepartmental programs have allowed staff and faculty to reach more students than ever. It has allowed an expansion of reach and better use of limited resources to create bigger projects. Most importantly, the institution is developing a culture that can make communication easier within any campus or division within the university. A staff member can call a colleague that is several states away about an issue due to relationships formed with that colleague during a summit. A recruiter can talk about a program offered at the Singapore campus because she learned about it through staff retreats. These changes are constantly being monitored and improved on a continuous basis. Initial response from students is positive. Several students have expressed appreciation that all diplomas have become standardized across campuses, particularly students who attend satellite campuses and felt their degree was somehow of less quality than that of those in the residential campuses. The interdepartmental workshops, delivered fully online, have been well attended by students. Assessments of these programs have resulted in positive feedback from the students who appreciate the diversification of topics presented thanks to the increased collaboration.

CONCLUSION

As higher education institutions see the increased enrollment of online students, the services they provide must adapt to meet their needs. An American private university did this by implementing a three-phase collaboration model to better serve an evolving student population. The first phase involved buy-in from leadership and creating a valid justification for the collaboration efforts. The second phase involved taking the first steps to create a culture of collaboration across the institution. The third phase involved the development of programs that continued collaboration efforts through various campuses and departments to create tangible products promoting student success. It was important to analyze the *process* of collaboration, not just the end result, to make sure that there was a foundation that could outlast staff changes and restructuring of departments. Though still early in the process, initial results of collaboration have been positive. Online students have reacted positively to the changes, and employee morale has also improved thanks to increased channels of communication. Other universities are encouraged to evaluate their own collaboration processes and look for areas of improvement using the three-phase model.

REFERENCES

Clinefelter, D. L., Aslanian, C. B., & Magda, A. J. (2019). *Online college students 2019: Comprehensive data on demands and preferences*. Louisville, KY: Wiley Edu, LLC.

Kezar, A. (2001). Organizational models and facilitators of change: Providing a framework for student and academic affairs collaboration. *New Directions for Higher Education, 116*, 63–74. doi:10.1002/he.34

Kezar, A. (2005). Redesigning for collaboration within higher education institutions: An exploration into the developmental process. *Research in Higher Education, 46*(7), 831–860. doi:10.1007/s11162-004-6227-5

Kuh, G. D. (1996). Guiding principles for creating seamless learning environments for undergraduates. *Journal of College Student Development, 27*(2), 135–148.

Newton, D. (2019). More than half of online college students may be in inferior schools, programs. Retrieved from https://www.forbes.com/sites/dereknewton/2019/03/30/more-than-half-of-online-college-students-may-be-in-inferior-schools-programs/#7220a1b03d6e

Paterson, J. (2019). More than half of online learners want to change careers. Retrieved from https://www.educationdive.com/news/more-than-half-of-online-learners-want-to-change-careers/556307/

ENGAGING STUDENTS IN ASYNCHRONOUS ADVISING USING THE DYNAMIC STUDENT DEVELOPMENT METATHEODEL: TOWARD A CRITICAL APPROACH

Pietro A. Sasso and Tyler Phelps

ABSTRACT

Online courses and self-directed and asynchronous learning may not be the best for everyone. Individuals possess a number of different learning styles and life circumstances when they enter higher education. Technology is but one answer to addressing these diverse needs and providing choices to students. Technology should be employed in a way that does not replace this system of choice but enhances it and provides individuals with other opportunities for achieving educational goals. The ideal for higher education lies somewhere in-between the purely digital and purely traditional modes of educational delivery. Lost in this capitulation of higher education to the enrollments of distance education is student success. This chapter will explore challenges to distance education student retention and persistence, disseminate the theoretical construct of the Dynamic Student Development Metatheodel, and apply specific student success strategies to distance education. These strategies include intrusive advising and asynchronous advising techniques. This chapter will conclude with how these advising techniques and strategies can facilitate increased student persistence through engagement with academic advisors using asynchronous approaches that move beyond the traditional temporal, didactic strategies employed by most higher education institutions.

Keywords: Advising; student development; asynchronous advising; academic advising; technology; cloud advising; Dynamic Student Development Metatheodel; meta model; significant other; technology.

INTRODUCTION

American postsecondary education institutions are *loosely coupled* through peer-reviewed accreditation, best practices, and continued partnerships in research. It is additionally coupled through its common mission. The notion of a common mission is somewhat of an artifact given the evolution of the American university into a multiversity, a term coined by Clark Kerr in the 1960s and referring to institutional evolution to large universities focusing on research at the undergraduate and graduate levels (Kerr, 2001). The role of the traditional American four-year institution has historically been to create and disseminate new knowledge and serve a repository for existing and historical knowledge (ACE, 1949). However, that historical role has evolved as the multiversity has taken new form in an attempt by colleges and universities to serve an increasing number of stakeholders while at the same time facing financial pressures caused by decreased federal and state appropriations and the inability to create additional revenue streams to satisfy budgetary needs.

Whether it is as an economic engine or an entrepreneurial endeavor, the traditional college and university still primarily focuses on the traditional 18- to 24-year-old, full-time enrolled, residential student (Frederick, Sasso, & Maldonado, 2018). In serving the traditional college student, colleges and universities have been the purveyor of the middle class and a certifier of the professions as a continuation of being connected to the educational dream of bettering oneself and as an effective means of social class mobility. However, in attempting to satisfy the educational dream, institutions have fallen short of their practical potential as retention levels have remained stagnant despite increases in online enrollment over the last few decades (Frederick et al., 2018). To bolster student persistence levels, institutional retention, and college/university enrollment rates, institutions of higher education have made a fundamental attribution error that distance education would further buttress these needs with increased enrollments. Yet, higher education has made a similar assumption in admitting and supporting these students to facilitate institutional retention and student persistence toward graduation (Frederick et al., 2018).

To understand what appears to be the failure of institutions to meet their practical potential in producing highly qualified graduates, it is important to understand this existing higher education heuristic and its guiding paradigm which we term the *fundamental attribution error of higher education* (Frederick et al., 2018). This means that American higher education assumes it is more cost-effective to attract new students than attempt to retain current ones because there will always be more prospective students in an unlimited recruitment pool. Furthermore, there is an underlying assumption within attribution error as a paradigm of institutional decision-making.

In response to this fundamental attribution error of American higher education, repeated again with distance learners and online education, the authors of this chapter call for the implementation of a new student success model to be delivered through synchronous advising, referred to as *cloud advising* by Phelps (2019). The entirety of the student success model will be distilled, and considerations for programing related to implementation of the model are recommended by the authors. This chapter concludes with critical approaches in further implementing asynchronous advising approaches related to engaging college students online.

CONCEPTUAL FRAMEWORK

Even in accepting these realities, it is unreasonable to think that no current theories or models of college student development hold enough truth to render them untenable. As such, identifying common themes or factors within sets of theories and models could lead to a reliable assumption as to their validity to the degree that they can appropriately inform practice. This is precisely the intention of the Dynamic Student Development Metatheodel (DSDM). The DSDM was originally conceptualized in 2012 and further refined by Frederick, Sasso, and Barratt (2015).

The DSDM is designed as highly flexible to meet the unique needs of each student, while demanding few resources beyond those already available at most colleges and universities, as it calls upon the expenditure of time and attention from existing institutional "people" resources as opposed to an outlay of already limited dollars. Higher education decision-makers are being called upon to prepare graduates to assume positions of responsibility in the various communities into which they will enter, to improve the quality of the nation's workforce, to provide support to those with whom they will develop significant relationships, and, in general, to advance the quality of life for themselves and all those around them. To assist in both refining the definition of student success and providing functional as opposed to theoretical guidance, the DSDM is presented.

Constructs of the DSDM

Metatheodel
A "metatheodel" is defined as the joining of multiple (meta) theories (the) and models (odel) focused on a broad construct: in this case, the construct of college student development. If one examines a set of theories or models attending to the same construct, common elements will emerge. The concept behind a metatheodel is the identification and application of those common elements to inform practice by first defining common elements; establishing accurate operational definitions; the planning and engagement of appropriate supports, services, interventions, and programs (SSIPs); and actively assessing the outcomes of their application in practice. This is consistent with the notion of a *metatheodel*, a term created by the authors.

Growth, Learning, and Development (GLD)
The DSDM asserts that student GLD should be understood as an integrated phenomenon that best occurs within a set of assumptions, including that (a) GLD

is best supported within the confines of a trusting relationship; (b) GLD is an active as opposed to passive process; (c) the degree and level of GLD is improved as student internalization increases; and (d) on entry to college, students possess a definable and acquired set of qualities, skills, and attributes which can be improved upon as a result of their collegiate experience.

Significant Other (SO)

The role of the SO, a term first coined by Kegan (1982), evolves from highly directive in the early portion of a student's academic years to that of a mentor/guide in the middle portion of the academic lifespan and, finally, to that of a "sounding board" and informal advisor in the latter portion of a student's college career. Each stage of the DSDM calls for the SO to manage different overarching goals in students' lives. In as much as students have a profound need to connect with caring others, so do all of us, and when SOs realize that not only will they be meeting the needs of their students through the relationship, they too will find their own need for a sense of effectiveness, purpose, and connection with others will be satisfied through the SO–student relationship. Too, highly developed undergraduate students are a rich potential source for the necessary personnel to serve as SOs to students early in their academic careers. To be sure, upper-class students would actually be developing their skills of interdependency by serving as SOs. Upper-class students would be no different than older faculty or staff members as it relates to the support given to mentees as the elements of relationship management would be the same.

SSIPs

Each of the DSDM's stages calls for the development of SSIPs designed to assist advancing student growth in specific functional areas which include critical thinking, self-awareness, communication, diversity, citizenship, membership and leadership, and relationships (Barratt & Frederick, 2015). Through appropriate assessment, student weaknesses in specific behaviors can be identified and directed to where attention should be focused by the SO and student. Presentation of the functional areas as well as the behaviors used to define those areas is included as part of the formal training provided by SOs before their work with students begins. As work progresses, the SO and student alike will more than likely identify other behaviors in need of attention that may or may not fall within the seven functional areas. The SO and student can then define those areas to facilitate the development of behavioral responses to guide their ongoing work. Tailoring specific SSIPs for each student renders the DSDM a highly flexible and adaptable model and overcomes the inherent weaknesses found in typical manualized or one-size-fits-all programs.

SSIPs development should occur within a tripartite structure, which includes the experiences students have within the spheres of (a) academic emphasis, (b) co-curricular emphasis, and (c) environmental and process emphasis. Within each of the three areas, each has two overlapping levels, one for the overall campus community and one for the individual student. It is important to note that the three areas of academic, co-curricular, and environmental and process management spheres exist as overlapping as opposed to independent areas of emphasis. Changes to one will no doubt lead to changes in the others due to their unique relationship to one another.

Integration of the DSDM

Understanding the DSDM requires a new conceptualization of how traditional models and theories of college student GLD impact students. The DSDM is neither a model nor theory but a "superstructure" or psychological scaffolding at the institutional level within which the overall success in applying various models and theories can be accelerated and enhanced. The DSDM attends to students' perceptions of their lived experiences while enrolled and it is the "sense they make" of their experience that drives their ongoing decisions of remaining enrolled and the degree to which they will be actively involved in managing their own success.

We make sense of our lived experiences within the three domains of (a) cognition (how we think), (b) behavior (how we act), and (c) affect (how we feel). While cognition and behavior are important, and the two domains on which higher education tends to focus, it is the affective domain that exerts primary control over our decision-making. The affective domain is so strong that we often make decisions contrary to what would be cognitively supported.

The affective domain is best dealt with through relationships. Exacerbated by entering students' high degree of dependency, managing relationships between institutional personnel and students is a collaborative venture, but the initial responsibility of establishing and managing them falls primarily on institutional personnel. The tenets of the DSDM and application of any models or theories of student GLD are grounded in the relationship.

In their ongoing quest to support student success, higher education decision-makers have attended to "structure and throughputs" in such a way to positively affect student quality of life in terms of cognitive and behavioral GLD but have lagged in their attention to the affective domain of individual students' lives. Yet affectively based phenomena have the greatest of all domains' impact on critical decisions regarding academic performance, motivation to succeed, the decision of whether or not to remain enrolled through graduation, and the perceived quality of their "lived experience" while enrolled and after graduation.

Unless institutions develop SSIPs aimed at positively influencing students' affective domain, the probability of improving overall performance and ultimate graduation will remain where it stands today at their own institution as well as the nationwide six-year graduation rate of just over 55% (Frederick et al., 2018). And of those students who do graduate, many depart with less-than optimally developed skills than they might with a greater overall GLD.

Theoretical Foundations

By applying theoretically and empirically validated theories and models that attend to students' affective state within the superstructure of the DSDM, we can expect that not only graduation rates will improve, but the levels of students' actual performance while enrolled will improve as well. The key to employing theories and models is that of how well they are created, administered, and delivered to students and the DSDM provides a superstructure of student development within which appropriate, empirically based, individualized SSIPs can be created and effectively employed to meet desirable and adequately articulated outcomes: both aspirational and functional. Essentially, the DSDM provides an environment within which empirically based SSIPs can be employed with the greatest potential for positive impact.

The theoretical foundation of the DSDM is not limited to one domain or position of any identified theory. The model is individualistic in forming to the needs of the student. This allows the model to be shaped around the student where they are in development rather than a fixed model to which the student must be formed. In addition, the key is not for the institution to assess and interpret student experiences but for students to do so themselves. However, this cannot be accomplished in the absence of support and guidance of an SO.

By integrating complementary elements of the theories, the DSDM disrupts the current fragmented paradigm by defining student success as an intricate model of SSIPs and ongoing assessment. The current paradigm addresses students' cognitive and behavioral needs but fails to consider students' affective needs, such as sense of belonging, affiliation, and connectivity. This current paradigm also defines student success quantitatively while denying the complexities of persistence behavior that reflects students' engagement experiences in the college environment. Synthesis of theories allows for unique application of the DSDM in a way not currently addressed by any other model. Like never before, this provides a bridge to practice that allows one to shape the complexities of theory into a model that is purely focused on student sense of membership and belonging in the academy where processing along the affective domain is critical.

Few, if any, current student development theories or models exist which institutions can draw from to inform the holistic development of their students that positively affect both persistence through graduation and full-potential performance. Yet none have arrived at an ideal regression equation which fully informs the development of SSIPs to the degree that absolute predictability of success can be expected and replicated with other students across all developmental levels. Moreover, Reeves and Lose (2009) even cautioned against the development of one-size-fits-all approaches as decision makers might well be led astray by over-relying on regression as an accurate predictor of success.

The DSDM is based on a variety of human and college student development theories as well as college student support models. The following sections will address the theories incorporated into the metatheodel. The relevance for integration and application of the defined theories are presented in a summary table (see Table 1).

Engaging Students in Asynchronous Advising

Table 1. Summary of Theories Within the DSDM.

Theory	Summary	DSDM Contract
Chickering's Theory of Vectors (1969; later Chickering & Reisser, 1993)	The "vectors" suggest a degree of movement. This freedom of direction is intended to recognize that development is not linear and therefore some students may regress with regard to their individual maturation process	GLD
Astin's Model and Theory of Involvement (1984, 1999)	Assumes that the degree to which any meaning students perceive from involvement with the institutional community will trigger affinity which will positively affect retention, ultimate graduation, and performance	SSIPs
Tinto's Model of Student Departure (1987, 1993, 2012)	Depicts departure as a process of interaction between the individual's attributes, goals, commitments, institutional experiences, integration, and outcomes. The majority of students who depart from higher education are not struggling academically	DSDM stages
Pascarella's General Model for Assessing Change (1985)	Identifies several core components, including student input variables, structural and organizational characteristics, the institutional environment, interactions with agents of socialization, and quality of student effort	SSIPs
Bandura's Social Learning Theory (1977)	Asserted people learn from observing the behavior and outcomes of that behavior in others, which leads to modeling	SO
Baxter Magolda's Theory of Self-Authorship (1992a, 1998, 2001, 2009)	The theory of self-authorship, a developmental process, examines how one constructs meaning from events which occur in their individual environment	DSDM stages
Schlossberg's Theory of Marginality and Mattering (1989)	Proffers a lens through which one can examine how college students interpret their membership in the academy and how this interpretation relates to student success.	GLD
Kegan's Orders of Consciousness (1982)	Referred to an SO as one with whom a protégée can establish a trusting relationship and from whom the protégée can grow, learn, and develop under the guidance and mentoring of the other	SO
Glasser's Sense of Belonging (1998)	Basic safety needs of students and meeting cognitive development needs in many ways, they seem to have fallen short of meeting the needs of belongingness/love and esteem needs. Not attending to the basic needs of belongingness, love, and esteem will result in lower probabilities of meeting higher level needs	SO
Maslow's Hierarchy (1943)	Defined levels of need in a hierarchy with the most basic needs defined as physiological drives for air, food, water, and shelter and the highest need is self-actualization. When these needs are absent or blocked, the individual can feel inferior, weak, or helpless and can result in discouragement	SO
Perry's (1970) Theory of Intellectual and Ethical Development	Provided a framework of cognitive development in his nine-step progression of positions from dualistic to relativistic thinking. Perry used the term "position" as opposed to stage because it represents the positional view the student has when it comes to cognitive matters of right and wrong	GLD
Kuh's Theory of Student Engagement (Kuh, Schuh, Whitt, & Associates, 1991)	Emphasized the importance of out-of-class experiences where a great deal of learning occurs. Student and faculty/staff relationships are essential to facilitate student success using intentional developmental approaches focusing on student learning	SSIPs

DSDM Stages

Stage one: Dependency
The broad goal of Stage one is to assist in student identity development; the early establishment of positive habits; the creation and maintenance of a meaningful relationship with the SO; acclimation to the institutional environment; and, finally, the development of an effective goal strategy.

Stage two: Independence
Stage two is designed to assist student GLD through the state of independence. Self-agency, critical thinking, communication skills, appreciation for differences in others, community stewardship, working with others, and relationship management are learned through meaningful interaction with and modeling positive behaviors of the SO and in the active participation in the wide variety of activities available within the institutional community.

Stage three: Interdependence
This stage is designed to support the advancement of students to the level of interdependence. They should have a clear understanding of their strengths and weaknesses and be focused on intentionality, all of which are supported and developed as a result of earlier work in Stages one and two. Interdependence finds students having moved past being overly reliant on others or too focused on the self. Interdependent students find themselves capable of and wanting to help those around them, whether to meet individual or group goals or to engage in altruism with the intent of contributing to the betterment of both self and others.

PROFESSIONAL STANDARDS FOR ADVISING

Universal Design (UD) in Academic Advising

The concept of Universal Design in Education (UDE) has provided an inclusive approach to student learning and removal of barriers in the academic environment (Burgstahler, 2008; Dukes, Morris, & Walker, 2018). Research on UD approaches to academic advising has not only enriched asynchronous delivery but also promoted individualized approaches to student learning (Burgstahler, 2008; Dukes et al., 2018; Shaw, Kampsen, Broad, & Albecker, 2008). By implementing such universal techniques in higher education, practitioners have provided supportive academic environments and acknowledged individual differences in student learning (Burgstahler, 2008).

Vanderheiden and Tobias (1998) define UD as

> the process of creating products (devices, environments, systems, and processes) which are usable by people with the widest possible range of abilities, operating within the widest possible range of situations (environments, conditions, and circumstances), as is commercially practical. (p. 1)

According to the Assistive Technology Act of 1998, "universal design" is defined as:

> A concept or philosophy for designing and delivering products and services that are usable by people with the widest possible range of functional capabilities, which include products and services that are directly usable (without requiring assistive technologies) and products and services that are made usable with assistive technologies. (p. 112, STAT 3634, 17)

Universal Design in Higher Education (UDHE) has spawned varying frameworks such as Universally Designed Teaching (UDT), Universal Instructional Design (UID), Universal Design for Learning (UDL), Universal Design for Instruction (UDforI), and Universal Design of Instruction (UDI) (Dukes et al., 2018). Each approach has intended to provide students with a holistic, individualized experience.

The primary purpose of UD in academic advising "is to provide equal access to effective advising and advising services for all students using an approach that consider each student's unique and individual needs regardless of demographics" (Shaw et al., 2008, p. 233). Influenced by student development theory, a UD approach to academic advising considers all aspects of individuals' identities, including physical and cognitive abilities (Burgstahler, 2017).

In applying online technologies and the DSDM to academic advising, professionals must be conscious of best practice. For the design and implementation of asynchronous advising, Phelps explored professional organizations' expectations for student services; specifically, the scholar was guided by principles set forth by The Council for the Advancement of Standards in Higher Education (CAS) and NACADA: The Global Community for Advising.

CAS (n.d.) was developed in 1979 "for promoting standards in student affairs, student services, and student development programs." CAS (n.d.) has identified itself as "the pre-eminent force for promoting standards in student affairs, student services, and student development programs." Academic advising has been identified as one of the professions for which CAS Standards have been developed (CAS, n.d.).

CAS Standards on Academic Advising Programs (AAP) has addressed multiple areas of the profession such as mission, programing, ethics, diversity, and technology. Standards identify "AAP must be intentionally designed" and driven by theory (CAS, 2014). In addition, AAP should be "designed to provide universal access" (CAS, 2014, Part II). Finally, CAS Standards for Academic Advising have identified programing should be "private and safe" as well as "convenient and accessible" to learners (CAS, 2014). Additional organizations have documented their expectations of advising; NACADA has established recommendations for institutions to engage.

In 2010, NACADA's Distance Education Advising Commissions developed standards for the organization which expects practitioners to advise distance learners. Two particular expectations addressed, "employ(-ing) a myriad of technologies in the delivery of distance education and related services" and "provide(-ing) appropriate student support services for distance learners as they would for students on campus" (NACADA, 2010).

IMPLICATIONS FOR PRACTICE

Integration within the theoretical foundation of the DSDM allows for a holistic approach to student development and success not addressed in isolation by any singular theory. The DSDM model is developed from common factors of the aforementioned theories. A lack of this incorporation would leave the model deficient in addressing students' needs for GLD. While not an exhaustive list, some common factors within the theoretical foundation of the DSDM include strong, trusting relationships with others in the college environment; orientation to individuals' needs for growth and change through assessment and feedback; involvement and influence of the environment on students' sense of belonging and mattering; and support of students' attainment of self-actualization.

Utilizing the Baxter Magolda's Epistemological Reflection Model (1992), the SO can help students move from absolute knowing in the first-year experience toward transitional knowing, catering to the affective domain by instilling a stronger sense of interpersonal and impersonal knowing. Baxter Magolda (1992) established a cognitive-structural model of reflection to facilitate self-authorship through meaning-making and reflection. This model is guided by six assumptions: (1) ways of knowing and patterns within them are socially constructed; (2) ways of knowing understood through naturalistic inquiry; (3) fluid use of reasoning patterns; (4) patterns are related to, but not dictated by, gender; (5) student stories are context-bound; and (6) ways of knowing are "patterns" (Baxter Magolda, 1992). These approaches help us consider how academic advisors can facilitate connection, facilitate student development, and use emerging SSIPs.

Technology and Academic Advising

Academic advising has been traditionally offered in a face-to-face format, due to components of interpersonal communication and relational development (Ohrablo, 2016); however, in recent years, advising has taken a greater presence in the online learning environment (Amador & Amador, 2014; Ambrose & Ambrose, 2013; Gaines, 2014; Habley, Bloom, & Robbins, 2012; Sotto, 2000; Steele, 2016a, 2016b). As online learning has continued to expand and reach new environments, advisors have explored manners to meet students' communication needs and expectations (Pasquini, 2011; Pasquini & Steele, 2016).

Development and integration of technologies in advising have given practitioners the opportunity to explore both synchronous and asynchronous channels of delivery (Amador & Amador, 2014; Ambrose & Ambrose, 2013; Gaines, 2014; Habley et al., 2012; Sotto, 2000; Steele, 2016a, 2016b). Applying varying technological mediums has allowed for greater opportunities for advising to occur (Leonard, 2008).

Using the DSDM, the SO serves a significant role to humanize the actual interactions between the student and the advisor. The SO should be a consistent advisor through the experience of the distance learner. Since the student is detached from a physical space of campus, the academic advisor as the SO provides this sense of belonging. The challenge is for the SO to help students develop affinity for the institution by facilitating strong and consistent rapport with their distance students.

Synchronous Versus Asynchronous Communication

Whereas synchronous communication occurs simultaneously between participants and is bound by time, asynchronous communication occurs at varying times and may involve differing locations of participants. Synchronous channels of communication require all involved parties to communicate in a simultaneous environment; such interaction allows for immediacy of a response. Specifically, participants are allowed to engage in real-time communication and share synchronous feedback. Examples of synchronous communication include face-to-face interaction, live videoconferencing, and telephony (Sotto, 2000). The ease of creating a virtual group or using Google Hangouts, Skype, Zoom, or other platforms open to simultaneous multiple users also makes it possible for discussion with students at other universities who are wrestling with the same academic 'questions.'

In contrast, asynchronous communication allows participants to communicate at times most conducive with one's schedule. Examples of online asynchronous advising methods has included email or other text-based messaging (Love & Maxam, 2011; Pasquini & Steele, 2016; Sotto, 2000), social media communication (Amador & Amador, 2014), "flipped advising" approaches (Steele, 2016a), and ePortfolios (Ambrose & Ambrose, 2013). Additional asynchronous communication examples have included web blogs, podcasts, and streamed online video (Habley et al., 2012).

Due to its flexibility of delivery, asynchronous email communication has been identified as the preferred primary method of interaction for academic advisors (Habley, 2004; Pasquini & Steele, 2016). Despite their popularity, text-based mediums such as email and instant messaging (IM) possess limitations; often times, typed messages are misinterpreted due to their "lack of visual and auditory cues" (An & Frick, 2006, p. 486). Specifically, scholars have acknowledged the text-based communication channel does not possess the interpersonal dynamics of face-to-face interaction (Ohrablo, 2016). In addition, email communication may not be best practice. "Although email is one of most commonly used (channels of communication), it can be relied on too heavily" (Leonard, 2008, p. 304). The scholar argued despite being a primary method of communication, one day, the medium will eventually become an outdated means of interaction (Leonard, 2008).

As alternatives, advisors could create a Facebook page or Google Hangout independent of their caseload to develop community which increases sense of belonging. Some advisors could also just simply choose social media as a way to build rapport among students. McCarthy (2010) found that Facebook provided a meeting place to enhance the learning experience and 92% of students participating in this class site agreed with the value for making stronger connections with other peers. By creating a Facebook page with strong privacy settings and a closed group for only class members, the discussions retained some selectivity.

Academic advisors still need discretion in monitoring the page that operates outside the security of the learning management systems (LMSs).

Miller (2016) championed social media for making it possible to go directly to an expert via Twitter and get almost instant response to a question. Miller (2016) considers the method of connection less important than the potential value of "building learning networks." While LMSs provide methods for live group or class discussion, the choice to use Facebook or other social media may be valuable for meeting students in the places they find most convenient and comfortable. Millenials and Generation Z students are already part of multiple Communities of Practice (Wenger, 2000) when supporting a cause, sharing a political position or surrounding a friend in need with encouragement. Their social media participation becomes a Community of Inquiry (Garrison, 2007) as they actively seek new "friends" among peers around the world who share a common interest, network with others who are developing a new idea or finding ways to better understand different cultural or social norms by dialoguing with others both near and far. Considering the high value that social media has for Millenials and Generation Z, incorporating these within the distance class builds on existing desire to connect in a way that is natural for this generation. When Social media is constructively applied, it can become the path to help students move from the independence stage (own ideas, shared with few) to the stage of interdependence (contribute ideas, work on ideas with others).

Advising From the Cloud

Encouragingly, many faculty and staff have been intentional in their application of technology in learning environments (Crawley & LeGore, 2009). Emerging approaches to academic support have included asynchronous advising. In this process, a student who engages in the process may access their advising video at any time with unlimited access. The theory is one of convenience and access as this meets the needs of distance education students who are often non-traditional student learners as they often have personal demands, commitments, or additional demands beyond the traditional classroom (Sasso & DeVitis, 2015). This approach to academic advising has a specific limitation as acknowledged by Phelps (2019) who examined the efficacy of asynchronous advising. Specifically, Phelps (2019) found that this advising modality may meet the needs of students who possess interdependence as noted within the DSDM but may not be beneficial to students who require synchronous face-to-face conversation and are within the dependent stage.

Further, Phelps (2019) explored students' perceptions of individualized, asynchronous advising via video. Phelps (2019) documented students' experiences with delayed video communication and advisement. The qualitative study provided insight as to how students engaged with "Advising from the Cloud" (Phelps, 2019, p. 89). Specifically, participants identified the asynchronous medium as a potential means of advisement via student and practitioner. This is referred to *cloud advising* by Phelps (2019) which was found to be successful in a small pretest–posttest evaluation of the method. Those students who engaged in cloud advising demonstrated preference for the medium but also wanted access to face-to-face advising in which Phelps (2019) noted that institutions may need to offer the duality of both synchronous and asynchronous "cloud" advising. These are both promising SSIPs which meet many of the tenets of the DSDM.

Student perceived asynchronous advisement via video as a convenient experience; however, these students also identified this method of communication lacked the ability for immediate feedback (Phelps, 2019). Benefits of asynchronous advising via video included transcending institutional and ability barriers and complementing scheduling demands of undergraduate students (Phelps, 2019). As participants noted, barriers in education and support vary from student to student (Phelps, 2019). Regardless of the obstacle a student faces, academic advisors must be conscious of the strategies and techniques available to meet students' needs which are consistent with the individualized approach of the DSDM.

Findings from this study by Phelps (2019) demonstrated that academic advising does not have to take place in a synchronous face-to-face setting. Naturally, not all students may be attracted to this method of advising; however, if such an approach provides a greater and more enriched experience for students, practitioners must consider the delivery method as a potential tool for connection and guidance. The task of the postmodern educator as the SO must be to identify barriers in learning and aid students in overcoming such obstacles. This approach follows a process of using video by the academic advisor (state of dependence) moves to developing an idea to implement the video response (state of independence). The SO as the academic advisor should also allow the student to initiate video queries (state of interdependence).

Phelps (2019) concluded that individualized asynchronous advising via recorded video is not meant to replace traditional face-to-face advising sessions; rather, the asynchronous strategy, or what this researcher has designated as "Advising from the Cloud," has the potential to meet the advising needs of diverse student populations. Simply, advising practitioners and higher education professionals must promote best practices and methods of connecting with their students. UD approaches in academic advising and higher education pedagogy encourage inclusive environments and support individualized strategies for learning.

Rather than provide services as a one-size-fits-all approach and engage the fundamental attribution error of American higher education, academic advisors must consider a holistic approach to student engagement. Advising professionals routinely explore methods of connecting with students in online environments; when browsing these options, practitioners must be cognizant of students' preferences for communication and learning. Specifically, technology has allowed individuals to custom design aspects of their life – entertainment streaming, realistic emojis, and online shopping have all been tailor-made based on an individual's interests and identities. Unfortunately, such an approach to learning has not yet been embraced by all higher education communities.

CONCLUSION

The DSDM helps us consider a holistic approach to student engagement. Burgstahler (2015) has noted, "UD (Universal Design) promotes an expanded goal to make products and environments welcoming and useful to groups that are diverse with respect to many dimensions, including gender, race, ethnicity, age, socioeconomic status, ability, veteran status, disability, and learning style". By incorporating an individualized approach to student success by means of the DSDM and asynchronous advising, higher education practitioners may meet students not only where they are but also when they are.

REFERENCES

Amador, P., & Amador, J. (2014). Academic advising via Facebook: Examining student help seeking. *Internet and Higher Education, 21*, 9–16.

Ambrose, G. A., & Ambrose, L. W. (2013). The blended advising model: Transforming advising with ePortfolios. *International Journal of ePortfolio, 3*(1), 75–89.

American Council on Education. (1949). *The student personnel point of view*. Washington, DC: Author.

An, Y., & Frick, T. (2006). Student perceptions of asynchronous computer-mediated communication in face-to-face courses. *Journal of Computer-Mediated Communication, 11*(2), 485–499.

Assistive Technology Act. (1998). Retrieved from https://www.congress.gov/bill/105th-congress/senate-bill/2432/text

Astin, A. (1999). Student involvement: A developmental theory for higher education. *Journal of College Student Development, 40*(5), 518–529.

Astin, A. W. (1984). Student involvement: A developmental theory for higher education. *Journal of College Student Personnel, 25*(4), 297–308.

Barratt, W. R., & Frederick, M. A. (2015). *University learning outcomes assessment (UniLOA) national report of means*. Retrieved from http://www.uniloa.com/wp-content/uploads/2015/11/NationalNormsPublic.pdf

Baxter Magolda, M. B. (1992a). *Knowing and reasoning in college: Gender-related patterns in students' intellectual development*. San Francisco, CA: Jossey-Bass.

Baxter Magolda, M. B. (1992b). Students' epistemologies and academic experiences: Implications for pedagogy. *Review of Higher Education, 15*(3), 265–287.

Baxter Magolda, M. B. (1998). Developing self-authorship in young adult life. *The Journal of College Student Development, 39*(2), 143–156.

Baxter Magolda, M. B. (2001). *Making their own way: Narratives for transforming higher education to promote self-development*. Sterling, VA: Stylus Publishing, LLC.

Baxter Magolda, M. B. (2009). *Authoring your life: Developing an internal voice to navigate life's challenges*. Sterling, VA: Stylus Publishing, LLC.

Burgstahler, S. E. (2008). Universal design in higher education. In S. E. Burgstahler & R. C. Cory (Eds.), *Universal design in higher education: From principles to practice* (pp. 3–20). Cambridge, MA: Harvard University Press.

Burgstahler, S. E. (2015). *Universal design in higher education: From principles to practice* (2nd ed.). Cambridge, MA: Harvard University Press.

Burgstahler, S. E. (2017). *Equal access: Universal design of advising*. Retrieved from https://www.washington.edu/doit/sites/default/files/atoms/files/EA_Advising.pdf

CAS. (2014). Standards and guidelines for academic advising programs. Retrieved from http://standards.cas.edu/getpdf.cfm?PDF=E864D2C4-D655-8F74-2E647CDECD29B7D0

CAS. (n.d.). About CAS. Retrieved from https://www.cas.edu/history

Chickering, A. W. (1969). *Education and identity*. San Francisco, CA: Jossey-Bass.

Chickering, A. W., & Reisser, L. (1993). *Education and identity* (2nd ed.). San Francisco, CA: Jossey-Bass.

Frederick, M. A., Sasso, P. A., & Barrat, W. R. (2015). Towards a relationship-centered approach in higher education: The dynamic student development metatheodel (DSDM). *New York Journal of Student Affairs, 15*(2), 2–27.

Frederick, M., Sasso, P. A., & Maldonado, J. (2018). *The dynamic student development meta-theory: A new model for student success.* New York, NY: Peter Lang Publishing.

Dukes, L. L., Morris, K. K., & Walker, Z. (2018). Universal design in higher education. In B. B. Frey (Ed.), *The SAGE encyclopedia of education research, measurement, and evaluation* (pp. 1757–1760). Thousand Oaks, CA: Sage Publications, Inc.

Gaines, T. (2014). Technology and academic advising: Student usage and preferences. *NACADA Journal, 34*(1), 43–49.

Garrison, D. R. (2007). Online community of inquiry review: Social, cognitive, and teaching presence issues. *Journal of Asynchronous Learning Networks, 11*(1), 61–72.

Glasser, W. (1998). *Choice theory: A new psychology of personal freedom.* New York, NY: HarperCollins.

Habley, W. R. (2004). *The status of academic advising: Findings from the ACT sixth national survey.* Manhattan, KS: NACADA.

Habley, W. R., Bloom, J. L., & Robbins, S. (2012). *Increasing persistence: Research-based strategies for college student success.* San Francisco, CA: Jossey-Bass.

Kegan, R. (1982). *The evolving self: Problem and process in human adult development.* Cambridge, MA: Harvard University Press.

Kerr, C. (2001). *The uses of the university* (5th ed.). Cambridge, MA: Harvard University Press.

Kuh, G. D., Schuh, J. H., Whitt, E. J., & Associates. (1991). *Involving colleges.* San Francisco, CA: Jossey-Bass.

Leonard, M. (2008). Advising delivery: Using technology. In V. N. Gordon, W. R. Habley, & T. J. Grites (Eds.), *Academic advising: A comprehensive handbook* (2nd ed., pp. 292–306). San Francisco, CA: Jossey-Bass.

Love, P., & Maxam, S. (2011). Advising and consultation. In J. H. Schuh, S. R. Jones, S. R. Harper, & Associates (Eds.), *Student services: A handbook for the profession* (5th ed., pp. 413–431). San Francisco, CA: Jossey-Bass.

Maslow, A. H. (1943). A theory of human motivation. *Psychological Review, 50*(4), 370–396.

McCarthy, J. (2010). Blended learning environments: Using social networking sites to enhance the first year experience. *Australasian Journal of Educational Technology, 26*(6), 729–740.

Miller, D. (2016, March 1). How online learning and social media are revolutionizing education. *Teachercast Live.* Retrieved from http://www.teachercast.net/2016/03/01/online-learning-social-media-revolutionizing-education/

NACADA. (2010). *NACADA standards for advising distance learners.* Retrieved from https://www.nacada.ksu.edu/Portals/0/Commissions/C23/Documents/DistanceStandards.pdf

Ohrablo, S. (2016). *Advising online students: Replicating best practices of face-to-face advising.* Retrieved from http://www.nacada.ksu.edu/Resources/Clearinghouse/View Articles/Advising-Online-Students-Replicating-Best-Practices-of-Face-to-Face-Advising.aspx

Pascarella, E. T. (1985). College environmental influences on learning and cognitive development: A critical review and synthesis. In J. C. Smart (Ed.), *Higher education: Handbook of theory and research* (Vol. 1, pp. 1–66). New York, NY: Springer Netherlands.

Pasquini, L. (2011). *Implications for use of technology in advising 2011 national survey.* Retrieved from https://www.nacada.ksu.edu/Resources/Clearinghouse/View-Articles/Implications-for-use-of-technology-in-advising-2011-National-Survey.aspx

Pasquini, L. A., & Steele, G. E. (2016). Technology in academic advising: Perceptions and practices in higher education. *NACADA Technology in Advising Commission Sponsored Survey*, 2013. https://dx.doi.org/10.6084/m9figshare.3053569.v1

Perry, W. G. (1970). *Forms of intellectual and ethical development in the college years: A scheme.* New York, NY: Holt, Rinehart, and Winston.

Phelps, J. T. (2019). *Asynchronous advising via video: A qualitative study of exploratory undergraduates' perceptions of universal design in academic advising.* Ph.D. thesis, ProQuest (13885536).

Reeves, E., & Lowe, J. (2009). Quantile regression: An education policy research tool. *Southern Rural Sociology, 24*(1), 175–199.

Sasso, P. A. & DeVitis, J. L. (2015). *Today's college student.* New York, NY: Peter Lang Publishing.

Schlossberg, N. K. (1989). Marginality and mattering: Key issues in building community. In D. Roberts (Ed.), *Designing campus activities to foster a sense of community* (New Directions for Student Services No. 48, pp. 5–15). San Francisco, CA: Jossey-Bass.

Shaw, M. E., Kampsen, A., Broad, C. A., & Albecker, A. (2008). Universal design in advising: Principles and practices. In J. L. Higbee & E. Goff (Eds.), *Pedagogy and student services for institutional transformation: Implementing universal design in higher education* (pp. 231–244). Minneapolis, MN: University of Minnesota.

Sotto, R. R. (2000). Technological delivery systems. In V. N. Gordon, W. R. Habley, & Associates (Eds.), *Academic advising: A comprehensive handbook* (pp. 249–257). San Francisco, CA: Jossey-Bass.

Steele, G. (2016a). Creating a flipped advising approach. *NACADA Clearinghouse*. Retrieved from http://www.nacada.ksu.edu/Resources/Clearinghouse/View-Articles/Creating-a-Flipped-Advising-Approach.aspx

Steele, G. (2016b). Technology and academic advising. In T. J. Grites, M. A. Miller, & J. G. Voller (Eds.), *Beyond foundations: Developing as a master academic advisor* (pp. 305–326). Hoboken, NJ: Wiley & Sons.

Tinto, V. (1987). *Leaving college: Rethinking the causes and cures of student attrition*. Chicago, IL: University of Chicago Press.

Tinto, V. (1993). *Leaving college: Rethinking the causes and cures of student attrition* (2nd ed.). Chicago, IL: University of Chicago Press.

Tinto, V. (2012). Completing college: Rethinking institutional action (Kindle ed.). Chicago, IL: University of Chicago Press.

Vanderheiden, G. C., & Tobias, J. (1998). *Barriers, incentives and facilitators for adoption of universal design practices by consumer product manufacturers*. Retrieved from https://www.researchgate.net/publication/270723895_Universal_Design_of_Consumer_Products_Current_Industry_Practice_and_Perceptions.

Wenger, E. (2000). Communities of practice and social learning systems. *Organization*, 7(2), 225–246.

ENGAGING WITH ONLINE GRADUATE STUDENTS THROUGH WRITING SUPPORT AND EMPLOYMENT

Jessica J. Jones

ABSTRACT

As online academic programs and online student populations continue to grow, it is important to consider the population of graduate-level students and what support they need from the university in order to be engaged and successful. This chapter will provide a review of the theory and research to show that there is a need for academic support for graduate-level students while also discussing how institutions have worked to create meaningful connections for students. Drawing on Astin's theory of student involvement, this chapter will discuss three ways that the University Academic Success Programs department at Arizona State University has worked to address that need and provide academic support to online graduate students: online graduate writing centers, online dissertation writing camps, and employment of online graduate students. Using interview examples from former student tutors, this chapter will show how these opportunities helped online graduate students feel valued, supported, and connected to the institution. This chapter will conclude by addressing limitations, areas for program growth and future research, and recommendations for practitioners to apply in their own institutions.

Keywords: Online; online student; writing; graduate students; support; retention; employment; academic support; student engagement; dissertation

In January 2007, I was that graduate student. I was taking an online class and felt that I was not getting the experience I wanted. The instructor was not very communicative and often late posting grades. I was trudging through the obligatory discussion board posts and responses. I struggled to work on the "group" project where each of us took a section and one person put all the pieces together. I finished the class with an A but was not sure what new knowledge I gained. The experience left me feeling disengaged and wanting more from my education. The catch? I was a traditional campus-based graduate student taking one online course while also taking two other in-person classes. Had I been solely an online student without many opportunities to make meaningful connections with others or to feel engaged by my coursework, I may have been one of the many students who does not complete their online degree.

As online programs grow and online student enrollment increases, online graduate students are a cohort who need targeted support while enrolled in degree programs. While developed with traditional campus-based students in mind, Astin's (1999) student involvement theory can still be leveraged as a model for online graduate students learning at a distance. The theory is based on the concept that the more physical and mental energies students put in to their educational experiences, the more successful they will be in the college setting. His theory considered the individual student's time and energy as a resource for the college but often a finite one. Students learning a distance still have their own resources of time and energy to invest in educational experiences, but they need options available to them to do so while enrolled in their degree program. Since students learning at a distance do not have the option of being physically connected to the university in the way Astin describes, faculty and administrators need to find new methods for students to make connections with their energies in and outside of the classroom. In a 2015 article, Lee, Pate, and Cozart brought a concern that only a fraction of students who enroll in online courses complete their degrees. They suggest some guidelines for assignments that "provide choice, rationale, and opportunity for personalization" (p. 59) to increase engagement in classes for online students. This approach to structuring assignments increased motivation for students which ultimately led to greater rates of completion of the course. Though providing these opportunities for engagement in individual classes can help bridge the gap of not being physically on campus, not being on a physical campus can still have an impact on students who

> need their own version of the "certainties" of bounded, campus space, while at the same time relishing their immersion in the networked, fluid, and fire spaces of the online mode. (Bayne, Gallagher, & Lamb, 2014, p. 570)

How each student will choose to create and define their space in relation to the university varies, but universities need to create and make available avenues by which students can reach out and become involved.

In a study done of online community college students who did not successfully complete their degrees, the primary reason for non-success was "I got behind and it was too hard to catch up" (Fetzner, 2013, p. 15). The advice these students would give to others relates predominately to various academic skills such as time management and organizational skills. They also gave advice about asking when you have questions and using other resources provided. After reviewing and sharing the survey results, Fetzner concludes that the results can be used to "assist the college in the enhancement, development, and assessment of online student support services, in an effort to support the success of all online students" (p. 18). Then Ross and Sheail (2017) discussed that when students encounter challenges in their programs such as time management or feelings of isolation, they often perceive those challenges as being solely due to the online modality. Since the challenges can be explained away and attributed to the online modality, students tend not to discuss the challenges with others or seek out support and resources to overcome said difficulties.

Knowing that an online student's time and energy is a limited resource, and also knowing that students will often see challenges encountered as a result of the online modality (Astin, 1999; Fetzner, 2013; Ross & Sheail, 2017), how can practitioners find ways to provide support for these students given those challenges? Kahn, Everington, Kelm, Reid, and Watkins (2017) researched how integrating reflection into the classroom impacted engagement. They concluded that reflection through various class discussions allowed students to engage in their work in a way that was meaningful to them as individuals and successfully manage the demands of the online learning environment. Creating those opportunities for reflection helped enhance engagement within the structure of classes, but there are many other opportunities for online students to enhance their engagement outside the classrooms just as there are opportunities for campus-based students. Providing spaces for collaboration and dialogue among peers, such as online forums with links to resources and activity spaces, as well as targeted academic coaching for online students has been found to have a positive impact on student engagement and persistence (Bondi, Daher, Holland, Smith, & Dam, 2016; Conway & Hubbard, 2004; Lehan, Hussey, & Shriner, 2018). There are various ways to support online students who are completing their degrees while not physically on campus to ensure they stay engaged through to graduation. Online graduate writing centers can be a resource where online students can invest their energy that not only provides academic support to students in graduate programs but also opportunities to help them feel connected and part of the university.

ONLINE GRADUATE WRITING CENTERS

In early August 2013, the Graduate and Professional Student Association (GPSA) at Arizona State University (ASU) reached out to the University Academic Success Programs (UASP) department with a request for targeted academic support for graduate students. GPSA asked the department to create a center that provided peer-to-peer writing support for the growing population of graduate students on campus and online. UASP's professional staff promptly devised a plan to create graduate writing centers that would open in September. This plan focused on creating structure, staffing, and marketing for the service.

First, it was determined how many graduate writing centers would be opened and on what campus locations. As a university with many physical campuses along with an online presence, administrators determined that four centers would be opened at the campuses where the largest populations of graduate students matriculated: Tempe, Online, Downtown Phoenix, and West. The model for how the centers would run was taken from UASP's current writing center structures that were in operation, with some slight adjustments given the graduate student population. The centers would provide one-on-one, appointment-based services for graduate students in any degree program, and the appointments would be 60 minutes in-person or 50 minutes online. In order to use the services, students would need to be enrolled in at least one graduate-level course at the university and the staff, called Graduate Writing Tutors (GWTs), would also be graduate students currently enrolled in programs at ASU.

After determining what the service would look like once in operation, a plan was devised for how to recruit, interview, hire, and train the GWTs. After writing and posting a job description, administrators sent emails to current students enrolled in master's, doctoral, or graduate certificate programs at ASU informing them of this opportunity. A new interview template and rubric were developed for this position, again taking inspiration from the forms already in use for writing tutors. Included were specific questions about applicants' past experiences with peer review and how those experiences would be applied to working with graduate-level students on their writing, or how they would work with a student on a thesis in a discipline outside their area of expertise. Training for this first group of GWTs was developed to be a half-day on a Saturday after classes had begun in order to train staff on department policies, expectations of their work, and tutoring strategies such as active listening, probing questions, and using a tutoring cycle.

The new service was marketed directly to faculty teaching graduate-level courses, GPSA networks, and students themselves, and the graduate writing centers officially opened in September 2013. The online graduate writing center has experienced growth every year, starting with offering 30 synchronous appointment hours per week to offering 95 synchronous appointment hours per week in 2019/2020. Though the services are open to all ASU students, online students have always been the largest percentage of users starting at 39% in 2013–2014 and growing to 83% in the 2018–2019 school year (UASP, 2014, 2019). This usage is compelling proof of the need to provide writing support for students enrolled in online graduate programs as an opportunity for engagement in academics while at the university.

Online graduate students are like all students in that they come from various backgrounds and, as a result, have various needs when it comes to writing support during their programs. Some graduate students are entering their programs directly after completing their undergraduate degrees or may be returning to college after several years in the workforce. They may be entering a discipline similar to the one they previously studied or be exploring an entirely new interest. They may be seeking to grow their personal knowledge, secure a degree to remain current in their field, or obtain a degree to be competitive for a promotion to further their career. Any student may experience imposter syndrome phenomenon that they do not belong and doubt their ability to be successful (Cisco, 2020). The online graduate writing center is a place where online students, who may be working on their degrees in solitude, can receive additional support on their writing projects at any stage while also connecting with another graduate student, a peer tutor at ASU. As an example of Astin's (1999) suggestion that students need to dedicate time to their academic experience, the online graduate writing center gives these students an opportunity to invest their energy in their educational experience, thus providing a way to be more successful.

ONLINE DISSERTATION WRITING CAMP

The online graduate writing center had great success, but another gap in services presented itself. UASP had been offering in-person, week-long Dissertation Writing Camps during June since 2012. These camps were designed to provide support for doctoral candidates working to finish their dissertations. Students and faculty continually asked if the camp was offered online as students from in-person programs would move out of state to complete degrees, begin working full-time, or otherwise could not commit to an in-person camp. Considering those needs, along with seeing the number of online doctoral programs growing, UASP decided to adapt the in-person camp to be offered virtually in 2016.

The driving goal for creating this online dissertation writing camp was to provide resources, support, and time to write for doctoral students working through this unique and often nebulous process of writing a dissertation at a distance. The process of completing a dissertation can be an isolating one (Ross & Sheail, 2017); completing it at a distance through an online program could heighten that sense of isolation. Knowing that research has found students completing their programs online may assume that challenges encountered are due to that modality and may not seek out support or resources, UASP's camp could be a valuable resource aiding doctoral students toward completion. Administrators decided to be strategic about designing the camp to not just provide resources and information but to hopefully generate a sense of community.

To ensure the camp's success, the in-person curriculum could not be simply taken and "put online"; instead, the knowledge of what had been successful for the in-person camp setting needed to be curated and adapted to be successful in an online modality. A main feature of the camp is that most of the workshops and meetings are offered in an "a-la-carte" model, meaning camp participants choose what to attend given what is most relevant to their individual needs in their writing process. This meant that a priority when designing the online camp was to continue providing that flexibility and choice to participants, particularly given that some would be participating from different time zones. Using the university's online learning management system (LMS), it was decided that for each synchronous component of the camp, there would also be an asynchronous component to allow participants to leverage the different aspects even if their schedules would not allow them to log on in real-time when an activity was scheduled.

One such instance of these synchronous and asynchronous options was the way in which a panel of faculty and recent graduates was set up to operate online. During the in-person camp, administrators invite three to five faculty members and recent graduates to attend an hour and a half long event where they would answer questions the camp participants had about the dissertation process. Rather than offering the panel as a one-day/one-time activity online, the decision was made to have the synchronous component be for each panelist to host an individual office hour during which camp participants could log on and ask their questions. The asynchronous component was that the panelists would include their biographies and answers to three to four questions from administrators about the process of writing a dissertation. Those biographies and answers would then be posted to the camp LMS site so that camp participants could read at their convenience.

Decisions about the structure of the camp workshop content also required intentional thought for successful online delivery. The in-person camp would typically offer two workshops per day as a live presentation. The online version strategically selected three topics that were recorded and offered in a flipped classroom model. Camp participants who were interested in that topic were encouraged to watch the recorded presentation in advance at their convenience. They could then log on during a scheduled time to discuss the topic or any questions they had with a facilitator and each other. The remaining topics that were part of the in-person camp were made available to online participants as either videos or resource handouts to ensure they were getting a comparable experience.

After determining the structure of offering the online dissertation writing camp and how resources would be shared with the participants, the focus shifted to considering the support components. As previously mentioned, most online camp activities would be considered "a-la-carte," but strategic messaging was sent to those who enrolled in the camp encouraging them to be logged on the first day of the camp for the welcome and goal setting session. That session curriculum was designed to not only go over logistical items, such as the camp schedule and technology tips, but to also learn more about the participants as individuals in order to assist with making realistic goals for the camp week and beyond. To scaffold that initial reflection and provide support throughout the week, there were morning writing reflections and closing check-out activities each day that participants could complete and synchronously discuss such as their ideal writing setting and what they accomplished that day. Participants were also encouraged to complete a daily reflection form online if they could not make the synchronous afternoon check-in activity that asked about what they accomplished that day and if there was anything they still wanted to discuss or learn more about. Those reflection forms were then read by a camp facilitator who responded with comments, shared resources, or answers to questions.

The final component of the camp design was to support individuals' actual writing to help drive forward their dissertation projects. The participants needed to know that, despite all these available workshops and activities, using their time to focus on their writing was encouraged in lieu of participating in a workshop or other scheduled activity. On the schedule, during all activities except the

Monday morning check-in, there was an alternative listing for "writing time." Online GWT staff were employed to provide one-on-one appointments to camp participants. During these appointments, participants were able to get feedback on their outlines, drafts, or revisions as they progressed on their writing. This three-pronged approach of providing resources, support, and time to write in an online environment helped the camp grow 420% from 5 participants in June 2016 to 26 participants in June 2019 (UASP, 2017, 2019).

The growth of participation shows how the camp is a valuable resource for online doctoral students by providing support and connections while they are working on their culminating projects. By providing workshops on topics such as "Planning for Long-Term Projects" and "Introduction to the Literature Review," some of the hidden curriculum for successful completion of a doctoral program is exposed. The chance to connect and dialogue with professional staff in UASP, faculty, recent doctoral graduates, and each other helps strengthen the sense of community that may be lacking when completing a degree at a distance. These opportunities will hopefully help online students avoid what Ross and Sheail (2017) identified as a potential concern for this group: feeling their experience is less valuable and ultimately inferior to those on campus.

EMPLOYMENT OF ONLINE GRADUATE STUDENTS

The online graduate writing center and the online dissertation writing camp have become hallmark programs of UASP for providing support to students enrolled in online master's and doctoral programs. But a key component of success of these programs is that they provide the opportunity to employ online graduate students. In the second semester of operation, the online graduate writing center was able to hire its first online student to work as an online GWT. The parameters for hiring an online student for the position are the same for hiring campus-based students: they must be currently enrolled students in a graduate-level program, have and maintain a 3.0 cumulative grade point average (GPA), submit a writing sample that demonstrates their ability to write at the graduate-level, and have a faculty member complete a referral with feedback on areas such as the students writing knowledge and ability to work with others.

After those minimum requirements are met, applicants are contacted to provide their schedule availability for the semester and to schedule an interview. The center has specific hours of operation, so the staff must be able to work during those times. Time zone differences have been the biggest challenge encountered with hiring remote workings, mainly due to the fact that Arizona does not participate in Daylight Saving Time. Administrators work to clearly communicate that work schedules are set to Arizona time, and that the local time for out-of-state staff changes in November and March. Candidate interviews are evaluated using a rubric to assess their technical knowledge of writing concepts, communication skills, and applied knowledge. Those who are offered the position work with the Human Resources Office to complete I-9 and other university required hiring paperwork, either at a reciprocal institution or with a notary, before mailing everything to the university's office to be processed. Once all paperwork is completed and processed, staff then go through training for the role before they begin tutoring.

Training evolved from the half-day training given when the center was first established. Online students employed as GWT staff living out of state are integrated into the scaffolded 14 hours of College Reading and Learning Association (CRLA) certified training (College Reading & Learning Association, 2018) that all campus-based staff experience; the only difference is that they attend using various online meeting technologies. Topics covered during this initial training include employment requirements such as expectations, payroll, and technology training, as well as philosophical topics like ethics, using a tutoring cycle, and assertiveness. After that initial training, new staff are scheduled to observe a peer online GWT who has worked for the center for at least one semester. After conducting two to three hours of observations, new staff complete an observation reflection form which has questions about what they noticed their peer doing when tutoring a student, things they think they will duplicate in their own tutoring interactions, and any follow-up questions they may have. Supervisors then read and respond to those reflections, commenting on and clarifying what the new tutor observed while answering any questions. Finally, when the new online GWT works their first shift, a supervisor is present in their online meeting room to provide additional support. This first shift observation is helpful for several reasons: to answer any questions about logistics that may have been forgotten due to cognitive overload, to give immediate feedback on their work, and to take notes and give more thorough written feedback within 24 hours.

The training just described takes place all within the first two weeks of the tutor starting their position. The ongoing management of these online tutors is a thread that continues throughout their employment. While there is a reliance on email for ongoing communication, there are several other tools in place to ensure that an online tutor living out of state feels supported in their work. All online tutors submit a report to their supervisor each week, and this tool is particularly valuable for establishing rapport with the online GWTs. The report asks staff to share a success they had that week, any challenges they encountered and how they overcame the challenge, how their academic classes are going, and if they have any questions or need anything from their supervisor. This ongoing reflection is helpful when the staff need to complete their semester self-evaluation form. Not only do they complete a self-evaluation reflecting on their accomplishments and developing goals, but they also complete a peer observation, and are likewise observed by a peer, as a way of intentionally learning from their colleagues. Beyond the mechanics of being hired and employed, the online GWTs form connections with each other, the students with which they work, and the greater university. Their employment has an impact on how they feel connected to the university not just while they are enrolled but also beyond the tenure of their employment.

I conducted an Institutional Review Board (IRB)-approved study to interview former ASU online GWT staff about their experiences working as online GWTs. Ten former staff members were contacted and four staff participated in a semi-structured interview conducted in the summer and fall of 2019. The interview consisted of 12 questions and was conducted live using the Zoom meeting platform. The interviews were recorded and transcripts were reviewed to find common themes. All names used in this chapter were anonymized.

When asked to reflect on their experience being employed as an online GWT, the former staff talked about how they were able to support other ASU online students when working with them on their papers. David and Ruth talked about how being online students themselves helped them know what kind of resources to encourage other ASU online students to use to support their academics knowing they would not have access to the physical campus. Sebastian also brought up the fact that being a peer of the online students gave him opportunities to listen, empathize, and validate their concerns by "being on the same level as them as someone who's going through the same things." Nicole described her ability to support other ASU online students through this personal connection as well:

> I think I was able to provide a good service in that a lot of ASU online students don't hear another person's voice. When tutoring, I was talking to them. There was an actual feel of connection. Yah, it was online, but I was reacting to them. I was responding. I was laughing at their jokes and they were laughing at mine. I was listening to them rant and rave. It was different than just typing something out and waiting for a response.

These connections were not just limited to the students whom they were tutoring. Many staff also talked about the connections they felt to their fellow tutors during their time of employment. David, who started his time as an ASU online student with the goal of forming meaningful relationships with people during his program, shared that "working in the writing center helped me to feel more a part of that community because I was interacting with other students, some of whom were on campus." He went on to share how he and the other tutors would use downtime before and after shifts to talk with each other in the online chat about their classes and getting ready to graduate. Since he worked for the center during his final semester before graduating from ASU, he said, "in that final semester I felt more connected to the larger community." Ruth and Nicole also talked about the connections they made with other tutors through staff meetings, staff parties, and group activities through chat. Working remotely while still being part of a team had some long-term impacts on some of the tutors. Sebastian talked about how he would work with other staff during shifts to discuss different techniques for tutoring or improving communication with students. He shared that even though he was living in another state, it never felt like he was there by himself because of the team around him. Sebastian also shared how "getting the teamwork and the communication skills and the time management skills while you're trying to do schoolwork" helped him show on his resume that he can manage multiple tasks and communicate effectively at a distance.

When discussing if their work as an online GWT helped in their future careers, all the staff had specific examples of how the position had made an impact. Nicole talked about how she is now working in the field of law where she has to not only do research but also review colleagues' writing in legal briefs and motions. She talked about how it is important to make things clear in the writing and also to be sure to cite information properly:

> I think learning more about citations with tutoring helped me immensely. I didn't really think about it until actually just now, just how much research is in our day to day lives, especially in the professional world.

Another key skill she talked about included that she was now often giving feedback to colleagues on the phone in her job and not face to face. David shared that not only did he feel his own writing improved by having to think about the nuances of writing in different ways, but that the position helped him secure his two positions postgraduation. He shared how in his first job, the interviewer indicated that having worked in a writing center showed that he had demonstrated competency for writing and writing mechanics. For his second position working as an adjunct professor for a community college, the online tutoring position helped show he had the required number of years of experience with teaching or training. He also shared that "the department chair liked the fact that I worked in a remote environment specifically because they are trying to ramp up their own technical writing online certification program." Ruth talked about how the experience inspired her to make a change in her current position:

> I had a kind of revelation. I've been a freelancer for a long time, like 19 years now. I actually went to her after ... and it was time for me to negotiate a new contract. And I said to [my boss], I have been on a staff for the first time in 19 years at ASU and feeling part of a team has been an incredible positive for me. And so, I actually proposed to that organization that they make me a staff member so that I could be part of their publication team instead of being someone a little bit on the outside.

Ruth concluded by sharing that they are working on implementing that for the next year and that it was a surprise to her that she was so satisfied being part of a staff where the collaboration on the team was real and inspiring.

These interview examples are a small insight into the ways employment as a tutor while being enrolled in an online graduate degree can have an impact on feeling connected to a university, even at a distance. This opportunity for greater involvement not only impacted the online students' experiences while attending the university and finishing their degree but also had long-term positive impacts on their career paths after graduation.

Through running online graduate writing centers, facilitating online dissertation writing camps, and providing employment opportunities for online graduate students, UASP at ASU is providing support for online graduate students in various ways to increase their overall engagement with the university. The online graduate writing centers are creating an opportunity for online graduate students to invest time in their academics in a peer-to-peer setting while also allowing for potential personal, real-time connections. By participating in the online dissertation writing camp, online doctoral students can not only have a structure to help them dedicate time to working on their culminating writing projects but may also help curb the feeling that their online experience is less valuable than an in-person experience. Throughout both experiences, online graduate students can be student employees at a distance which provides experiences to enhance their skills both while employed and after graduation.

LIMITATIONS

There are some limitations in the research that was done, along with areas for further program growth and future research. One limitation of this chapter is that only four students agreed to be interviewed, thus providing a limited perspective. Similarly, the students who agreed to be interviewed were selected from a group of ASU online students who did work as GWTs. It could be argued that the type of student who is going to seek out and apply for an experience such as this is already positively inclined toward being more involved with the university. Finally, this chapter describes what one department at one institution is currently doing programmatically for its online graduate students. Not only are online academic programs and online faculty doing many things to ensure engaging academic experiences, but there are other support programs and staff that are helping to contribute to online graduate student engagement and success. For the purpose of this chapter, the focus is solely on what UASP is doing as a unit.

AREAS FOR PROGRAM GROWTH AND FUTURE RESEARCH

Some limitations of this chapter also lend themselves as areas for future research. First, UASP only offers synchronous service support options, so there is no discussion about how engaging with an asynchronous tutoring service option may impact a feeling of engagement. While UASP does offer synchronous online writing tutoring to undergraduate students, the focus of this chapter was on graduate students who were enrolled in online degrees. Expanding the discussion to include undergraduate students would yield valuable insights. Technology is often changing and what was written about in this chapter took place predominantly using the meeting technology platform of Adobe Connect. However, in May 2019, ASU switched to using the service Zoom for meetings and tutoring services. Exploring the different technology that is utilized and whether or not it has an impact on engagement would be valuable to determine if any recommendations can be made regarding what components are necessary for educational engagement. When some think about who an online student typically is, a picture comes to mind as someone who tends to be older, is returning to school after being in the workforce, and has numerous demands on their time such as having partners, children, or full-time employment. As more students enroll in fully online degree programs immediately after high school or after completing a bachelor's degree, exploring the different types of students who enroll in online degrees would be valuable in order to learn what types of services each group may be looking for to increase their feelings of engagement.

In addition to exploring different types of student populations, different types of academic support and their respective impact on students could also be investigated. UASP has been offering online subject area tutoring for undergraduate students since 2013 but has more recently started offering additional options for online Supplemental Instruction (SI), as well as online Graduate Statistics

Tutoring. As those newer programs grow and evolve at ASU, as well as other institutions, more research can be conducted in those specific service areas to measure impact on engagement for online students.

RECOMMENDATIONS FOR PRACTITIONERS

While there are limitations to the information presented in this chapter and many avenues to explore for future research, there are still opportunities for departments and institutions to start implementing their own online writing support services for online graduate students. In order to decide on the logistics of the program, consider questions such as:

1. Will it be appointment-based, drop-in based, or a mixture of both?
2. What will the structure of an appointment be as far as time and what can be discussed?
3. Will the service be synchronous, asynchronous, or a mixture of both?

Then there are also some decisions to make with regard to the technology used, such as:

1. If going with an appointment-based model, what technology will you use for scheduling appointments?
2. What technology will you use for tutoring, be it synchronous or asynchronous? Is it the same system for scheduling or will it be different?
3. What challenges may students encounter when trying to use the necessary technologies or what barriers may exist? If barriers do exist, how might you address them?

And finally, think about the recruiting, hiring, and training processes for any student staff who will provide the service. Consider things like:

1. What equipment would the student staff need (e.g., computers, dual monitors, headsets, webcams, tablets, etc.)?
2. Can you hire student staff who live out of state, and does your human resources department require you to complete additional steps?
    a. If out-of-state staff are hired, how do you ensure they have the equipment and infrastructure to be successful?
    b. If they do not have something you have deemed necessary for your service, like a reliable internet connection or a web camera, how do you provide that for them?
3. What qualities are you looking for in student staff and how do you create a job description and interview questions to help hire students who have those qualities?
4. What training and onboarding is necessary for the job? On what topics do you train in terms of employee expectations, technology, and tutoring philosophies and strategies?

These areas to consider and questions to answer are by no means exhaustive, but they can help those interested in starting online graduate writing centers consider some necessary pieces and identify key stakeholders while working through the process. Ultimately, working to create a center that provides writing support to online graduate students can help a department and institution provide an opportunity for those students to engage in a meaningful way. This engagement increases their connection to the university which can lead to better retention and overall success as they work toward graduation and their future endeavors.

REFERENCES

Astin, A. (1999). Student involvement: A developmental theory for higher education. *Journal of College Student Development, 40*(5), 518–529.

Bayne, S., Gallagher, M. S., & Lamb, J. (2014). Being 'at' university: The social topologies of distance students. *Higher Education, 67*(5), 569–583. https://doi-org.ezproxy1.lib.asu.edu/10.1007/s10734-013-9662-4

Bondi, S., Daher, T., Holland, A., Smith, A. R., & Dam, S. (2016). Learning through personal connections: Cogenerative dialogues in synchronous virtual spaces. *Teaching in Higher Education, 21*(3), 301–312. https://doi-org.ezproxy1.lib.asu.edu/10.1080/13562517.2016.1141288

Cisco, J. (2020). Using academic skill set interventions to reduce imposter phenomenon feeling in postgraduate students. *Journal of Further & Higher Education, 44*(3), 423–437. https://doi-org.ezproxy1.lib.asu.edu/10.1080/0309877X.2018.1564023

College Reading & Learning Association. (2018). International tutor training program certification (ITTPC): ITTPC certification requirements. Retrieved from https://www.crla.net/index.php/certifications/ittpc-international-tutor-training-program. Accessed on April 6, 2020.

Conway, J. I., & Hubbard, B. C. (2004). Completing the picture: The development of online activities and involvement opportunities. *Online Classroom*, 7–8. Retrieved from http://search.ebscohost.com.ezproxy1.lib.asu.edu/login.aspx?direct=true&db=aph&AN=12123867&site=ehost-live

Fetzner, M. (2013). What do unsuccessful online students want us to know? *Journal of Asynchronous Learning Networks, 17*(1), 13–27.

Kahn, P., Everington, L., Kelm, K., Reid, I., & Watkins, F. (2017). Understanding student engagement in online learning environments: The role of reflexivity. *Education Technology Research & Development, 65*(1), 203–218. https://doi-org.ezproxy1.lib.asu.edu/10.1007/s11423-016-9484-z

Lee, E., Pate, J., & Cozart, D. (2015). Autonomy support for online students. *Techtrends: Linking Research & Practice to Improve Learning, 59*(4), 54–61. doi:10.1007/s11528-015-0871-9

Lehan, T. J., Hussey, H. D., & Shriner, M. (2018). The influence of academic coaching on persistence in online graduate students. *Mentoring & Tutoring: Partnership in Learning, 26*(3), 289–304. https://doi.org/10.1080/13611267.2018.1511949

Ross, J., & Sheail, P. (2017). The 'campus imaginay': Online students' experience of the masters dissertation at a distance. *Teaching in Higher Education, 22*(7), 839–854. https:/doi.org/10.1080/13562517.2017.1319809

University Academic Success Programs. (2014). *Online graduate writing center end of year data report 13–14*. Tempe, AZ: Jessica Jones.

University Academic Success Programs. (2017). *Online graduate writing center end of year data report 16–17*. Tempe, AZ: Jessica Jones.

University Academic Success Programs. (2019). *Online graduate writing center end of year data report 18–19*. Tempe, AZ: Jessica Jones.

STUDENT TRANSITIONS: ACADEMIC SUPPORT FOR POSTGRADUATE ONLINE DISTANCE STUDENTS

Louise Connelly and Donna Murray

ABSTRACT

The academic needs of postgraduate online distance students are often very diverse. Typically, the students will be over 35 years old and studying part-time, while juggling other commitments, such as family or employment. Therefore, providing academic support which is targeted and meets their needs is paramount for enhancing the student experience and ensuring that they have the best possible chance of succeeding at postgraduate level. The academic support can be positioned into three transitional stages: into, throughout, and exiting their studies. Typically, during the first stage (entering the university), the main concern for the student is around academic expectations and getting started. During the second stage (while studying), there will be a variety of academic needs, ranging from assignments to literacy skills. In the third stage (exiting the university), this will typically be related to employability or going onto further study. This chapter presents an academic transitions roadmap (ATR) that can be used by institutions, in order to provide targeted academic support that is aligned with the three stages. By implementing the ATR, there is the potential for enabling students to become more confident while on their academic journey, and ultimately, this contributes to enhancing the student experience.

Keywords: Academic support; distance learners; masters; online; pedagogy; plagiarism; postgraduate; roadmap; support; transitions

Academic support, informal peer support, and social networks are necessary to ensure attrition rates remain low, students maintain their well-being, and succeed at their studies. Universities will invest considerably in providing support and services which align with the academic journey of the student. It is generally accepted that students may need academic support (Thompson & Mazer, 2009). However, this may vary greatly from one institution to another.

Furthermore, based on our experience in higher education, it has become apparent that the definition of academic support may differ depending on the individual or institution. It may include provisions offered by university services, some of which are enablers of academic achievement such as the disability office, the library, an academic study unit, or computing services. There may also be less formal support networks available, for example, student peer support facilities, societies, or a student association. For the purpose of this discussion, our focus will be on the formal academic support pertaining directly to the students' studies; academic requirements of their degree; and those offered by university departments, with a specific focus on a central academic study unit. Therefore, we are defining academic support as "resources, information, or individuals which will enable the student to engage with their programme of study and feel confident and equipped academically."

While the provision of academic support in higher education is not without its issues, the challenge of providing this to a diverse cohort of postgraduate (master's level) online distance learners (ODL) requires careful consideration as to the most appropriate model of delivery, as well as how to evaluate the effectiveness of the academic support. One of the most noticeable differences of this particular cohort, compared to on-campus students, is that they are typically mature students, with the majority being over 25 years old, studying part-time, based in different time zones, and juggling other commitments, such as family or employment (Sheail, 2018). Therefore, providing academic support which is differentiated, and targeted to meet their needs, is paramount for enhancing the student experience and ensuring that they have the best possible chance of succeeding at postgraduate level (Nichols, 2010).

In order to gain a better understanding of the postgraduate online student cohort and to ascertain what academic support is needed at different stages of the degree, we undertook a mixed-method approach, which included a literature review, an evaluation of existing support (workshops and online resources), as well as surveys (responses $n = 17$) and follow-up interviews ($n = 2$), to a specific group of online distance students from one Master of Science (MSc) program, at a Scottish university.

Our findings indicate that academic support can be positioned into three transitional stages, namely on entering the university, while studying, and on exiting the university (LaPadula, 2003; Tobbell, O'Donnell, & Zammit, 2010). Typically, during the first stage (entering the university), the main concern for the student is around academic expectations. During the second stage (while studying), there will be a variety of academic needs, ranging from different types of assessments (exams, reflective writing, essays, case reports, dissertations, etc.) to improving digital and time management skills. In the third stage (on exiting the university), this will typically be related to helping students articulate their academic journey.

First, we will present an academic transitions roadmap (ATR) that can be used by other institutions, in order to provide an academic support package that is targeted and aligned with the three stages. A suggested portfolio of academic support topics is outlined in the roadmap, including how to succeed at postgraduate level, critical thinking, presentation skills, academic writing, dissertations, digital skills, time management, as well as one-to-one academic support. The discussion of the ATR focuses on the practical ways in which it can be delivered locally at a devolved school/faculty level, and/or at a central university level, via a study skills or academic support department.

The ATR presents a holistic model for delivery, whereby educators should consider collaborating with and/or signposting the support offered by other departments, such as study skills, the library, digital skills, and the careers service. By implementing the roadmap, there is the potential for assisting students to become more confident while completing their academic journey. Ultimately, this type of intervention and support contributes to enhancing the student experience and may help lower attrition rates which can be higher in online programs compared to on-campus programs (Baxter, 2012; Rovai, 2002). It is possible that the ATR will not suit every institution due to finance limitations or expertise availability. The intention is that institutions consider modifying the ATR model specifically for their ODL students to ensure that the uniqueness of this cohort is carefully considered, their needs are met, and to ensure equivalency with on-campus support.

To enhance the understanding of the ATR model, each transitional stage will be discussed in detail, including the rationale for the provision of different types of support. We will draw from the survey and interview data gathered, to emphasize the student expectations and requirements, thus instilling the "student voice." The discussion concludes with a number of recommendations, alongside possible considerations for developing this approach further.

METHODOLOGY

The development of the roadmap arose due to the rapid growth in the number of postgraduate students, particularly the online distance cohort, at a research-intensive university. It became apparent that there was a requirement to offer academic support to online students in specific ways which facilitated their engagement, and that replicating the on-campus support would not be appropriate. Specifically, due to the profile of the cohort, and the need to deliver academic support both asynchronously or synchronously, but at a distance and potentially targeted at different time zones. We argue that these areas need to be addressed in order to avoid "campus envy" and to avoid the ODL student feeling that they are not enveloped in the authentic university experience (Bayne, Gallagher, & Lamb, 2013). The concern of equivalency in support offered to on-campus and online students is aptly highlighted in a survey response when asked "Before starting the programme did you have any concerns or requirements in relation to academic support" (question 8), where the student stated "I did wonder if online distance learning would offer the same level of academic support that on-campus learning offers its students." Ensuring the online model is not a deficit model is paramount to ensure that there is equivalency in experience and support. The ATR model can help to identify what provision is available or lacking, and where there are gaps in academic support, institutions can develop the provision to meet the needs of their students.

During 2017–2018, we examined a specific online distance learner cohort from a specific MSc program, in order to determine whether the academic support could be categorized in a way that would make sense to students and allow staff to have clarity about what was required at different stages in the academic journey. In doing so, we intended to demarcate transitional stages in relation to academic support needs. The project received ethical approval and was undertaken in 2017–2018.

The UK university, in which the research is positioned, has 9,781 postgraduate students, with 3,403 of these being online distance students and 496 based in the school being discussed in this chapter. As the support may vary between schools, and even at program level, a small cohort from a particular MSc program was selected to survey and asked to self-select for a small number of follow-up interviews. In doing so, this provided a sample group to address the following research questions:

- What academic support is needed?
- Does the academic support vary throughout the student journey?
- Are students aware of the academic support offered by the university (communication strategy)?

We approached the data gathering in two stages. Stage one was the issue of a survey in semester one of 2017, to a specific MSc program that had 70 students enrolled on it. Seventeen students completed the survey (24%). The survey contained 13 quantitative and free-text questions. This included demographic questions to enable us to identify possible correlations between academic support needs in relation to age, geographic location, and English as a first language.

Stage two was a semi-structured interview with two students (a second-year and a final-year student), who volunteered to help us understand the academic support requirements and associated challenges particular to an online distance student. The semi-structured one-hour interviews were hosted and recorded via Blackboard Collaborate and later transcribed. The interviews provided an opportunity for the research team to explore themes in more depth and, where useful, refer to the results of the data collected from the survey. The interviews were independently analyzed by the researchers and a number of themes emerged, which will be explored later. Both interviewees also provided an insight into their preference for how support is communicated to students, which helped us to review the communication strategy for academic support.

Due to the small cohort examined in this research, we are cautiously optimistic of the results, as they align with our own experiences of working with students, as well as anecdotal evidence, current research on academic support (Hebdon, 2015; Nichols, 2010; Thompson & Mazer, 2009), and online distance learning (Baxter, 2012; Bayne et al., 2013; Sheail, 2018). However, it is worth noting that the small sample size includes a gender bias (82% female, 18% male), which could have an impact on the findings presented here, especially in relation to motivational factors, where research has indicated a correlation to gender (Meece, Glienke, & Burg, 2006). Furthermore, 47% of survey respondents were between 22 and 30 years old, 35% were between 41 and 50 years old, and nearly 11% were between 51 and 60 years old. This is typical of the ODL cohort and is representative of many ODL programs (Bayne et al., 2013; Harrison, Harrison, Robinson, & Rawlings, 2018; Sheail, 2018).

DISCUSSION

This section presents our findings that have led us to consider academic support through the lens of a transitions model. The data from the surveys and interviews have informed the development of the ATR model, as well as the broader recommendations for supporting online distance students and academic support needs. Before we can evaluate the students' needs and reflect on the data, it is important to understand the motivational factors for students engaging with academic support. From there, we will consider possible communication factors that can influence the uptake of the support. Thereafter, we will focus on the three transitional stages and the specific support included at each stage.

Motivation and Communication

The UK Higher Education Academy Retention Grants Briefing Program presented an insight into the reasons for progression or attrition factors of postgraduate students. Some of the factors include those we outline here, such as support for easing students transitioning into postgraduate studies, building communities and relationships between staff and students, and facilitation of communication (HEFCE, 2010).

Before developing or expanding existing academic support provision, it is important to consider the motivational factors of why students will and will not engage with the support. Baxter (2012) refers to the link between resilience, motivation, and student identity. Considering these themes, intrinsic and extrinsic motivational factors may contribute to engagement with academic support, similar to the influence of these factors within a course; however, there may be more nuanced considerations such as confidence, self-efficacy (the ability to judge self-performance and belief in one's ability to succeed), anxiety, or a reflection on previous grades (Bandura, 1977). One of the direct challenges that an ODL student faces which could impact on their level of motivation is that they are often busy juggling a variety of commitments, as 82% of survey respondents stated that they are employed while studying. In addition, as interviewee two highlighted when asked what resources or workshops had she engaged with and she stated that it was limited, as "I've just been so busy ... you know when I stop having to get up at 6:00 in the morning to check the horses." This is not atypical, as many students have other commitments that may impact on how they structure their time, and as Sheail (2018) acknowledges, online learning is not "the ubiquitous promise of anytime, anywhere" (p. 464), as the structure of content and deadlines requires the student to be adept at simultaneously managing their personal, professional, and study life, even if the quality of the time may be variable (Sheail, 2018, p. 476).

In addition, the student may seek out and engage with academic support resources as they directly relate to a specific assessment/assignment or as a result of reflecting on previous grades that were not as high as expected, as interviewee one states: "Sometimes I did what I thought the assessment wanted ...," but this wasn't reflected in the feedback or grade. She then reflects on this and states "if I could tell people don't assume you know" and considers what academic support would have been useful to her at the time of the assessment. This highlights the importance of providing resources in relation to assessments and interpreting feedback, as well as signposting to and delivering the resource at the appropriate time in the academic year.

The importance of promoting and communicating the academic support on offer needs to be seriously considered, even more so with a cohort that may feel isolated, based in different time zones, and studying while juggling other commitments. Unlike the on-campus cohort who may network face to face (F2F), there needs to be a more targeted approach for ODL students. This was reinforced by the interviewees, who stated that positive modes of communication are email, announcements via Blackboard Learn (as the announcements are also received via email), website, induction welcome page, and serendipitously via live lecture sessions (which are also recorded). As shown in the discussion below, there are positive steps that can be taken to help promote academic support, especially as students transition into the university. For example, email, a newsletter, virtual learning environment (VLE), or virtual classrooms. Without targeted communication and throughout the time the student is at the university, there may be information overload at the wrong time or missed opportunities to engage with support at key points in their studies. When implementing the ATR model, it is crucial to consider the adjoining communication strategy, which may include social media, announcements via the VLE, or email. In doing so, this will assist with uptake and engagement with the resources and reinforce that support is offered.

ATR

To date, research on academic transitions and support has primarily focused on undergraduates or on-campus postgraduates; however, we can extract elements that complement the ODL academic support provision. A similar ATR model has been considered by other scholars such as Thompson and Mazer (2009), who developed the Student Academic Support Scale (SASS) "as a method of assessing the frequency, importance, and mode of communicating academic support among college students" (p. 433). Their research focused on undergraduate students, and some of their findings are pertinent to the discussion here, specifically motivational factors and modes of communication. They also discuss the importance of peer support, which is not an area we explored in detail but could be in the future. Their findings indicated that F2F support was preferable (p. 453). However, this is not always possible in the online context, although the virtual classroom may go some way to provide the F2F communication style and enhance the sense of identity, presence, and mitigating feelings of isolation (Harrison et al., 2018).

Others have also undertaken a similar venture, such as Hebdon (2015), who focuses on academic support for students transitioning from vocational education to higher education. The Learning Academic Skills Support (LASS) program aims to provide a "student-centred support programme, tailored to students' needs" (Hebdon, 2015, p. 120). The LASS program is focused on undergraduate students, and there are noticeable similarities to the development and implementation of support that we offer. For example, the provision aligns with certain stages in the students' academic journey. However, where it differs is in relation to embedding it within the curriculum of a specific program, whereas our model is typically implemented by an academic study skills unit (but this doesn't prohibit the embedding of provision directly into curriculum). The ethos of their venture aligns with ours as "it provides a model for support within the context of the whole student experience, delivered at times when students need it most," and this is what we are keen to promote (Hebdon, 2015, p. 127).

Where our model significantly differs from the LASS and SASS models is that the ATR model targets online distance students (typically 3–6 years part-time intermittent study). Therefore, this requires a flexible approach that meets a wide range of needs, as well as challenges. Based on the research and review of existing support in our institution, there is now a full suite of support for ODL students. This is a mixture of MSc program-based support and central provision via the academic study skills unit or other units, for example, the library. Where support is offered at a central, university level, this allows students the opportunity to learn from their peers in other disciplines, which can be missing when support is contained solely to specific MSc programs.

As mentioned earlier, communication of the ATR is vital. In our instance, the academic support offering is communicated centrally and via programs so that there is "normalisation" of the need for support. This provision continues to expand in line with the development and growth of ODL postgraduate programs and will be reviewed, refined, and redeveloped over time (Fig. 1).

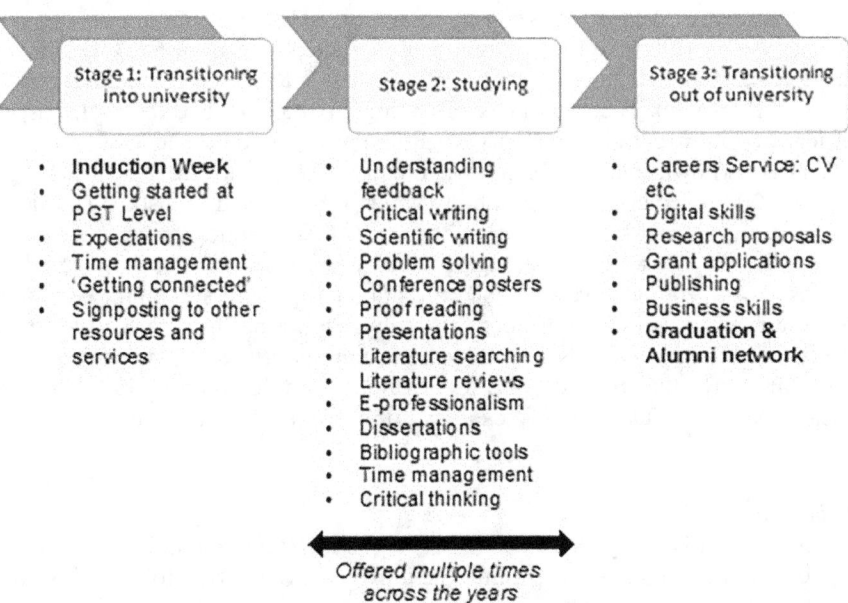

Fig. 1. Academic Transitions Roadmap.

Stage 1 – Transition into University

A theme that commonly arises when examining the ODL experience is community, which can be bound with the university or the specific program (Bayne et al., 2013; Rovai, 2002) and is also posited by Cahill, Bowyer, and Murray (2014) who state that "support strategies need also to foster a sense of belonging to the institution, the student's cohort group and discipline" (p. 199). This is a fundamental element to the first transitional stage and needs to be considered alongside the design and implementation of the academic support offered. Furthermore, the globally diverse cohort may experience or engage with academic support which is influenced by their cultural, environmental, or personal experience, and this needs to be considered in the "pedagogical framework" and contextualization of the learning resources when designing and delivering academic support (Harrison et al., 2018, pp. 480–481). Therefore, we need to consider transitioning into the university in the following interlinked contexts: development and integration into a community, induction, and academic support.

Community

Feeling isolated can be a common occurrence for ODL students (Rovai, 2002) and yet community building may not manifest until much later, if at all, or it may be focused at a program level. However, both the program and university can assist with facilitating the development of a strong community for the ODL cohort. Simply, this can commence in the transition stage with the induction process (also known as Fresher's Week or Welcome Week). Longer term, it can be embedded via coursework, such as group work, or via ongoing social activities, to ensure students maintain the sense of community. However, caution may need to be exercised with synchronous group work activities, if the specific ODL cohort has technical challenges such as an intermittent internet connection (Harrison et al., 2018, p. 490). The importance of community building and the related aspect of identity construction, which occurs through interaction and engagement with others, is acknowledged by Delahunty, Verenikina, and Jones (2013) who highlight Rovai's (2002) depiction of community which is connected to a socio-emotional investment, in order for a community to work. This includes the complexities of developing a sense of trust, belonging, similar expectations, and shared goals or values (Rovai, 2002). If we are to succeed at building successful online communities, we need to carefully consider this alongside the pedagogical and technical design of activities that will help to facilitate community development. It is therefore imperative that the expertise of learning technologists are drawn upon to ensure the successful design of academic support for ODL students.

Induction

The induction is a key aspect of the ATR, as it is fundamental for setting the scene and inducting the student into the university. In relation to the cohort that we examined, 53% were entering first year of their studies. On transitioning into their program, they are given access to a program "Base" course on Blackboard Learn, where there are links to academic support, program-specific information, for example, the handbook, as well as university regulations. They will have access to this course for the duration of their studies, as the intention is to not only provide an induction space but also act as a community hub for the students and academics, as well as a space to signpost academic skills resources.

In order to facilitate the social and community aspect, there are a range of induction activities, such as pinning information to a private virtual map, which highlights location and their expectations from the course and addresses some of the challenges highlighted by Rovai (2002). There is also a virtual corkboard/wall (Padlet.com), where students post a short biography and photo, and this instills a sense of identity which Delahunty et al. define as "socially constructed, being forged through human involvement in social activity" and the interaction is "mediated by language" (2013, p. 255). Identity curation is intertwined with community formation and can be enabled by instilling a sense of identity online through activities such as those mentioned above as well as being mediated through text-based activities (e.g., discussion boards). Activities such as virtual welcome sessions during induction week sets the tone for the academic and pastoral support for the ODL student and addresses the notion of "transition shock" (Nelson, Kift, Humphreys, & Harper, 2006, p. 3), as well as other transitions, such as language transition which is highlighted by Zhao (2014) in the study of Chinese students transitioning into postgraduate studies. Although only 25% of our study stated that English wasn't their first language, this may be higher on other MSc programs or in other institutions and should be a consideration when developing academic support.

Academic support
The ATR allows for a "just-in-time" approach to academic support, for example, students are offered support when they will require it, rather than having to figure this out on their own. There are a number of academic support topics that are crucial at Stage one – transition into university, if students are to succeed at postgraduate level. These include academic conduct (including plagiarism), getting started at postgraduate level (setting expectations), and getting connected (technologies). By addressing these topics early on and providing resources, it will avoid delayed engagement with the academic context and/or highlight where there are gaps in knowledge or experience.

Academic Conduct (Plagiarism)
One area that we are acutely aware of and can be a challenge for all institutions, as well as confusing for students, is the definition of plagiarism. We have addressed this by embedding it within the wider definition of "good academic practice," which is more fitting to developing and supporting students. To enable this, during induction week, there is a self-directed learning activity, where the student can take a quiz and receive immediate feedback. This provides them with definitions

of plagiarism; highlights ambiguous poor academic practice; and, in doing so, clearly outlines the expectations and regulations of the institution. This "good academic practice" quiz has now been implemented into a number of online postgraduate inductions, as it has been useful across disciplines.

Getting Started at Postgraduate Level
The university has invested heavily in ensuring online students are supported; there are "Getting Started" guides and checklists that the student can engage with, to ensure they feel confident of the practicalities of university life and support on offer. This is particularly important, as many may have not studied online before, and this can be a cause of anxiety, as one student highlighted when asked what they were concerned about: "Doing the whole course online, as this is something I have not done before." Or as another student highlighted,

> I was concerned that I would not have the help to conduct research. When I was in university 30 years ago we physically went to the library and pulled journal and text etc. Today I know things are different and I will need support on this. (Question 8)

Knowing that students have such anxieties means that universities can easily address them early on.

In addition to university practical support, the academic study skills unit also provides online workshops (via Blackboard Collaborate), asynchronous resources via the "Study Hub" (a website of resources), and one-to-one support via Skype or Blackboard Collaborate. It is important to communicate the different resources on offer via different means, as students may feel overwhelmed in this early stage.

Getting Connected (Technologies)
For many ODL students, studying online can be daunting, as there may be a fear of technology or what is expected online. The survey asked about levels of confidence in relation to technologies and software packages (question 10.12), and 18% stated they are "very confident," 47% stated "quite confident," with 35% stating "not confident." This is a significant number of students who have identified that they are not confident and in order to address this, at a university and program level, there has been investment in support. At a program level, this particular cohort has access to a section called "Getting Connected," on their VLE, which highlights the resources and technologies they will need for getting started with their studies. Furthermore, it is important to gain a better understanding of where students source information about technologies (question 11.12), and nearly 59% stated that they would access the information via the VLE, and nearly 12% sourced information via the academic study skills department, and 47% looked for sources elsewhere. Speculatively, this may be from an Information Technology department or a search engine. This information is particularly useful for refining the communication strategy, addressing anxieties, and for the development of technology resources.

Stage 2 – Transition – During Studies

If students have successfully transitioned into the university, they will have a greater familiarity with the academic support on offer to them. However, as many ODL students may be studying part-time and intermittently, they will engage with their studies for a longer duration than the on-campus cohort. Consequently, academic support provision may change during this time. In addition, there may be different academic support needs at different points during their studies. It is during this transitional stage that it is important to have a breadth of resources, support, and frequent communication.

In order to understand what the students may be feeling at this transition stage, we asked in the survey "what do you think will be or has been the biggest challenge for you, academically?" (question 9). The responses included time management, the challenge of engaging with resources and content fully online, critical reading and writing, and sourcing information. These concerns were further reinforced in relation to a series of questions about confidence and specific topics. For example, we asked how confident they felt in relation to "critical reading, for example, critiquing a paper or reading at postgraduate level." In total, 82% stated that they felt "quite" or "not" confident in relation to this. Only 18% stated that they were "very confident."

Unsurprisingly, the question about levels of confidence in relation to understanding data and statistics was also similarly scored. What was reassuring to see was the levels of confidence in relation to understanding assessment feedback, with 29% stating "very confident" and 65% stating "quite confident." An interesting outcome appeared with the levels of confidence in relation to time management. With students about to start first year, 35% stated they are "very confident" and 12% stated "quite confident" about time management. Levels of confidence decreased in later years. This may be due to expectations shifting over the duration of their studies or the challenge of balancing studying and other commitments; further research is needed to fully understand this.

Another academic area where students indicated lower levels of confidence overall was "dissertation e.g. project management and writing." This may relate to self-efficacy or a lack of awareness of what academic support is on offer. As the dissertation is a large component of the MSc, the findings have influenced the investment in academic support in this area, including resources and synchronous workshops on writing a dissertation, bibliographic tools, and more.

A number of themes emerged during the interviews which align with the survey results and literature review, including the type of support in which students are particularly interested, for example, proof reading (participant two – final-year student), and scientific writing (participant one – second-year student). There were three students identified in the survey, who were in their dissertation year, who highlighted specific support provision needed, including statistics, research methods, critical writing, and literature searching. While many postgraduate programs will provide a research methods course, there may be anxieties around these topics, and the ATR can highlight additional resources, workshops, or one-to-one provision, to ensure students feel more confident in this final stage of their studies.

The interviews provided a greater insight into what academic support the students had engaged with, why, and at what point in their studies. Interviewee one stated that

> I accessed anything I could, time management ... writing for scientific papers, critiquing scientific papers, and I mean anything they offered that wasn't filled up, I got a seat on it and went to that.

This raises a number of points. Significantly, this student was very aware that the university offered ODL students a range of support and that the majority of it was offered by a specific academic study skills support department. However, the challenge was securing a place on the courses/workshops, as they "filled up." Unsurprisingly, the demand for support often outstrips availability. Unfortunately, many universities have limited finances or academic skills staff to meet the demands; however, there are other means in which academic support can be provided, for example, through video tutorials, peer support schemes, or online resources. Successfully planning the range of topics and how they can be delivered, and when (as they need to be delivered a number of times throughout the academic year), requires forethought into the best pedagogical and technical approach, as well as financial and resource implications.

Stage 3: Transitioning Out of the University

The intention of the university academic skills support unit may not directly include careers support, or seeking funding for further studies, or entering into the business world. However, it would be remiss if the ATR did not highlight other resources which will enable the student to transition successfully out of the university.

Furthermore, there may be specific areas that the academic skills unit can provide in this transitional stage, such as "how to publish a dissertation." It is stage three that demonstrates that the ATR can be used to highlight other university departments in addition to the academic skills unit. It is important to acknowledge this stage of the ATR, as it provides a conclusion to the academic stage of the students' journey and reinforces the sense of community through the alumni cohort. Providing the ATR model from transition to exiting out of the university provides an opportunity for institutions to highlight the provision offered by other departments at different times of the student academic journey, thus presenting a holistic model of provision.

CONCLUSION AND RECOMMENDATIONS

This study has provided a richer understanding of a small cohort of students and their academic support requirements. As a result, a number of themes have emerged, including what support they most needed and at what stage in their academic journey. In addition, the need for support was aligned with the level of confidence that they highlighted in relation to different topics.

The ATR provides a model in which a university can clearly plan and deliver academic support for ODL students. The support should be targeted at the right time and delivered in a flexible manner. In addition, to ensure students are adequately supported and to address anxieties, it has been demonstrated that facilitating the development of a community and ensuring there is an adequate induction into the university will ensure a greater chance of success. To further enhance the academic support offered, and to ensure uptake of the support, it is imperative that there is an associated communication strategy, both centrally and locally. In doing so, this will reinforce the normalization of support and ensure students (and academic staff) are aware of the support on offer.

Therefore, to implement an ATR, we propose the following recommendations:

1. Identify support needs specific to your cohort, taking account of the topics presented here.
2. Identify limitations in delivery related to your specific ODL cohort, for example, technical limitations or financial or resource implications in your institution.
3. Consider the wider context of online learning, including the facilitation and benefits of developing a community.
4. Engage with other colleagues, such as learning technologists and other support departments, to ensure a holistic and well-designed provision can be offered.

The intention of this research is to enable other educators to consider the recommendations put forth here, as well as adjust and implement the ATR model to suit their specific cohort of students. Longer term, we aim to evaluate the effectiveness of the ATR model in order to refine it further, as well as dialogue with and collaboratively share best practice with other institutions, in order to gain a better understanding of the academic support requirements for ODL students. As the needs of students and the digital landscape changes, so too should our provision of academic support.

REFERENCES

Bandura, A. (1977). Self-efficacy: Toward a unifying theory of behavioral change. *Psychological Review, 84*(2), 191–215.

Baxter, J. (2012). Who am I and what keeps me going? Profiling the distance learning student in higher education. *International Review of Research in Open and Distance Learning, 13*(4), 107–129.

Bayne, S., Gallagher, M. S., & Lamb, J. (2013). Being 'at' university: The social topologies of distance students. *Higher Education,* 67, 569–583.

Cahill, J., Bowyer, J., & Murray, S. (2014). An exploration of undergraduate students' views on the effectiveness of academic and pastoral support. *Educational Research, 56*(4), 398–411.

Delahunty, J., Verenikina, I., & Jones, P. (2013). Socio-emotional connections: Identity, belonging and learning in online interactions. A literature review. Technology, Pedagogy and Education, *23*(2), 243–265.

Harrison, R. A., Harrison, A., Robinson, C., & Rawlings, B. (2018). The experience of international postgraduate students on a distance-learning programme. *Distance Education, 39*(4), 480–494.

Hebdon, S. (2015). Embedding support for students transitioning into higher education: Evaluation of a new model. *International Journal of Training Research, 13*(2), 119–131.

Higher Education Founding Council for England (HEFCE). (2010). Retention grants briefing programme number 3. Retrieved from http://www.hefce.ac.uk/

LaPadula, M. (2003). A comprehensive look at online student support services for distance learners. *American Journal of Distance Education, 17*(2), 119–128.

Meece, J. L., Glienke, B. B., & Burg, S. (2006). Gender and motivation. *Journal of School Psychology, 44*(5), 351–373.

Nelson, K., Kift, S., Humphreys, J., & Harper, W. (2006). A blueprint for enhanced transition: Taking an holistic approach to managing student transition into a large university. Paper presented at the 9th first year in higher education conference – Engaging students, Gold Coast, Australia.

Nichols, M. (2010). Student perceptions of support services and the influence of targeted interventions on retention in distance education. *Distance Education, 31*(1), 93–113.

Rovai, A. P. (2002). Building sense of community at a distance. *The International Review of Research in Open and Distance Learning, 3*(1), 74–85.

Sheail, P. (2018). Temporal flexibility in the digital university: Full-time, part-time, flexitime. *Distance Education, 39*(4), 462–479.

Thompson, B., & Joseph P. Mazer (2009). College student ratings of student academic support: Frequency, importance, and modes of communication. *Communication Education, 58*(3), 433–458.

Tobbell, J., O'Donnell, V., & Zammit, M. (2010). Exploring transition to postgraduate study: Shifting identities in interaction with communities, practice and participation. *British Educational Research Journal, 36*(2), 261–278.

Zhao, W. (2014). *Journeys towards masters' literacies: Chinese students' transitions from undergraduate study in China to postgraduate study in the UK*. Unpublished Ph.D. thesis, The University of Edinburgh, Scotland.

SUPPORTING ONLINE STUDENTS IN US-BASED PROFESSIONAL DOCTORAL PROGRAMS

Melora Sundt and Leslie Wheaton

ABSTRACT

What contributes to US professional doctoral student success in the online space is the subject of this chapter. The online doctoral student occupies two underserved categories of higher education students: doctoral students and online students, both of which have historically low graduation rates (Bawa, 2016; Stone, 2017). A number of US online doctoral programs have significantly higher graduation rates than normal, demonstrating that it is possible to create highly successful online doctoral programs. In this chapter, we apply the R. E. Clark and Estes (2008) conceptual framework of human performance to understanding the factors contributing to doctoral student success in online programs. We look at three stakeholder groups, faculty, staff, and students, and review the factors and solutions that could allow each group to contribute to doctoral student success. This review of the literature is informed by examples drawn from two online professional doctoral programs for which the authors either designed and taught courses, and chaired dissertations, or were enrolled in as a student.

Keywords: Online learning; professional doctoral program; doctoral students; doctoral degree; feedback; student support; motivation issues; knowledge and skills issues; organizational issues; student retention

THE CONTEXT FOR ONLINE US PROFESSIONAL DOCTORAL EDUCATION

Each year, hundreds of thousands of students return to universities in the US to study in a doctoral program. A small but increasing percentage of those students, approximately 25%, choose to attend online doctoral programs (Carnegie Project on the Education Doctorate (CPED), 2016; National Center for Education Statistics (NCES), 2017).

Completing a doctoral program is difficult. Doctoral attrition rates in the United States (approximately 44%) rival six-year undergraduate attrition rates (NCES, 2017). The *online* doctoral student has the unfortunate luck of falling into two underserved categories of higher education students: doctoral students, which have an average graduation rate that has not moved beyond about 56% in decades (Olive, 2019), and online students, who also trail national average graduation rates (James, Swan, & Daston, 2016). This chapter addresses the conditions that contribute to online doctoral student success in the United States and provides suggestions for students, faculty, and staff to increase the likelihood of program completion.

Relative to the number of undergraduates, the small number of doctoral students online could prompt us to ask, "Why care about their retention?" Doctoral students aspire to faculty positions, to lead research labs, to influence national policy, to manage clinical care, or to lead organizations. In short, they are our next generation of researchers and leaders (National Science Board, 2018). When only about half of them successfully complete their programs, dreams – of the institution, the nation, and the student – are deferred, opportunities lost, to paraphrase the poet Langston Hughes (1951). This chapter's authors have attended, built, taught in, or advised a number of US professional doctoral programs that are experiencing very high completion rates – 85%–92%. Understanding the strategies they use could help other programs improve.

The US Professional Doctoral Degree

The requirements for the professional doctorate vary by discipline, but usually these degrees are known for preparing leaders who can apply research to problems of practice (CPED, 2016). Their final deliverable, if one is required, is often a capstone project, an example of applied problem-solving in their respective field. Some professional doctorates have no culminating deliverable, but the related profession may require the passing of a board exam (e.g., the MD and medical boards, or the JD and the bar exam). Enrollment in professional doctoral degrees in the United States tends to be larger than in PhD programs. More professional doctoral programs than PhD programs are currently online (CPED, 2016; Ma, Dana, Adams, & Kennedy, 2018). For these reasons, supporting students in online professional doctoral programs is the focus of this chapter.

Diversity of Online Experiences

"Online" refers to a variety of program structures and experiences. Sundt (2012) described the range: (a) from completely asynchronous to completely synchronous and (b) from entirely online to blending online and onground[1] experiences. The doctoral programs the authors have worked with are hybrids, using both asynchronous and synchronous resources and meeting online at least once during a term. Some also bring students to the physical campus at least once during the program. With this context in mind, this chapter turns to understanding the challenges to increasing online professional doctoral student retention.

CONCEPTUAL FRAMEWORK

Think of doctoral degree completion as a type of human performance – there are conditions that must be present and behaviors that must be initiated for a student to successfully complete a doctoral program. R. E. Clark and Estes' (2008) theory of human performance identified three categories of factors influencing success. These are (a) the participant's knowledge and skills related to the goal, (b) the participant's motivation, and (c) the level of organizational support and resources available. Correctly identifying the specific influencers, such as specific skills, or beliefs or resources, allows one to create better support strategies, because the solutions for a knowledge gap are different from those for a resource gap (Shaw, Burrus, & Ferguson, 2016). In this section, each of these factors is described generally, and in the following section, this theory is applied to three institutional stakeholders – faculty, staff, and the doctoral students – involved in doctoral student success in online programs.

The Role of Knowledge and Skills

For a person to be successful in achieving a performance goal, such as graduating from a doctoral program, R. E. Clark and Estes (2008) assert that the person must have the requisite knowledge and skills. They need to understand the goal and expectations of the task and know how to do the task. If the person does not have the knowledge or skills needed, then various types of training, such as providing job aides, workshops, and opportunities for practice and feedback, are the optimal solutions (Schraw & McCrudden, 2006).

The Role of Motivation

Motivation, according to R. E. Clark and Estes (2008), consists of three key factors: self-efficacy, task value, and mental effort. Self-efficacy refers to a person's confidence in their ability to succeed in doing a task (Bandura, 1997; Pajares, 2006). Task value refers to the belief that a task is worth doing – that doing the task will contribute to one's larger goals (Eccles, 2006). Mental effort refers to a willingness to persist in attempting the task, including a willingness to seek out and apply new strategies for completing the task when old strategies do not work (Anderman & Anderman, 2006).

R. E. Clark stated (personal communication, 2017) that of the three factors, motivation is foundational. A person may know how to do a task and have the resources needed, but if the person does not believe the task is important, or does not have confidence in their ability to do the task, or is unwilling to apply the effort needed to persist to completion, the task will not be completed. Motivation can be heavily influenced by organizational factors, described next, but training, a common response to a performance gap, will generally not influence motivation, unless it provides information about the priority and value of achieving the task.

The Role of Organizational Factors

Successful performance also depends on the context, or the "organization" in which the person is attempting the goal (Gallimore & Goldenberg, 2001). This factor, according to R. E. Clark and Estes (2008), is comprised of resources, such as time, tools, and space. It also refers to an alignment of incentives and policies with achieving the goals, consistent communication from an organization's leadership, and the presence of supporting processes such as providing effective feedback on attempts to achieve the goal (AlDahdouh, Osorio, & Caires, 2015). A third element is organizational culture, including the degree to which an organization values the goal. "Organization" can include cultural and social norms, such as those belonging to one's family or the larger society within which the person functions, not just those of formal organizations. While some goals can be achieved in the absence of these organizational factors, most are much harder to achieve without this support.

Stakeholder Groups

The student may interact with stakeholders outside the institution who influence their success, such as family, friends, or an employer. Because this chapter centers on universities, the three stakeholder groups addressed in this chapter are students, faculty, and student affairs staff.

FACTORS INFLUENCING ONLINE DOCTORAL DEGREE COMPLETION

Factors Impacting the Student

Knowledge and Skills the Student Needs

Clarity of the Goal. Online doctoral students need to know what milestones are needed to graduate, including what a dissertation or capstone is, and how one constructs its component parts (Locke & Boyle, 2016). Because the dissertation or capstone is often work product unique to US doctoral programs, most students may not have encountered assignments of this magnitude before.

In contrast, many faculty are expert in constructing research studies and dissertations. Sullivan, Yates, Inaba, Lam, and Clark (2014) found that most experts have automated the steps involved in "doing" their area of expertise, and they tend to leave out as much as 70% of the necessary steps when explaining their processes to others. They may also assume, incorrectly, that doctoral students understand the structure and purpose of the dissertation or capstone (Ames, Berman, &

Casteel, 2018; Schraw & McCrudden, 2006). It is not unusual, therefore, to find that many doctoral students know less about creating a dissertation than faculty expect.

Academic Cultural Capital. B. R. Clark (1987) wrote extensively about the variations in community culture between institutional types and academic disciplines. It can be challenging for doctoral students to engage effectively with their department's and their discipline's culture, particularly if their doctoral institution is different from other institutions they attended (Bégin & Géarard, 2013). Learning how to navigate the relationship with one's chair and dissertation committee, for example, is an important step toward degree completion (Orellana, Darder, Pérez, & Salinas, 2016). Cultivating this relationship and interpreting cues from a distance can put additional pressure on online doctoral students, as the traditional means for connecting – dropping by the faculty member's office, for example – can work differently online, depending on the technology being used for the program (Evans, 2015).

Self-regulation. Getting a doctoral degree is often compared to running a marathon. It can require greater persistence, and therefore motivation, than previous degree experiences (Shaw et al., 2016). Doctoral students need to manage their motivation, keep themselves working on their assignments, and writing their drafts (Yukselturk & Bulut, 2007). They also need to hone their ability to manage competing time commitments, particularly students who are working while enrolled (Bawa, 2016). While not having to drive to campus can save time, it can also contribute to a feeling of "out of sight, out of mind." To combat this isolation, students need to feel as though they are part of a supportive community and have the resources necessary to succeed (Rovai, 2002).

Academic Skills. Multiple skill sets contribute to the doctoral student's success; academic writing, inquiry and research skills, and statistical analysis skills being the primary set for doctoral students. Students in online doctoral programs may be older and more non-traditional than those attending onground doctoral programs (Radda, 2012). Studies suggest that older students may need help refreshing their writing and analytic skills, and with adapting to heavy reading expectations (Brown, 2017; Evans, 2015). They also need to know how to access campus resources online, resources which may not have adapted yet to serving online students.

Facility with Technology. Perhaps the greatest skill challenge is mastering the technology needed to be an online doctoral student (Harrison et al., 2017). Like other online students, doctoral students need to be able to navigate the campus learning management system (LMS) to attend courses, meet with their chair, and meet with study groups. They need to become comfortable with all of their interactions for their doctoral program occurring virtually.

Balancing Work and Family Expectations. If students are enrolled in a professional doctorate, they may be working and have family obligations (Rockinson-Szapkiw,

Spaulding, & Lunde, 2017). Knowing how to juggle these competing priorities is a skill, particularly when the student is not traveling to a campus and therefore could be more accessible to the demands of work and family (Bawa, 2016).

Motivational Issues
Self-efficacy. Doctoral students do better when they have confidence in their ability to do the work or "be a doctoral student" (Baltes, Hoffman-Kipp, Lynn, & Weltzer-Ward, 2010). Studies have identified a lack of confidence as becoming more acute as a student progresses through the academic degree ladder (from bachelor's to master's to doctoral student) or intensifying among students who are returning to being a student after a long gap (Cope-Watson & Betts, 2010; Rockinson-Szapkiw et al., 2017). Online students also need to feel confident in their ability to work in a virtual setting, a confidence that increases as their skills increase.

Task Value. All doctoral students will perform better if they believe that the individual steps required, such as completing a draft, are worth doing. They are more likely to see the value in the individual steps and tasks if they understand the goal (part of the knowledge gap, discussed earlier). Similarly, they need to be able to prioritize the completion of their academic work over other obligations. Those who struggle may not see the relevance of what they are doing, either toward graduation or to their career goals (Olive, 2019; Yukselturk & Bulut, 2007).

Mental Effort. Mental effort refers to a person's willingness to persist and try alternative strategies when their initial efforts to achieve a goal fail (Anderman & Anderman, 2006). Mental effort is about persistence and grit, but it is also about creativity and flexibility as finding solutions to barriers does not mean just doing more of the same thing. Much has been written about persistence and grit as characteristics of successful students (Pajares, 2006). The number of barriers a person encounters can influence their level of effort; continuing to encounter challenges to one's success can wear down one's willingness to persist.

Organizational Issues
Lack of Structure and Support. The low completion rates of doctoral degrees are partly related to a failure to complete the dissertation rather than a failure to complete coursework (Bagaka's, Badillo, Bransteter, & Rispinto, 2015). With most traditional doctoral programs, the student experiences a noticeable lack of structure once courses are finished and are often left to figure out much of the dissertation process on their own (Baltes et al., 2010).

This lack of structure, including a lack of communication about the chair's or institution's expectations and timelines, contributes to attrition (Ames et al., 2018). The relationship with one's advisor also contributes to doctoral student success (Olive, 2019; Rigler, Bowlin, Sweat, Watts, & Throne, 2017). Students who feel supported by their chair, who find the chair to be responsive to questions, tend to complete at higher rates than those who struggle to develop this relationship.

Financial Aid. The cost of a doctoral program, when the cost burden becomes too high compared to other financial priorities, is a leading factor of attrition (Rigler et al., 2017). Online students tend to receive less aid than onground students, and aid for doctoral (all graduate students actually) students is less available than aid for undergraduates (Deming, Goldin, Katz, & Yuchtman, 2015). Institutions may be less likely to offer assistantship packages to online professional doctoral students if the work requires presence on campus, or if the student is already working, or because of a perception that online students cannot contribute in the same way when working remotely.

Campus Climate and Sense of Belonging. The research has indicated that in addition to weak academic preparation, a key contributor to attrition from doctoral programs is feeling isolated (Rockinson-Szapkiw, 2012) and/or that one does not belong (Berry, 2017; Black, Dawson, & Priem, 2008; Evans, 2015). In poorly designed online programs, that sense of isolation can be exacerbated by a lack of contact with peers, procedures and schedules that seem unaccommodating to the student's needs, and unresponsive staff or faculty.

Student-centeredness of the Program. A doctoral program can be student-centered or faculty centered (King, 2016). A student-centered program will work to schedule classes, faculty office hours, and access to university services during times that work for most students. An online doctoral program expands the demographics of students attending; they can live in time zones that are very different from the physical campus or the faculty (Evans, 2015). A 5 p.m. class can be accessible for students on the east coast in the United States but cut into work hours for students in the central and pacific time zones, not to mention students in Asia or Europe. Similarly, a financial aid office that closes at 5 p.m. EST will be difficult for students outside of that time zone to access.

Accessibility of Campus Resources. Sometimes when a program goes online, the rest of the campus is slow to adapt. Library resources, including research librarians, need to be accessible online. Not all necessary documents may be available online, and some may require in-person signatures. Language on the university website such as "drop by our office" or "can't wait to see you on campus" may sound welcoming to the onground student but requires the online student to "read themselves into" the message.

In particular, online programs have created a new challenge for college mental health services in the United States: how to serve students who do not live in the state in which the college is located. Not only does this increasing population increase demand on existing services, but counseling centers also may be restricted from serving many of those students because of licensing regulations.[2] The lack of national reciprocity for mental health services across states leaves many online students facing a gap in services. Some universities have, regretfully, ignored the issue, putting nothing in place to serve out-of-state, online students experiencing psychological distress. Others have begun outsourcing mental health services.

Solutions for Students

Programs with higher online doctoral completion rates do the following to mediate potential student knowledge, motivation, and organizational gaps:

Create a Robust Online Orientation Program. The orientation program should introduce students to the program, establish the goals, reveal the pathway of courses they need to complete, and focus on demystifying the dissertation or capstone (Bawa, 2016; Stone, 2017).

Create a Toolkit. Borrowing from the concept of job aides, some programs create a one-stop location for essential program information. Some programs call this a digital "toolkit" and include in it frequently used contact information, the program's course schedule, and tips for using the different technology tools.

Utilize Success Coaches. A student affairs staff member who can access the LMS analytics can be invaluable in setting up early warning "flags" to trigger outreach to students. The staff member can work with students to learn how to navigate university systems – both procedural and technological (Pifer & Baker, 2016).

Create a Student Portal, or Better Yet, a Virtual Student Union (VSU). Create a central space for students to connect with one another, university resources, faculty, and staff. The toolkit, mentioned earlier, can be located in the VSU. The VSU can serve as a gateway into all university resources and, with a little design work, can become a meeting place for faculty and students, student organizations, and student study groups. It can stream program and university information and connect students to their academic advisors and/or faculty.

Offer Webinars on Professional and Academic Topics. An advantage of using an LMS is the ease with which an information session can be created. Faculty and staff can respond almost immediately to information gaps they discover and set up workshops online to address student needs. Due to the variety of time zones in which a cohort of students may live, live webinars may not always be accessible, but recording them will enable students to access them at their convenience.

Offer Opportunities to Practice Key Skills and Get Timely Feedback. Within the design of the program, faculty can create opportunities to deconstruct key concepts and skills, and find ways to allow students to practice those, getting corrective, constructive feedback as they do so. Another advantage of the online space is the opportunity to use interactive learning experiences to explain steps and concepts, check for knowledge, and practice. The faculty generally know where students are likely to struggle in the program. Providing thoughtful, diverse learning activities – some asynchronous, some in groups, some recorded – can help scaffold those skills for students and increase the likelihood that they will master the content.

Address Common Skill Deficiencies as they Emerge. Some programs host virtual or in-person writing weekends. Faculty identify a weekend and make themselves available with office hour sign up slots through a program like youcanbook.me to meet one-on-one with students, set very short writing goals ("What will you finish by this afternoon?"), and provide quick review and feedback sessions. Another hosted a regular "Dissertation Boot camp," a residential experience that students paid extra for which involved gathering in a hotel near campus and working with the school's writing advisors on sections of their dissertation (Locke & Boyle, 2016).

Jumpstart Community Building. In several of the programs with high graduation rates, program staff create opportunities for students to engage with one another and with faculty (Berry, 2017; Stone, 2017). Feeling like one is not alone when facing a barrier can be a motivator to persist (Rockinson-Szapkiw, 2012). Most programs the authors have worked with have found ways to facilitate students connecting to one another, by assigning group work, encouraging the use of social networking tools, or creating virtual meeting spaces, like the VSU. A community coordinator can review student profiles and encourage students with like interests to connect with one another. The coordinator could create "meet ups" for students from common geographic regions and looks for opportunities to create informal webinars between faculty and students to highlight research interests or discuss a current event. They find ways to connect alumni or students to encourage them and mentor them through the program.

Provide as Much Structure as Possible. Data suggest that the biggest drop off in enrollment in doctoral programs comes during the typically unstructured dissertation phase (Bagaka's et al., 2015). Some programs have discovered ways to assure guidance and provide structure throughout that process (Ames et al., 2018). One program took the basic components of their dissertation and embedded them into the course sequence so that students engaged with the dissertation throughout the program. Another used advisories – an advisor who worked with a small group of online doctoral students to check in with them on their progress, help them set and keep timelines. Some programs insist that the chair serve in this capacity, but there is some value in supplementing the chair with an advisor trained to assist in this way.

Reorient the Program and Services to be Student-centered. These programs survey students to find common convenient class times. They audit website language, and university services and processes to ensure online accessibility and inclusion. They conduct satisfaction surveys of students and apply the findings to program revisions.

Factors Impacting Student Affairs Staff's Success in Helping Doctoral Students Graduate

In many US universities, the student affairs staff working with online doctoral students are to be located in the student's academic department, rather than located centrally. These departmental staff play a key role either as facilitators of or barriers to doctoral student satisfaction and success (Barnes & Randall, 2010).

The role of student affairs staff in supporting online doctoral students can range from orienting and onboarding students to the program and technology and providing basic academic and registration guidance, to providing skills support such as writing or data analysis coaching, providing counseling, and helping students navigate the university's maze of processes, offices, and deadlines.

Knowledge and Skills
Goals and Responsibilities. Staff need to know that online doctoral student success is a priority for the institution. They also need to know their specific goals and responsibilities relative to supporting online doctoral students. Programs that work with an Online Program Manager (OPM) may be collaborating with OPM staff who also support students. An OPM is a firm a university hires to take on some of the tasks involved in creating and maintaining an online degree program, such as recruitment, instructional design, and/or student support. Clarity of roles across these two teams is critical to providing optimal student services.

Facility with Technology. Staff supporting online doctoral students need to be technically proficient (Anderson & Dron, 2011; Berry, 2017). They need to be able to schedule virtual office hours, run virtual webinars, navigate the LMS, and provide information such that an online student does not have to come to campus (e.g., to sign a form).

Communication Skills. Staff need to communicate program information to students (Anderson & Dron, 2011). They need to demonstrate effective meeting management, empathy, listening, and problem-solving skills via videoconferencing tools. Learning to be responsive across multiple time zones and setting effective boundaries are important and sometimes new communication skills for staff working with online students.

Student Development Knowledge. Staff who understand the research regarding the needs of adult learners and the stresses facing doctoral students, many of whom may be working, will likely be more effective in supporting those students (Harrison et al., 2017).

Motivation Issues
Task Value. Staff working with an online doctoral program need to believe that the initiative to take the program online is worthwhile and valued by the institution (Eccles, 2006). They need to believe that doctoral students benefit from staff interaction and can succeed, and that therefore their jobs are worthwhile.

Self-efficacy. Staff need to have confidence in their ability to assist doctoral students in the online program and have confidence in their ability to navigate the virtual space effectively (Yukselturk & Bulut, 2007).

Organizational Structural Issues

Alignment of Incentives. Earlier in this chapter, the authors established that aligning incentives with goals and intended outcomes increases the likelihood that individuals will attempt those goals. In this case, the degree to which the department communicates the value and priority of online doctoral student success, including the importance of going online, and the value of the student affairs role at the doctoral level will influence staff performance (Radda, 2012). Aligning incentives and resources with supporting doctoral student success will influence the degree to which staff focus on practices that contribute to doctoral student success.

Feedback. Receiving timely, constructive, and specific feedback regarding their work relative to supporting doctoral students will help staff become more effective (Stone, 2017).

Resources. Launching and effectively sustaining a successful online doctoral program is hard work. It takes additional time, sometimes new staff, funding, and sometimes better equipment. Often a new online program gets added to the responsibilities of existing staff with no additional resources. This strategy is understandable when the potential growth of the program is unknown, and extra financial resources have yet to be realized until the program gains enrollment traction; however, this strategy can demotivate staff if they equate the new program with more work and no additional resources.

Solutions for Student Affairs Staff

Provide Onboarding for Staff. Onboard staff members who are expected to work with online doctoral students. Ensure staff understand the program, the goals, the technology, and what is expected of them.

Provide Resources. Resources can include time, tools, and funding. First, consider establishing and monitoring reasonable student-to-staff ratios for advising and outreach. Online students can be more demanding and more communicative than onground students, so ensure the program is adequately staffed to be responsive. Staff working with online students need the relevant technology to connect with students through videoconferencing.

Demonstrate that the Program and the Team Supporting it are Valued. Successful programs normalize and mainstream the program by doing things like including updates about the online program on regular school agendas. They regularly recognize the staff supporting the program. They communicate with alumni, who may be concerned about brand dilution. Helping alumni accept and value the online doctoral program can help the student affairs staff get alumni support for initiatives, like mentoring, that can contribute to online doctoral student persistence.

Factors Influencing Faculty's Success in Helping Doctoral Students Graduate
Many of these factors and solutions discussed so far also apply to faculty, who need to understand how the technology works, value taking the program online, and have sufficient resources. In the final section about faculty needs, the authors focus on those specific to the faculty role that are in addition to the factors and solutions already discussed.

Knowledge Issues
While faculty may be experts in their disciplines, working with online students in a virtual environment may pose new knowledge challenges. Knowledge in two areas, pedagogical practice and the needs of online students, are central to supporting doctoral students.

Pedagogical Practices
Online learning experiences are similar to classroom-based experiences in that they both consist of two domains: what students do together with the instructor (synchronous time) and what they do on their own time (asynchronous time). For faculty to successfully support doctoral students, they need to know how to adapt instruction to the virtual space, including how to optimize asynchronous resources and how to facilitate learning in live, virtual classrooms (AlDahdouh et al., 2015).

A second pedagogical factor is the faculty member's degree of awareness of how much information they have automated, given their expertise in a subject (Schraw & McCrudden, 2006). Faculty can focus on deconstructing procedures and explanations, especially when teaching early in a doctoral program, to ensure they make the implicit explicit in their instruction.

Third, while faculty have much anecdotal experience teaching, US higher education is not known for formally preparing faculty to teach (Pifer & Baker, 2016). For example, unlike primary and secondary schoolteachers, faculty teaching in higher education may never have been exposed to the evidence base about learning and therefore may only coincidentally apply the science of learning to their instruction. Knowing more about how to sequence learning experiences and how to design learning experiences to improve retention and avoid cognitive overload could improve the learning outcomes of their doctoral students.

Student Development
As with pedagogy, many faculty have an intuitive understanding of student development derived from their years of working with students. But knowing more explicitly what the research says about the needs of adult learners, doctoral students and online students could improve faculty's ability to support online doctoral students (Black et al., 2008). In particular, faculty need to understand common developmental issues for doctoral students, such as how coming back to a doctoral program, or enrolling in the online environment, can raise feelings

of inadequacy among otherwise very competent professionals, and how those manifest or become exacerbated in a virtual environment. Finally, they need to understand the negative impact of alienation among online and doctoral students, and what they and their institution can do to combat those feelings.

Motivation Issues

Task Value. The degree to which faculty believe that online doctoral education can be successful and is a good use of their time will influence how effective they are with their students (Eccles, 2006). Some may think that doctoral education and laboratory-based or clinically based education are impossible to do well in the virtual environment. Yet the technology to support these areas is changing and improving year over year. Nevertheless, if the faculty member does not see the value of taking the doctoral program online, or believe it can be done well, they will be less likely to succeed in supporting online doctoral students. Their belief in the value of the online experience may also influence the degree to which they prioritize their work with online doctoral students over competing demands. Online doctoral students cannot "stake out" a professor's office, persisting until they get a chance to meet. Instead, they rely on the responsiveness of the professor to their email, chat, and text inquiries. Faculty may be more likely to make themselves available and responsive when they value the online experience and their online doctoral students.

Self-efficacy. Some programs, as they expand into the virtual space, also add faculty, some of whom may be new to doctoral instruction and advisement. Their confidence in their ability to work with doctoral students could be expected to influence their success (Pajares, 2006). Similarly, the faculty member's level of confidence in their ability to work well in the virtual environment will influence their success (Harrison et al., 2017).

Organizational/Structural Issues

Incentives. We previously discussed how the degree to which the incentives of the university and the department reinforce the importance of a high doctoral completion rate in the online program will influence the time and effort staff, and now faculty, apply to working with their online students. If the institution's incentives deprioritize working with online students and/or professional doctoral students, faculty may spend their energy elsewhere.

Resources. Faculty's most precious resource is time – time to prepare for class, time to review student work, time to conduct research, apply for grants, and draft publications. Teaching online takes time, as does advising doctoral students (Yukselturk & Bulut, 2007).

Learning how to navigate the virtual environment takes time. Therefore, finding ways to provide sufficient time (if that is ever possible) for the faculty working with online doctoral students will help them better serve those students. Similarly, getting them the resources they need, such as a teaching assistant, may increase the likelihood of their success.

Policies/practices. Finally, faculty may experience little success working with online doctoral students if they have to struggle under oppressive policies or practices (Berry, 2017). The number of students for whom a faculty member is responsible, in class and as an advisor, matters. The number of courses the faculty member is expected to teach matters. Policies that are not well thought through can create unbearable working conditions and demotivate the faculty who support the online program.

Solutions for Faculty
Create Onboarding Programs for the Faculty Either Building or Teaching in an Online Doctoral Program. These programs should address the pedagogical and technological skills needed to be successful as an instructor in an online doctoral program and provide ample opportunities to practice. Much of the technological skills overlap with those needed by staff, so opportunities to repurpose content or to collaborate abound.

Recognize and Reward the Faculty Working with Online Doctoral Students. Recognition could be informal mentions at faculty meetings, in newsletters, and more formally as part of the tenure review or other promotion process for non-tenure track faculty. Rewards can include recognition in formal awards ceremonies for exceptional teaching in the online doctoral program.

Provide Sufficient Resources. Just as a new online program can be added to a staff member's responsibilities, the building of a course for the program can be simply added to a faculty member's load without providing sufficient resources. A better approach is to provide release time for faculty building courses for the online doctoral program. As the advising or teaching load increases, provide graduate assistants to assist with research or teaching responsibilities.

Examine Current Policies and Practices for Barriers to Faculty Participation in the Online Program. Teaching load expectations and section sizes can influence the faculty experience which can then influence faculty's ability to be supportive of their doctoral students. It is important to balance financial assumptions about section size and teaching loads with the faculty experience and ensure program policies make it possible for faculty to be successful.

Integrate Part-time Faculty into the Academic Community. As online doctoral programs grow and exceed the capacity of the incumbent faculty, new faculty, either full time or part-time, may be hired. Sundt and Chung (2017) describe supportive practices and policies, such as creating a merit and promotion system that includes all faculty regardless of full- or part-time status; including the voice of part-time and adjunct faculty on faculty governance groups; and including all faculty in professional development opportunities. It is possible to include these academic colleagues such that they feel welcome and part of the community without threatening the concept of tenure. *The result will be more confident and satisfied faculty who are better able to serve the online doctoral program.*

CONCLUSION

Themes/Lessons from the Review

Online Doctoral Students Have Unmet Needs
Online doctoral students fall into two neglected categories of students: doctoral students and online students. For too long, institutions have made a faulty assumption that graduate students, by virtue of having completed an undergraduate degree, no longer need assistance or as much assistance (Locke & Boyle, 2016). Universities may also assume that online students, because they are not visiting the campus, have no need for student services. Neither is true. Doctoral students bring complex family and work situations into their educational experience, and online doctoral students bring the added challenge of needing to connect with their advisor, yet may be unable to get to the campus, due to geography, work, or other obligations. Programs that successfully graduate high rates of their online doctoral students have designed their programs to serve that intersection of need: online and doctoral.

Some Solutions Lie Within the Student, But Most Involve the Other Stakeholders
Using the R. E. Clark and Estes (2008) Knowledge–Motivation–Skills human performance model to explore the factors impacting key stakeholders' ability to support online doctoral students reveals that while many of the solutions and support involve the doctoral student directly, implementing only those, while necessary, would be insufficient. The online doctoral student's success is also influenced by the preparation and support of the two primary stakeholders engaged with that student: the student affairs staff member and the faculty (Pifer & Baker, 2016). Ignoring the needs of these two stakeholders will place all the responsibility for success on the student – putting that student at a disadvantage.

Many of the solutions require implementation by the institution – either faculty or staff. For them to implement these solutions, they need to be aware of the need, know how to implement them, believe they are important, and have the necessary resources.

Further, while most research has recognized the importance of a supportive faculty member, we also need to recognize the more invisible structural and organizational factors that will impact both the faculty member and the online doctoral student. It will not work well to have an administration say it wants a successful online doctoral program and then not align its resources, rewards, policies, and procedures with supporting that program.

If Student Success Goals are Clearly Articulated and Prioritized, Programs Find Ways of Improving Student Outcomes
When student success is prioritized, meaning that students, faculty, and staff are prepared, and all the organizational factors are made to align with the goal of student success, there is a likelihood that we can increase the graduation rates of doctoral students generally and online doctoral students specifically (Pifer & Baker, 2016).

NOTES

1. We use the term "onground" rather than "on-campus" because a number of programs have begun creating virtual ecosystems such that the "campus" is comprised of both virtual and onground environments. Using "campus" to refer to only the onground experience is no longer accurate.
2. State regulations typically prohibit "inter-jurisdictional" counseling, meaning mental health treatment by someone who is not licensed in the state in which the therapy is occurring, which has been interpreted as being where the client (student) lives. The United States does not have a national license or reciprocity among states (https://www.zurinstitute.com/telehealth-across-state-lines/). Eight states have signed PSYPACT, a reciprocity agreement for psychologists, effective January 1, 2020: Illinois, Georgia, Arizona, Utah, Colorado, Nebraska, Missouri, and Nevada (https://cdn.ymaws.com/www.asppb.net/resource/resmgr/psypact_docs/psypact_press_release_4.23.2.pdf).

REFERENCES

AlDahdouh, A., Osorio, A., & Caires, S. (2015). Understanding knowledge network, learning and connectivism. *International Journal of Instructional Technology and Distance Learning, 12*(10). Retrieved from https://ssrn.com/abstract=3063495

Ames, C., Berman, R., & Casteel, A. (2018). A preliminary examination of doctoral student retention factors in private online workspaces. *International Journal of Doctoral Studies*, 13, 79–107.

Anderman, E., & Anderman, L. (2006). Attribution theory. Retrieved from http://www.education.com/reference/article/attribution-theory/

Anderson, T., & Dron, J. (2011). Three generations of distance education pedagogy. *The International Review of Research in Open and Distributed Learning, 12*(3), 80–97.

Bagaka's, J. G., Badillo, N., Bransteter, I., & Rispinto, S. (2015). Exploring student success in a doctoral program: The power of mentorship and research engagement. *International Journal of Doctoral Studies, 10*, 323–342.

Baltes, B., Hoffman-Kipp, P., Lynn, L., & Weltzer-Ward, L. (2010). Students' research self-efficacy during online doctoral research courses. *Contemporary Issues in Education Research, 3*(3), 51–58.

Bandura, A. (1997). *Self-efficacy: The exercise of control*. New York, NY: W. H. Freeman.

Barnes, B., & Randall, J. (2010). Doctoral student satisfaction: An examination of disciplinary, enrollment and institutional differences. *Research in Higher Education*, 53, 47–75.

Bawa, P. (2016). Retention in online courses: Exploring issues and solutions – A literature review. Sage Open, 6(1). https://doi.org/10.1177/2158244015621777

Bégin, C., & Géarard, L. (2013). The role of supervisors in light of the experience of doctoral students. *Policy Futures in Education, 11*(3), 267–276. https://doi.org/10.2304/pfie.2013.11.3.267

Berry, S. (2017). Building community in online doctoral classrooms: Instructor practices that support community. *Online Learning, 21*(2), n2.

Black, E. W., Dawson, K., & Priem, J. (2008). Data for free: Using LMS activity logs to measure community in online courses. *Internet and Higher Education, 11*, 65–70.

Brown, C. G. (2017). The Persistence and Attrition of Online Learners. *School Leadership Review, 12*(1), 7.

Carnegie Project on the Education Doctorate (CPED). (2016). The framework. Retrieved from http://www.cpedinitiative.org/page/AboutUs
Clark, B. R. (1987). The academic life: Small worlds, different worlds. *Educational Researcher*, 18(5), 4–8.
Clark, R. E., & Estes, F. (2008). *Turning research into results: A guide to selecting the right* performance solutions. Charlotte, NC: Information Age Publishing, Inc.
Cope-Watson, G., & Betts, A. S. (2010). Confronting otherness: An e-conversation between doctoral students living with the Imposter Syndrome. *Canadian Journal for New Scholars in Education/Revue Canadienne des Jeunes Chercheures et Chercheurs en Éducation*, 3(1), 1–13.
Deming, D. J., Goldin, C., Katz, L. F., & Yuchtman, N. (2015). Can online learning bend the higher education cost curve? American Economic Review, 105(5), 496–501. doi:10.1257/aer.p20151024
Eccles, J. (2006). Expectancy value motivational theory. Retrieved from http://www.education.com/reference/article/expectancy-value-motivational-theory/
Evans, H. (2015). International postgraduate students and peer learning. *Journal of Pedagogic Development*, 5(3), 32–43.
Gallimore, R., & Goldenberg, C. (2001). Analyzing cultural models and settings to connect minority achievement and school improvement research. Educational Psychologist, 36(1), 45–56.
Harrison, R., Hutt, I., Thomas-Varcoe, C., Motteram, G., Else, K., Rawlings, B., & Gemmell, I. (2017). A cross-sectional study to describe academics' confidence, attitudes, and experience of online distance learning in higher education. *Journal of Educators Online*, 14(2), n2.
Hughes, L. (1951). Harlem or a dream deferred. In L. Hughes, E. Pound, P. Taylor, H. Smythe, & M. Smythe (Eds.), *Montage of a dream deferred*. New York, NY: Henry Holt and Company. Retrieved from https://www.encyclopedia.com/education/educational-magazines/montage-dream-deferred. Accessed on April 15, 2021.
James, S., Swan, K., & Daston, C. (2016). Retention, progression and the taking of online courses. Online Learning, 20(2), 75–96.
King, K. P. (2016). Facilitating the doctoral mentoring process in online learning environments. In K. Peno, E. S. Mangiante, & R. Kenahan (Eds.), Mentoring in formal and informal contexts (pp. 77–96). Charlotte, NC: Information Age Publishing, Inc.
Locke, L. A., & Boyle, M. (2016). Avoiding the ABD abyss: A grounded theory study of a dissertation-focused course for doctoral students in an educational leadership program. The Qualitative Report, 21(9), 1574–1593.
Ma, V., Dana, N., Adams, A., & Kennedy, B. (2018). Understanding the problem of practice: An analysis of professional practice EdD dissertations. Impacting Education: Journal on Transforming Professional Practice, 3(1). Retrieved from https://impactinged.pitt.edu/ojs/index.php/ImpactingEd/article/view/50/78
National Center for Education Statistics (NCES). (2017). Fast facts. Retrieved from https://nces.ed.gov/fastfacts/display.asp?id=40
National Science Board (2018). Science and Engineering Indicators. Retrieved from https://nsf.gov/statistics/2018/nsb20181/report/sections/higher-education-in-science-and-engineering/highlights
Olive, J. (2019). The impact of longitudinal action research on doctoral student retention and degree completion. *The Qualitative Report*, 24(3), 470–482. Retrieved from https://nsuworks.nova.edu/tqr/vol24/iss3/3
Orellana, M. L., Darder, A., Pérez, A., & Salinas, J. (2016). Improving doctoral success by matching PhD students with supervisors. *International Journal of Doctoral Studies*, 11, 87–103.
Pajares, F. (2006). Self-efficacy theory. Retrieved from http://www.education.com/reference/article/self-efficacy-theory/
Pifer, M. J., & Baker, V. L. (2016). Stage-based challenges and strategies for support in doctoral education: A practical guide for students, faculty members, and program administrators. International Journal of Doctoral Studies, 11(1), 15–34.
Radda, H. (2012). From theory to practice to experience: Building scholarly learning communities in nontraditional doctoral programs. *Insight: A Journal of Scholarly* Teaching, 7, 750–753.
Rigler, K. L., Jr, Bowlin, L. K., Sweat, K., Watts, S., & Throne, R. (2017). Agency, socialization, and support: A critical review of doctoral student attrition. Paper presented at the third international conference on doctoral education, University of Central Florida.

Rockinson-Szapkiw, A. J. (2012). Investigating uses and perceptions of an online collaborative workspace for the dissertation process. *Research in Learning Technology*, *20*(3). Retrieved from https://journal.alt.ac.uk/index.php/rlt/article/view/1297

Rockinson-Szapkiw, A. J., Spaulding, L. S., & Lunde, R. (2017). Women in distance doctoral programs: How they negotiate their identities as mothers, professionals, and academics in order to persist. *International Journal of Doctoral Studies*, *12*(7), 50–72.

Rovai, A. P. (2002). Building sense of community at a distance. The International Review of Research in Open and Distance Learning, *3*(1). 10.19173/irrodl.v3i1.79.

Schraw, G., & McCrudden, M. (2006). Information processing theory. Retrieved from http://www.education.com/reference/article/information-processing-theory/

Shaw, M., Burrus, S., & Ferguson, K. (2016). Factors that influence student attrition in online courses. *Online Journal of Distance Learning Administration*, *19*(3), 211–231.

Stone, C. (2017). *Opportunity through online learning: Improving student access, participation and success in higher education*. Perth: The National Centre for Student Equity in Higher Education (NCSEHE), Curtin University. Retrieved from https://www.ncsehe.edu.au/publications.

Sullivan, M. E., Yates, K. A., Inaba, K., Lam, L., & Clark, R. E. (2014). The use of cognitive task analysis to reveal the instructional limitations of experts in the teaching of procedural skills. Academic Medicine, *89*(5), 811–816.

Sundt, M. (2012). Common misperceptions of online education. *USC Rossier Show and Tell*, October 12.

Sundt, M., & Chung, M. (2017). Models for online faculty staffing and support. *White paper*. Retrieved from msundt@noodle.com

Yukselturk, E., & Bulut, S. (2007). Predictors for student success in an online course. *Journal of Educational Technology & Society*, *10*(2), 71–83.

MEDICAL VERSUS SOCIAL MODELS OF DISABILITY: INCREASING INCLUSION AND PARTICIPATION OF STUDENTS IN ONLINE AND BLENDED LEARNING IN HIGHER EDUCATION

Nathan Whitley-Grassi, Bryan J. Whitley-Grassi, Shaun C. Hoppel and Melissa Zgliczynski

ABSTRACT

In this chapter, the authors examine the challenges presented by supporting higher education students with disabilities in an online learning environment and put forth a discussion and recommendations for delivering literacy supports to geographically disparate students in fully online courses by embracing the social model of disability and universal design principals as opposed to the typical medical model of disability that it pervasive in educational systems. Under the Americans with Disabilities Act of 1990, educational institutions are required to promote auxiliary aids and services. Broadly defined, these aids are meant to enhance communication, inclusion, and participation of people with disabilities. The discussion of the resources put forth in this chapter begins with an exploration of the evolving consensus on the nature of disability and the standard (medical) model for providing accommodations and supports for students with disabilities, which was developed before the rise of online and blended learning environments. Next, the authors explore the problems inherent in the use of the medical model and highlight how the social model and universal design for learning can be utilized to empower learners and enhance their learning experiences in online and blended learning environments.

The discussion returns to the importance of inclusion, participation, and engagement for students with disabilities no matter the modality of learning. This chapter concludes with a comparison of two models of support and recommended changes for implementation of best practices to enhance literacy supports in online learning environments.

Keywords: Social model; medical model; universal design for learning; assistive technology; disability; access; virtual assistive technology; Americans with Disabilities Act; CAST.

Too often when we think of creating inclusive and equitable online and blended learning in higher education, we focus on skills deficits in relation to medically diagnosed physical and/or mental disabilities. This model only offers assistance to a small group of students based on an identified lack of ability that is static. This model does not support the greater number of students who may have undiagnosed disabilities or suffer from marginal skills deficits that would also benefit from the use of assistive technologies (ATs) and best practices under universal design for learning (UDL) guidelines. This medical model is rooted in outdated notions of what it means to have differing abilities, especially when engaging in online and blended learning. This chapter presents updated scholarship for expanding the constrictive concept of a medical model of disability and expands discussions on the real and immediate benefits to all students by embracing a social model of disability and supporting UDL guidelines in all online and blended learning environments.

By discussing the concept of Disability 3.0, which examines student support services in modern contexts of education technologies and their place in online and blended learning, the authors will build an argument that higher education must embrace a social model of disability in order to provide the least restrictive and most supportive model of service to all students engaged in online and blended learning. Discussing the broader tent of a social model disability and how it benefits all students in a flexible and more fluid manner provides support to the implementation of UDL in online and blended learning environments to strengthen student outcomes and foster greater access to assistive tools and educational technologies to students with disabilities and their differently abled peers who, likewise, may benefit from those same resources being open and accessible to them, thus increasing equity among all learners.

We will examine a case study from a college in New York where instructional technologists devised a pilot study to attempt to solve the issue of access to ATs through remote means for students enrolled in online and blended learning instead of traditional campus-based courses. This case study identifies several key considerations in the planning and rollout of online and blended learning programs that are rooted in a social model of disability and grounded in UDL guidelines. Additionally, recommendations for best practices based on the analysis of the pilot program offer considerations for higher education administrators considering this option or examining ways to increase accessibility and equity for all students enrolled in online and blended learning. This chapter concludes with further consideration for researchers in the field of instructional technology, disability services, and online and blended learning.

DISABILITY 3.0

Disability in online and blended learning is fundamentally different than in physical spaces, which necessitates a difference in level, scope, and nature of student support services. Wood, Dolmage, Price, and Lewiecki-Wilson (2014) analyzed current accessibility standards in writing composition learning environments and set forth a definition of "Disability 1.0" as an implicit agreement among educators, workplace supervisors, and society in general that the disabled should be included in typical life activities such as attending college, seeking gainful employment, and having a family. Think of this as the "foot in the door" approach where pioneering persons with disabilities begin to participate fully in higher education, even if they needed to be litigious to make it happen, with the direct support of their peers. The authors defined "Disability 2.0" as chiefly represented by the reasonable accommodation model that seeks to make up for deficiencies that bar access to persons with disabilities. This approach may even involve a "checklist for compliance" (Wood et al., 2014, p. 147). In a post-Americans with Disabilities Act of 1990 (ADA) world, the accommodation model continues to be the dominant way to be inclusive of persons with disabilities. A major deficit of this model, however, is that it makes accessibility the exception, not the norm, and continues to "isolate disability within the body or mind ... disability as a set of symptoms rather than a social process" (Wood et al., 2014, p. 147).

In order to move beyond "Disability 2.0" in the context of higher education, faculty must embed accessibility into courses through the UDL guidelines and build "access and accommodation as recursive projects that exist before, throughout, and even after a course" (Wood et al., 2014, p. 148). The authors sat forth a number of examples of such recursive processes including small group brainstorming sessions and adapting assignments to involve more freedom and individual choice. The authors tied UDL to the rhetorical concepts of *metis* (wisdom plus cunning) and *kairos* (appealing to place or time, timeliness) and expound the fact that writing composition workshops may be used to "build a shared responsibility between instructors and students," ultimately leading to fully accessible and inclusive coursework through an iterative process (Wood et al., 2014, p. 149). Regarding writing composition, moving beyond checklists and individual accommodation is to think about disability differently and engage students in a way that is multimodal and involves the students' perspectives directly. For the purposes of creating a meaningful auxiliary aid in an online or blended learning environment, which was the aim of the Virtual Assistive Technology Lab (VAT Lab) pilot program, it is necessary to operate under this "Disability 3.0" definition and to move beyond checklists and individualized action to better align with an ongoing shift in understanding the nature of disability represented by the "medical" and "social" models.

MEDICAL VERSUS SOCIAL MODEL OF DISABILITY

Despite the need to rethink disability as it intersects with online and blended learning environments, many institutions remain ideologically stuck in the legally enshrined reasonable accommodation model. The Public Broadcasting Service (PBS), a large media entity, published resources that essentially framed disabilities in the context of an existence of an impaired person or child, rather than an inaccessible society. In a section on its website devoted to learning disabilities, the site directed parents of young children with disabilities to AT that could potentially be used as an auxiliary aid. The site initially informed parents of their child's rights to inclusive education as well as access to auxiliary aids and services under the ADA. PBS defined AT as any specialized device, either "low" or "high-tech," that assists an individual in accessing learning. The definition is intended to be ambiguous and inclusive of many aids that "increase, maintain, or improve capabilities" (PBS, n.d.). The site was further divided into categories based upon different learning disabilities. The fact that the website categorized children by their disabilities shows an adherence to the "medical model" of disability, a model that uses an impairment or functional limitation as a major identifying characteristic, with the implication that the disability is an inherent characteristic of the individual, contained solely with them. An extension of this logic is that any solution should be directed to correct for the individual deficiency. This model is opposed by the "social model" of disability, which instead places the focus on barriers that exist in the environment for those who have a different experience than the norm. A possible analogy used to explain this concept could be that a wheelchair user is not disabled in their mobility until they come across a flight of stairs without a ramp, and in the social model, it is the stairs that pose the problem as well as the lack of accessible alternative rather than the focus on the person as being wheelchair "bound" and as such needs to find some way to cope with the stairs or request some sort of reasonable accommodation. With the presence of a ramp, there is no functional limitation and no need for accommodation. To summarize, the social model puts forth that disability is caused by the way society is organized, rather than a person' impairment or difference. Disability is viewed as an aspect of diversity and a piece, rather than a defining characteristic, of an individual's identity.

The topic of medical versus social model of disability has ethical implications beyond issues of UDL and reasonable accommodation in online and blended learning environments. In the "medical model," if the focus of the limitation is on the individual's physical or mental state, then at the heart of this issue there remains the specter of potential discrimination against individuals who could at some point express a disability because of idiosyncrasies in their genome or may have future functional limitation due to existing disability which has not yet manifested. US lawmakers are aware of this concern in so far as to take action to protect this minority. The Genetic Information Non-discrimination Act of 2008 (GINA) is a relatively unknown US law passed in 2008 to protect against this type of genetic discrimination. Green, Lautenbach, and McGuire (2015) analyzed the law in terms of providing a spectrum of protection, allowing people to take advantage of genetic testing, research, technologies, or new therapies without fear of exclusion or reprisal. The authors posited that GINA covers asymptomatic people with underlying potential genetic disease but creates a gap between those covered by this law and the ADA, which covers those who actively experience functional limitations to daily activities. Also, those who have "manifest or diagnosed disease but are not yet disabled were essentially left out of the employment protections offered by both GINA and the ADA" creating an at-risk population (Green et al., 2015, p. 397). This potentially at-risk population of those with ADA qualifying conditions who are not yet experiencing functional limitations could easily overlap with the student population at an institution, such as SUNY Empire, whose average students is much older than the undergraduate college norm (18–22) at 35 years of age.

Since GINA is not well known, cases of discrimination prevented by US law are hard to determine. Furthermore, since the law exempts insurance companies, the effectiveness of the law has been questioned. Ultimately, Green et al. (2015) contended that the status quo with insurance companies cannot stand and the way in which these companies pool risk must adapt to changes in the medical field. As genetic science evolves, our understanding moves away from a "genetic determinism" and, coupled with a move from the medical to social model of disability, parts of GINA and even the ADA may be rendered obsolete or ineffective in the realm of higher education. This calls into question a continued reliance on the "medical model" and strengthens calls for shifting to the "social model" by implementing the UDL guidelines in all higher education online and blended learning environments.

UDL

The basic mechanism through which the VAT Lab pilot program could actualize its "social model" foundation already existed in the UDL guidelines. Universal design originated in architecture as a means of building and designing environments that were useable by all peoples, including those with disabilities (Williamson, 2019). When applied to education, UDL refers to the attempt to open up the curriculum to be fully inclusive of students with disabilities before any disabled students encounter it. The educational equivalent of ensuring a new building is built with an access rampFfinn at all entry points. Ingram, Lyons, Bowron, and Oliver (2012) dealt specifically with UDL concerning online course accessibility, explaining that UDL is based upon an understanding of how the brain facilitates learning and identifies links to three synaptic networks: recognition, strategic, and affective.

These networks play an integral part in the learning process, and UDL guidelines seek to stimulate each by following its related principle. The first principle is to provide multiple means of representation in order to activate recognition networks, the "what" of learning. This includes gathering information, categorizing facts based on what we hear, see, and read. This requires information to be presented in different ways to make it accessible to the most students possible within a course. CAST (2011) suggested providing options for perception including ways to "customize the display of information," options for aural data, and substitutions for graphic data. Additionally, they suggested that providing options for verbal, numerical expressions, and representations to clarify "vocabulary ... syntax and structure supporting decoding of text, mathematical notation, and symbols" that encourages "understanding across language" and demonstrated through various modes (CAST, 2011). Including options for "comprehension" that "activate background knowledge ... highlight patterns, features, big ideas, and [significant] relationships" to guide "information processing, visualization, and manipulation," thus increasing transference and creating generalities "lead to resourceful, knowledgeable learners" (CAST, 2011).

Additionally, CAST (2011) suggested that instructors create "strategic, goal-direct learners" withing various means of "action and expression" that provide options for bodily movement that "vary the methods for response" and improve "access to assistive tools and assistive technologies." Varying the ways that students express and communicate learning via multimedia "build fluencies with graduated levels of support for practice and performance" (CAST, 2011). These steps will help to further develop "executive function" that guides "appropriate goal setting," strategic planning, and self-regulation, according to CAST (2011).

Finally, encouraging various "means of engagement" that support student interest by building in options for student voice and choice paired with autonomy and authentic learning by minimizing learning distractions to encourage sustained "effort and persistence," CAST (2011) suggested. This can be accomplished by making learning purposeful and increasing motivation through varying demands and levels of challenge across course assignments while "fostering collaboration" and a sense of "community" through increasing levels and methods of feedback including opportunities for self- and peer-assessment to increase self-regulation based on explicit teaching of personal coping skills and strategies within reflective practices (CAST, 2011).

The goal of the guidelines is to reach all learners by identifying the biological building blocks of learning and leaving room for creativity, innovation, and individual variance. In online and blended learning environments in higher education, instructors must provide multiple means for perception, multiple means of expression, and multiple means of engagement with course material. This process includes space for students with functional limitations, which are covered by one of the aforementioned multiple means.

Ingram et al. (2012) clearly expounded the point that the process of making course tools accessible in higher education does not lend well to innovation because making courses accessible by design "is a bad fit with the fact that many university professors are content area experts as opposed to experts in pedagogy" (p. 146). Another major point made in the article involved the reactive rather than proactive response to course accessibility. The authors explained that instructors frequently retrofitted existing materials upon first encountering a student with a disability; however, Ingram et al. (2012) additionally called for a more proactive approach by pointing out that "retrofitting can be frustrating and time consuming, and does not address the legal expectation that courses are accessible even when students with disabilities are not enrolled" (p. 151). They pointed to this switch as the necessary paradigm shift to begin making UDL common in curricula. Their research results demonstrated that UDL is "a good idea whose time has arrived," partly because "the trend in higher education delivery modes is changing" (Ingram et al., 2012, p. 151). The authors linked this change to increased diversity and globalism on university campuses as well as new ideas about instructional planning. The authors called for further research on specific educational technologies and their relation to UDL, but their focus remained on the theoretical aspects of realizing UDL. In order to move beyond theory and into practice, more evaluations of the effect of the proactive UDL style must be conducted across various disciplines. The areas of support, training, and creating campus consensus among various stakeholders are additional areas for future research that would continue to inform the process of evaluating overall levels of success for UDL initiatives. Lastly, the authors predicted that UDL would foster a new level of collaboration while simultaneously reducing barriers and provide increased robust online supports to a wide variety of learners, a goal in line with the purpose of the VAT Lab pilot program.

UDL is often enhanced by access to ATs. Deployed typically in higher education as reasonable accommodations under the "medical model," these tools have the potential to be transformative under the "social model" if more widely distributed. Alnahdi (2014) explored the role of AT in classrooms through a concise literature review reaching all the way back to 1996. The author identified three main points regarding the use of technology to help students with learning disabilities. They included identifying funding resources during the transition process and ensuring that students can acquire devices in a timely manner to benefit, and selecting any device or technology must be informed by the educational environment, coupled with proper training and support. Alnahdi (2014) further explained that the appropriateness of the device or tool is paramount and that the expense may not matter, nor how "high-tech" the tool is deemed. Alnahdi (2014) continued,

> it is much more efficient to look within the normal, existing technology to find useful devices or software for students with disabilities than to just focus on finding a specific technology designed specifically for people with disabilities. (p. 19)

He advocated, for example, practical approaches, which involve keeping it simple and providing access to aids that are built into operating systems already. He also cited highlighting and contextually aware spellcheck as examples of simple solutions that may address some needs for a wide array of students. The focus is on reducing barriers to learning rather than assisting specific students with identified disabilities by deploying an AT directly to them.

Alnahdi (2014) broke down AT into three subtypes: accessible webpages, accessible instructional software or materials, and accessible telephone or communication technologies. He believes that each subcategory requires a different level of nuance, but that all three types of AT must be present for there to be a benefit to students with disabilities. A specific case cited involved a study on the use of word prediction software among fifth-grade students (ages 10–11) with mild disabilities. The study ultimately demonstrated that there was a general increase in the number of words produced correctly in writing samples after iterative use of the word prediction software in short writing exercises. There was a lower occurrence of misspelled words and an overall increase in vocabulary. In order for the results of the study to be of maximum benefit, the word prediction software should be transitioned from fifth to sixth grade (average age of 11–12). Alnahdi (2014) clearly stated the importance of considering ATs in transitional services when students move between grades or between secondary to higher education.

Another vital concern is that teachers have knowledge of available technologies that can support their students. Teachers themselves must be able to receive training and have the funding to access and implement ATs into their classrooms. Alnahdi (2014) cited cost as a major prohibition to current use of ATs, followed by training opportunities. He explained the seven principles of universal design that should be considered when selecting an AT device. They are: (1) equitable use; (2) flexibility in use; (3) simple and intuitive design or interface; (4) perceptible information; (5) tolerance for errors; (6) low physical effort; and (7) awareness of learning methods and democratic processes when appropriate. He placed the responsibility for applying these factors on the teacher, but as previously discussed, in higher education, the instructor may not be the best arbiter of such a change. This VAT Lab pilot program was designed to include input from faculty, professional educational technologists versed in pedagogy, and information technology professionals to collaborate in order to achieve the principles laid out by Alnahdi (2014), who stated that low-tech tools should always be the first option over high-tech tools or more expensive tools, that educators should search among available tools and devices first before looking for devices specifically made for educational purposes or for specific disabilities since expensive choices are not always the best choice, and lastly small adjustments to existing technologies will often make a huge difference. These principles informed the process of selecting an AT for the pilot program in our VAT Lab.

The advancement of services entitled to persons with disabilities in the United States has tended to grow not only through direct US legislation like the ADA, but through "Dear Colleague" guidance letters often written jointly by the departments of education and justice to advise institutions on best practices and offer guidance on how to resolve matters of access for students with disabilities. The evolution of AT software has been affected by this process through the development of gradually evolving standards elucidated in "Dear Colleague" letters. An example of one such letter and subsequent policy is the one written in response to complaints of discrimination against those with sensory disabilities using Amazon's Kindle eBook reader and their lack of compatibility with extant screen reading technologies. This "Dear Colleague" letter by Perez and Ali (2010) served as official communication between the federal government and all national universities and colleges explaining that use of emerging technologies, such as e-readers, must be accessible to individuals with disabilities. This letter also serves as guidance for the best practice that all instructional technologies be accessible. The original complaint stemmed from the required use of the Kindle DX in a curriculum that excluded a blind student from being able to access the required readings because at that time the Kindle did not have a text-to-speech (TTS) function to read words aloud. The law is careful to include that the policy does not extend only to e-readers but to all emerging technologies used in instruction. The authors end with the following:

> The DCL encourages colleges and universities to take steps to ensure that they refrain from using electronic book readers, or other similar technology, that is inaccessible to individuals who are blind or have low vision to the extent that a reasonable accommodation or modification for this type of technology does not exist or is not available. Technology is the hallmark of the future, and technological competency is essential to preparing all students for future success. Emerging technologies are an educational resource that enhances learning for everyone, and perhaps especially for students with disabilities. Technological innovations have opened a virtual world of commerce, information, and education to many individuals with disabilities for whom access to the physical world remains challenging. Ensuring equal access to emerging technology in university and college classrooms is a means to the goal of full integration and equal educational opportunity for this nation's students with disabilities. With technological advances, procuring electronic book readers that are accessible should be neither costly nor difficult. We would like to work with you to ensure that America's technological advances are used for the benefit of all students. (Perez & Ali, 2010)

The ultimate goal of the VAT Lab at SUNY Empire was to integrate the guidance from the "Dear Colleague" letter on accessible emerging technology and the principles of the UDL guidelines into an enterprise-wide system of support for students with disabilities. A secondary goal was the help students decide which AT tools to use by curating a short list of software that accounted for various areas of functional limitation.

THE VAT LAB AT SUNY EMPIRE

For those students attending blended or face-to-face classes, the common support model in place to would provide supports to students on institutional resources, usually in a computer lab. The AT Lab at SUNY Empire involved a rework of an existing office to create a physical AT resource room located at one of the campuses of the college in New York. This physical space was designed with accessibility in mind and had a dedicated space for students with disabilities to interact with AT to support literacy skills and ultimately promote academic equity by leveling the educational playing field.

The AT Lab was provisioned with several software products commonly in use by students registered with the Office of Accessibility Resources, including Read & Write Gold, Dragon Speaking Easily, JAWS, and Inspiration 9. These tools represent some of the most common and powerful tools in the auxiliary aids and services toolkit. The AT Lab is a valuable tool assuming that you are a student who comes to campus and has the familiarity and/or training required to use the power and proprietary tools, which is often only made available in response to a diagnosis (medical model).

This raises issues of access for online students. Planning is currently underway to implement just-in-time aid by allowing students to access the tool from their remote locations on their own devices via a college-provided virtual private network (VPN). Through the development of the VAT Lab pilot program, students could test the capabilities of the tools, experiment, and learn how these tools could support their learning needs alongside scaffolded, accessible written training materials. Educational technologists from SUNY Empire curated a list of ATs that addressed four areas of functional limitation due to disability and created a virtual machine with those technologies readily available. The four areas were literacy (Read and Write Gold), word processing (Dragon Naturally Speaking), notetaking (Sonocent Audio Note taker), and visual enhancements (ZoomText and JAWS screen reader).

Licenses for the software were acquired with institutional funding and the virtual machine was established in order to test for further and wider distribution. The online VAT Lab passed initial testing via the educational technologies, but more work is required due to issues with deployment. As a result, the VAT Lab pilot program was not in place to respond to the COVID-19 pandemic and the sudden influx of online students. The VAT lab is now moving to a more stable Cisco-based virtual environment to reach a broader audience of students. The VAT Lab program also brought up unanticipated questions and concerns regarding access to the peripherals needed specifically for Dragon Naturally Speaking, which presupposed access to a microphone and the sustainability of maintaining licenses for these tools to a broader student population.

ACCESS AND EQUITY: TOOLS AND RESOURCES TO SUPPORT ONLINE STUDENTS

Given some of the logistical and financial issues raised in the discussion of the AT and VAT labs, another possible approach may be to create and curate a list of (preferably free) resources and tools (including apps) that could be made broadly available to anyone with need, rather than requiring a diagnosis to access services. This would empower students to self-select from tool that they feel would help them be more effective in creating and explaining the meaning of their learning. This approach embraces both the social model of disability and UDL principles as it places options and choice in how students approach their learning in their hands without employing the medical diagnosis as a "ticket to ride" in order to gain access to supports, and supports that are prescriptive and may not take personal preferences into account. This section will present several broad categories of assistive tools that are available to learners at little or no cost and could be recommended as a suite of tools to all learners to choose to utilize.

Reading and reading comprehension tools can assist those students who may want assistance with reading problems, limited vocabulary or echolalia, difficulty in understanding similes, metaphors, humorous, ironic or sarcastic language, and information acquisition, interpretation, and application. AT tools such as optical character recognition (OCR) and TTS are common solutions to some of these issues. TTS allow learners to identify text that would be read aloud. Thus, it would allow learners to have their text played to them for audio only or read along with the text consumption. OCR tools convert text in image files such as scans of printed text as a PDF into a format that can be read by the computer for screen readers, TTS programs, and often edited or modified on computer software. These ATs are under the medical model are often prescribed to learners with visual impairments and/or processing disorders.

Both of these tool types allow learners enhanced freedom on how they engage with materials in a variety of formats. Many learners even those without the diagnosis could greatly benefit from access to these resources. Applying the UDL model to design of resources and classes, best practices would include presenting content that would be in a flexible format making TTS much more accessible. If the content is presented in an accessible way, the need for OCR is greatly reduced, as OCR is more of a remediation tool, than something that on its own that can improve literacy and comprehension learners.

There are a number of applications and toolbars that can be downloaded for web browsers that can create addition control over the user experience for the learner. Some of these can be seen listed in Fig. 1. The recent popularity of "dark mode" in Windows, Mac, and many mobile platforms illustrates that many people have preferences for the ability to vary the contrast or backlighting of their computer working experience. These tools are often prescribed for various visual impairments including color blindness or light sensitivity. Adding these resources to our list allow learners to choose settings that create pleasant and less stressfully learning environments while working online.

Planning tools like those that are listed in Fig. 1 are often prescribed for students with attention disorders, cognitive impairments, and issues with creating connections between ideas in the medical model of disabilities. Like those tools mentioned above, these tools can prove to be a valuable resource to many learners who self-select to employ them in their learning regardless of their diagnosis.

UDL AND VAT LAB CASE STUDY

If UDL is the viewed as the skeleton supporting the structure of auxiliary aids, then AT may, likewise, be viewed as the muscle, since they support the action of learning in a just-in-time manner. In online and blended learning environments, instructors following the UDL guidelines should provide options for perception, multiple means for expression, and multiple means of engagement within the course. As previously suggested, the UDL model might include the idea of creating a curated set of resources that when leveraged effectively could give all learners a greater ability to perceive, express, and engage in varied ways by self-selecting resources that the learner feels would be beneficial to their learning process remains

Online Services	Assistive Toolbars	Contrast/ Magnification	Text-to-Speech
• RoboBraille	• MyStudyBar • PortableApps.com	• ScreenTinter • VuBar • Virtual Magnifying Glass	• Balabolka • Dspeech
Screen Reading	**Audio Recording**	**Planning**	**Additional Resources**
• Non Visual Desktop Access (NVDA) • Thunder	• Audacity	• FreeMind • XMind	• Emptech • AbilityNet • ATHENA • The Innovative Educator • SPELD SA

Fig. 1. Freeware Tools for Disabled Learners. *Source*: Adapted from Oxford Library Guides at Bodleian Libraries University of Oxford.

at the root of the social model of disability. These ATs should be made available to students on a more open basis, thus moving away from the currently used "medical model" of disability, which presently requires students in the United States to have a diagnosis of impairment and supporting documentation detailing functional limitation. If these types of resources were offered more broadly, then any students who could potentially experience a barrier to perceiving, expressing, or engaging in their learning could choose to utilize these resources to create a new way to interact with the course or material. This is especially important at colleges and universities that serve non-traditional students as they may have never received a formal disability diagnosis in the K-12 system (ages 6–18), or they may exist in the legal limbo between coverage by GINA and the ADA.

CONCLUSIONS

Higher education institutions in the United States will likely remain ideologically stuck in the legally enshrined reasonable accommodation model for the foreseeable future, continuing to only support students with "medical model" solutions if changes are not implemented at the institutional level. Those institutions that are willing to embrace the social model of disability could easily do so by creating UDL aligned materials, resources, and pathways to support their students to get support. This support could take the form of proprietary resources such as those used in the VAT Lab or in a curated set of open source or freely available tools as presented in Fig. 1.

This proposed embrace of a social model of disability would represent a required investment to be implemented at higher education institutions. There is significant cost as well as policy and logistical needs associated with this type of student support. In the examples from SUNY Empire, educational technology staff would need to collaborate with staff from accessibility resources in the creation and curation of software and applications be made available through the VAT Lab or to curate and maintain the list of recommended tools. In addition, students and faculty would need to be educated further about the UDL guidelines and available resources that would be made available to all students. This would need to include both a UDL minded approach to course offerings and support that engaged with these tools as well as a less prescriptive approach to ATs than is currently used (i.e., "you have this diagnosis, use this tool"). In this case, each item or group of items in this collection of tools would need some recommendation about the specific barriers it could be used to overcome. In addition to the staff costs associated, there may be a need to acquire additional funding for new software, applications, and other resources to properly administer licenses and support to students. Students may require multiple training sessions as they learn how to use, diagnose, and solve problems arising from using these tools and resources.

Students, particularly non-traditional students (those outside of the general age range of 18–22) who are often drawn to online courses for their flexibility in scheduling, come to college with varying comfort levels in terms of technology due to age and life experiences. These students may require additional training and support to learn even the most basic computer skills. It can cause students great frustration as they navigate learning new technical skills as they are immersed in the content and learning of their courses. With these students, the more training and support that can be provided before they begin their courses, the better. For some, using the AT unaided may add an additional layer onto the already high demand for digital literacy inherent in online curriculum. Some students, however, may come to college already familiar with certain applications such as Google Docs, which have built-in accessibility features. Additionally, accessibility features that are available both on their computers and smartphones, such as talk-to-type capabilities, are important to know and utilize with the IT support. All these factors should be taken into consideration when providing supports to the students in online and blended learning environments.

The suggestions made in this chapter during a transitional time where law and its interpretations have not fully caught up with best practices in online and blended learning through the delivery of ATs and that the field of support for students with barriers to access remains a complex issue to explore with very real educational and personal costs to higher education students. Adding the component of digital literacy support in an online or blended learning environment can be both a great equalizer for students and a new challenge to an institution's existing student support model. One takeaway from this discussion is the revelation that in addition to the hidden development and maintenance costs, there is a need for clear logistical planning and implementation of UDL methods for student support in relation to the use and purpose of ATs being recommended at the institution. In other words, multiple departments need to make a coordinated effort to design the online learning environment and learning content with a UDL mindset that works with the resources being made available to students, thus easing their selection and integration by learners. This can be attained through strategic planning, collaboration, and communication across the entire campus community engaging students, faculty, and staff in advance of the deployment of pilot programs.

REFERENCES

Alnahdi, G. (2014). Assistive technology in special education and the universal design for learning. TOJET: The Turkish Online Journal of Educational Technology, *13*(2), 18–23. Retrieved from https://eric.ed.gov/contentdelivery/servlet/ERICServlet?accno=EJ1022880

CAST. (2011). *Universal design for learning guidelines version 2.0*. Wakefield, MA: Author.

Green, R. C., Lautenbach, D., & McGuire, A. (2015). GINA: Genetic discrimination and genomic medicine. *New England Journal of Medicine, 372*(January), 397–399.

Ingram, R., Lyons, B., Bowron, R., & Oliver, J. (2012). Higher education online course accessibility issues: Universal design. *Review of Higher Education and Self Learning*, *5*(16), 143–154.

Perez, T., & Ali, R. (2010, June 29). Dear colleague letter: Electronic book readers. Retrieved from http://www2.ed.gov/about/offices/list/ocr/letters/colleague-20100629.html. Accessed on June 17, 2020.

Public Broadcasting Service. (n.d.). Assistive technology information for parents. Retrieved from http://www.pbs.org/parents/education/learning-disabilities/strategies-for-learningdisabilities/assistive-technology. Accessed on February 11, 2016.

Williamson, B. (2019). *Accessible America: A history of disability and design*. New York, NY: University Press.

Wood, T., Dolmage, J., Price, M., & Lewiecki-Wilson, C. (2014). Where we are: Disability and accessibility: Moving beyond disability 2.0 in composition studies. *Composition Studies*, *42*(2), 147–150.

ABOUT THE AUTHORS

Jeremy Anderson is a Founding Associate Vice Chancellor, Strategic Analytics at Dallas College. He leads teams in developing and executing a vision for data-informed decision-making across the College in service of student access and success and organizational effectiveness. His background is in Teaching, Instructional Design, and Analytics in secondary and higher education. He earned his BS in History Education from Central Connecticut State University, MS in Educational Technology from Eastern Connecticut State University and EdD in Interdisciplinary Leadership from Creighton University.

Lynn Boyle is a Program Director for the BA Childhood Practice and BA Childhood Studies. She particularly enjoys working with students as they begin their studies and supporting students to participate through the widening access agenda. She was the Lead Officer for Transforming the Experience of Students through Assessment (TESTA) for nine years which focuses on developing best practice in assessment and feedback based upon a review and student feedback. She is currently a Professional Doctorate student. Her study is based around the Self Perception of Childhood Practice students, on the first year of the BA Childhood Practice in Higher Education.

Heather Bushey is an Associate Dean of Advising and Student Support at Bay Path University. Her past roles have included managing the enrollment and professional advising functions and serving as the Project Manager for a Department of Education Fund for the Improvement of Postsecondary Education (FIPSE) grant. She holds an EdD from Northeastern University in Higher Education Administration, a Master's in Public Administration from American International College, and a Bachelor's Degree in Human Development and Family Studies from the University of Vermont. She teaches Women's Leadership courses at The American Women's College, Bay Path University's undergraduate division for adult women learners. Her research interests include the engagement of online learners and how it contributes to retention and a quality educational experience.

Louise Campbell, PhD, is a Lecturer in Education at the University of Dundee. She is the Professional Graduate Diploma in Education (PGDE Secondary) Convenor and Pathway Lead for the Supported Induction Route, which is an alternative route into secondary school teaching. Much of her work is in Initial Teacher Education, and she is the Subject Lead for the PGDE Secondary English program. She also works with research postgraduate students both on campus and via distance learning. Prior to commencing her work in higher education, she was a Secondary Schoolteacher. Her research interests include effective pedagogies, innovative learning spaces, the development of learners' twenty-first-century skills, and philosophy of education.

Louise Connelly has an MA (Hons) in Religious Studies, an MSc in Information Management and Library Studies, a Postgraduate Diploma in Digital Education, and received her PhD in Religion, Media and Culture at the University of Edinburgh in 2012. She is a Senior Fellow of the Higher Education Academy (SFHEA). She is currently a Senior E-Learning Developer and Vice-Convenor of the Human Ethical Review Committee (HERC) at the Royal (Dick) School of Veterinary Studies at the University of Edinburgh. Her research interests includes internet research and ethics, the use of social media in an education environment, digital education, and academic support for online distance students.

Maura Devlin is an Associate Vice President and Dean of Undergraduate Studies at Bay Path University, where she oversees the academic teaching and learning and advising functions that serve Bay Path's entire undergraduate student body, including traditional, residential students and adult students earning bachelor's degrees primarily online. She is the Project Coordinator of a Department of Education's Title III grant, "Learning for the 21st Century: Reshaping the Student Experience," whose goals are to develop guided pathways, reframe student support, and leverage integrated technology to support the student learning experience. She earned a PhD in Educational Policy and Leadership from the University of Massachusetts, a Master of Public Policy and Administration from the University of Massachusetts, and a Bachelor of Arts in International Relations/French from Colgate University.

Michele Forte, PhD, LMSW, is the Manager for SUNY Online Student Supports. Her interests related to this position include the development and implementation of holistic student supports, leveraging faculty expertise to inform student success, and curricular and advising innovation in distance education and advising. She is also an Associate Professor of Human Services and a licensed, community-based mental health clinician. She has presented at regional, state, national, and international conferences on mechanisms to ensure student persistence and academic success.

Amanda J. Gould is a Vice President of Learning Innovation, Analytics and Technology at Bay Path University. Motivated by a passion for implementing systematic and data-driven approaches to both operational and learning arenas to impact student success, she has served as Project Director for multi-million dollar grants to drive innovative initiatives to advance teaching and learning practices to better serve under-represented populations. Currently, She is the Project Director for a grant project funded by the Strada Education Network to develop innovative solutions aimed at increasing the linkages between education and employment and to promote more women into technology fields. She received her undergraduate degree in Sociology and Communications and a graduate degree in Sociology from Boston College.

Dr Jaimie Hoffman is an Enthusiast of all things online education and technology from leveraging technology to enhance process efficiency to building online student communities. With over 20 years of experience in higher education, she spent the first 15 years of her career in student affairs/services which serves as the foundation for her experience and passion for making a difference in higher education. She has also served as a full-time and Adjunct Faculty Member in face-to-face, blended, and online (using synchronous and asynchronous technology) modalities. She earned her Bachelor of Arts in Music from California Lutheran University, Masters of Education in Higher and Postsecondary Education from Arizona State University, and her Doctorate of Education in Leadership from the University of California Los Angeles.

Shaun C. Hoppel, MA, trained in the use of assistive and adaptive technologies at the Center for Assistive Technology (CAT) located at SUNY Buffalo. He has served as Coordinator of Auxiliary Aids and Services in the Office of Accessibility Resources at SUNY Buffalo and has over seven years of experience working with faculty, staff, and students on issues related to accessible technology, including assessment and training of disabled students and training for faculty on best practices for creating accessible course materials. In his role as Educational Technologist at SUNY Empire State College, he has tested software and course components for accessibility and led an accessibility project group within Educational and Emerging Technologies.

Jessica J. Jones is currently a Program Manager in University Academic Success Programs at Arizona State University focused on supporting online tutoring services. She considers herself a lifelong learner and embraces opportunities to research and learn new information about impact on the success of others. During her years working as a higher education professional, she has worked as a Coordinator for Student Engagement at Arizona State University, a Resident Director at the University of Nevada-Reno, and a Hall Director at the University of South Dakota. These various positions have given her experience with program and event coordination, student and employee engagement, recruitment, event planning, tutoring, online education, and applying theory to work.

David A. Joyner, PhD, is an Executive Director of Online Education & OMSCS in Georgia Tech's College of Computing. As of spring 2021, the program has over 11,000 students from 120 countries and over 4,500 alumni. He has personally taught several classes in the program, amounting to over 15,000 students in the past five years. His research focuses on online education and learning at scale, especially as they intersect with for-credit offerings at the graduate and undergraduate levels. His emphasis is on designing learning experiences that leverage the opportunities of online learning to compensate for the loss of synchronous collocated class time. This includes leveraging artificial intelligence for student support and assignment evaluation, facilitating student communities in large online classes, and investigating strategies for maintainable and interactive presentation of online instructional material. As part of his work, he teaches online versions of CS6460: Educational Technology; CS6750: Human-Computer Interaction; CS7637: Knowledge-Based AI; and CS1301: Introduction to Computing. He has received several awards for his work in teaching online, including the 2019 USG Regents' Teaching Excellence Award for Online Teaching, 2018 Georgia Tech Center for Teaching & Learning Curriculum Innovation Award, and the 2016 Georgia Tech College of Computing Lockheed Excellence in Teaching Award.

Molly A. Mott, PhD, has extensive experience in student success in both virtual and traditional environments. She has presented at regional, state, national, and international conferences on distance learning and leads efforts across her university system to promote student access and completion.

Kristyn Muller, PhD, works within her university system as the Impact Analyst to evaluate the effectiveness of the services they provide to support online learning, analyzes how online learning impacts the system's overall goals, and develops ways to share data to inform the continuous improvement of system-wide online learning practices. She has presented at state, regional, and national conferences about the system's efforts to ensure online learning quality and promote student success.

Donna Murray has a BSc (Hons) in Horticulture from the University of Strathclyde, and a PhD in Botany from the University of Nottingham, and is a Senior Fellow of the Higher Education Academy. She is the Head of Taught Student Development in the Institute for Academic Development at the University of Edinburgh leading a team which supports 35,000 students in their academic development. Her research interests include self-efficacy, third-space professionals, and online learning.

Dr Roland Nuñez currently serves as the Director of Educational Opportunity Programs at Lake Sumter State College. He has over a decade of higher education experience, including roles such as Campus Director for Embry-Riddle Aeronautical University and Director of Student Development at University of Science and Arts of Oklahoma. He obtained his Master's and PhD in Educational Leadership at Oklahoma State University. His research emphasis and prior publications include online engagement, educational entertainment and innovation, and Hispanic college student development. He currently teaches Statistics and Research Courses in an online and hybrid format, allowing him to explore new strategies for online education and engagement.

Dr Tyler Phelps is a Director of Academic Advising at Eastern Illinois University and College Instructor. He has worked in academic advising and student success for more than 15 years in which he pioneered his "cloud advising" asynchronous model as a part of his own research. He has presented at conferences nationally and internationally with NACADA about university retention.

Dr Shelley Price-Williams is an Assistant Professor of Postsecondary Education at the University of Northern Iowa. Her research interests center on non-cognitive factors of college student development and persistence, inclusion of nondominant groups in the college environment, and multicultural organizational development. She holds two decades of experience in student and academic affairs spanning program development and management as well as academic advising, career counseling, and assessment.

Dr Pietro A. Sasso is an Assistant Professor at Southern Illinois University Edwardsville. He has Written and Co-edited seven textbooks, Authored approximately 50 scholarly publications, and Facilitated over 40 conference presentations. He has a continuous research agenda that has evolved to address: (1) the college experience; (2) student success; and (3) educational equity across cocurricular spaces. He has served as a college administrator and researcher of higher education for more than 15 years.

Rachel Scott has been passionate about the world of online education since high school when she took her first distance learning course and saw the potential for online learning to be both accessible and engaging. She has worked within the world of distance education and higher education in a variety of capacities over the past nine years, serving as an LMS Administrator, facilitating faculty training on LMS setup, providing 1:1 faculty coaching and support, spearheading the development of online training modules for a local non-profit volunteer network, and supporting undergraduate students in a remote support staff role before moving into the OPM space. She received her Master of Science in Education, Student Affairs Administration from the University of Wisconsin, La Crosse, where she focused her capstone research on the student support needs of online students.

Dr Melora Sundt is the Chief Academic Officer for Noodle Partners, a service provider supporting universities as they develop great online programs. Prior to joining Noodle, she was a Professor at the USC Rossier School of Education, and a Senior Advisor to the Center for Drug Evaluation and Research (CDER) at the US Food and Drug Administration (FDA). Before partnering with the FDA, she was the Executive Vice Dean for USC Rossier School of Education and Chaired the design teams that created USC Rossier's blended MAT@USC, Global Executive EdD, and EdD in Organizational Change and Leadership programs. She taught in USC Rossier's degree programs for more than 20 years and Chaired numerous doctoral dissertations. She blogs regularly about teaching online, organizational change, and preventing sexual assault.

Lorraine Syme-Smith is a Lecturer in Education at the University of Dundee. Working primarily in College Sector Education on the Teaching Qualification in Further Education, her students are lecturers currently employed in further education colleges, adult, and higher education. She has worked in tertiary education for nearly 30 years, principally in further and higher education as well as in the voluntary sector. Working with students on distance learning programs, she has in-depth experience of the use of virtual learning environments and other software in education and for learner support. Her research interests include online learning, learner motivation, the use of teaching observations, and equality and diversity in education.

Dr Leslie Wheaton has served the world of education for the past 25 years first as an Educator, then as an International Director of a non-profit educational organization, before becoming an Academic Director helping universities create interactive, collaborative, engaging, and innovative learning online. Throughout her career, she has presented on national and international stages on various topics relating to engagement and learning. Her personal and professional background is influenced by her educational, personal, and professional experiences throughout the United States and abroad. She has worked with every level of education spanning pre-kindergarten through higher education applying her knowledge of brain research and the science of learning coupled with her expertise in engagement. Her focus on social justice is ever-present as she develops and redefines educational and organizational structures and systems by providing knowledge and skills, motivation, and organizational support needed to successfully reach goals. She holds a BA from the University of North Carolina-Chapel Hill and an MA in Education from San Francisco State University and the University of Washington, respectively. Her administrative credential is from the University of Washington's Danforth Program. She received her Educational Doctorate in Organizational Change and Leadership from the University of Southern California.

Bryan J. Whitley-Grassi, MS, is a Professional Development Specialist at the Orleans/Niagara BOCES Center for School Improvement and Professional Development specializing in social studies and educational leadership, Culturally Responsive-Sustaining Education (CR-SE), and online/blended learning, a former Social Studies Teacher, Instructional Technology Coach, and Curriculum Coordinator. He is an Adjunct Professor of Sociology at Niagara University and an Officer of the Board of Directors for the New York State Council for the Social Studies with over 10 years' experience teaching online/blended classes at the secondary and university levels. His research interests include LGBTQ+ history, social studies education, virtual learning, political sociology, and public policy decision-making.

Nathan Whitley-Grassi, PhD, is the Interim Director of Educational and Emerging Technologies at SUNY Empire State College. In addition, he serves as the college's Electronic and Information Technology Accessibility Officer and an Assistant Professor. He has over 10 years' experience focused heavily on Program Management, Faculty Development, and Research, particularly in the use of program/learning assessment, design, and educational technologies to increase access to high-quality learning opportunities for all students. His office also works with the office of Accessibility Resources to implement technology support accommodations to students at SUNY Empire. In addition, he Co-manages SUNY Empire's award winning "emergency accessibility course review process" which identifies courses with students with accessibility issues enrolled in them and triggers an individually focused instructional design accessibility review of all course materials. His research interests include increasing access to STEM experiences through innovative technology integration, educational assessment, faculty development, and increasing access to learning opportunities for students with various barriers to access. These barriers can be related to dis/ability, cost, geography, or time.

Dr Autumn Willinger, coming from a family of lifelong learners, is a Believer in the Transformative Power of Education. She received two Master's degrees, one online and one face-to-face. These experiences contributed to her interest in best practices in adult online learning, which later became the focus of her research and dissertation. Her goal is to provide university staff and faculty the tools and support needed to offer meaningful and accessible opportunities for adult learners. A former Teacher and Administrator currently working in the field of Online Program Management, she received her MS in Information Services from the University of North Texas and both her MS in Education and an EdD in Organizational Leadership from Pepperdine University.

Melissa Zgliczynski, MEd, has over 10 years of experience working with students with disabilities. She is currently the Director of Accessibility Resources and Services at SUNY Empire State College where she oversees the day-to-day operations of the Office of Accessibility Resources and Services. In addition to providing accommodations and resources for students with disabilities, the office is also focused on providing professional development for faculty and staff on topics related to supporting students with disabilities. At her previous institution, she served as Director of Students with Disabilities where she began an academic support program for students with learning differences. She is an Active Member of the Collegiate Consortium of Disability Advocates, which is an organization of secondary and postsecondary professionals who provide trainings and resources for students and families of students with disabilities. She has presented on topics such as universal design, supporting students with learning differences, and campus collaboration with disability services at local, state, and national conferences.

NAME INDEX

Abrami, P. C., 92, 95
Akbulut., Y, 89
AlDahdouh, A., 164, 172
Aleksandrova., Y, 67
Ali, A., 32
Ali, R., 186–187
Allen, E., 14
Allen., I. E, 4, 30, 89
Alnahdi, G., 185–186
Amador., J., 126–127
Ambrose., G. A., 126–127
Ames, C., 164, 166, 169
An, Y., 127
Andercheck, B., 93
Anderman, E., 163, 166
Anderman, L., 163, 166
Anderson, T., 62, 66, 170
Andrusyszyn, M. A., 89
Aoun, J., 15
Arriaga, R., 47
Aslanian, C. B., 4–5, 14, 104
Aslanian, C., 89
Astin, A., 135
Atan, H., 93

Badillo, N., 166
Bagaka's, J. G., 169
Bailie, J. L., 6–7
Baker, V. L., 168, 172, 175–176
Baltes, B., 166
Bandura, A., 94, 123, 151, 163
Barnes, B., 169
Baum, S., 14
Bawa, P., 165166, 168
Baxter Magolda, M. B., 126
Baxter, J., 149, 151
Bayne, S., 134, 149, 151, 153
Bégin, C., 165
Bejerano, A., 15
Benton, D., 49

Berman, R., 164
Bernard, R. M., 92
Bernstein, E., 15
Berry, S., 167, 169–170, 174
Bettinger, E. P., 19
Betts, A. S., 166
Bhimdiwala, A., 90
Bilgrien, N., 47
Black, E. W., 167, 172
Blanchard, A., 93
Blaschke, L., 63, 69
Bloom, J. L., 126
Boerner, H., 19
Bond, L. T., 89
Bondi, S., 135
Boudreau, C. A., 17
Bowen, W., 15
Bowlin, L. K., 166
Bowron, R., 183
Boyle, M., 164, 169
Bradley, C. L., 93
Bransteter, I., 166
Brauer, A., 92
Brindley, J. E., 5
Brinthaupt, T. M., 93
Brown, C. G., 78, 165
Brusilovsky, P., 89
Brychan, T., 92
Buhr, E. E., 64
Bulut, S., 165–166, 170, 173
Bures, E. M., 95
Burg, S., 151
Burgess, M., 91
Burnsed, B., 14
Burrus, S., 163
Busby, R. R., 17

Caires, S., 164
Camacho, I., 47
Cameron, E. A., 82

Camus, M. S., 93
Cannon, J., 19
Cardak, C. S., 89
Casteel, A., 165
Chickering, A. W., 123
Chingos, M., 15
Chung, M., 174
Cisco, J., 137
Clark, B. R., 165
Clark, R. E., 10, 163–164
Clinefelter, D. L., 4–5, 20, 104
Clinefelter, D., 89
College Development Network, 65
College Reading & Learning Association, 140
CollegeAtlas.org, 4
Conole, G., 61
Conway, J. I., 135
Cook, J., 93
Cook, S. M., 36, 38
Cope-Watson, G., 166
Covey, S., 19
Cozart, D., 134
Cragg, C. E., 89
Crawley, A., 6–7, 128
Cross, L. K., 81–82

Daher, T., 135
Dalal, H. A., 20, 22
Dam, S., 135
Daniels, L. M., 64
Darder, A., 165
Dare, L. A., 5
Daston, C., 162
Dawson, K., 167
Deane, B., 37
DeBard, R., 79
Deci, E. L., 63
Delahunty, J., 154–155
DeVitis, J. L., 74, 84, 128
Diaz, S., 91
Dittmann, W., 89
Dolmage, J., 181
Dougherty, K. D., 93
Downes, S., 61, 68
Dron, J., 62, 66, 170

Dundar, A., 90
Dupin-Bryant, P. A., 89
Dweck, C. S., 89, 94

Eccles, J., 163, 170, 173
Edwards, M., 16
Elliott, E. S., 94
Else, K., 165, 170, 173
Estes, F., 10, 163–164, 175
Evans, H., 165, 167
Everington, L., 135

Farrugia, C., 38
Faulconer, J., 40
Ferdman, B. M., 37
Ferguson, K., 163
Fetzner, M., 6–7, 134–135
Finkelberg, R., 47
Fontaine, S. J., 36, 38
Fox, L., 19
Fraser, J., 89
Frederick, M., 74, 83–84, 118, 121
Frick, T., 127
Fry, R., 76
Fuller, M. B., 63
Furst-Bowe, J., 89

Gaines, T., 126
Gallagher, M. S., 134, 149
Gallimore, R., 164
Gammel, H. L., 17
Garrison, D. R., 8, 128
Géarard, L., 165
Geissler, J., 40
Gemmell, I., 165, 170, 173
Geri, N., 94–95
Getzlaf, B., 16
Ginder, S. A., 30
Giroir, B., 34
Glasser, W., 74, 81
Glienke, B. B., 151
Goegan, L. D., 64
Goel, A. K., 47
Goel, A., 46–47
Goldenberg, C., 164
Goldie, J. G. S., 61

Name Index

Goodchild, A., 67
Goodman, J., 44, 46
Grace, M., 74, 76, 78–79, 81, 84
Gravel, A., 34
Gravel, C. A., 81–82
Graziano, R., 47
Green, R. C., 183
Gustafsson, N., 47

Habley, W. R., 126–127
Harper, W., 155
Harrison, A., 151, 153–154
Harrison, R. A., 151, 153–154
Harrison, R., 165, 170, 173
Hartnett, M., 61, 63–64, 69
Hassan, H., 93
Haynie, L., 76
Hebdon, S., 153
Henderson, S., 63
Herbert, M., 32
Hess, J. A., 82
Hill, A., 61, 63
Hoffman, J., 6
Hoffman-Kipp, P., 166
Holland, A., 135
Hollins, T., 17
Holzweiss, P. C., 64, 68
Howe, N., 74–77
Howells, K., 67
Howland, J., 18
Hubbard, B. C., 135
Huie, F., 90
Humphreys, J., 155
Hurt, N. E., 93
Hussey, H. D., 135
Hutt, I., 165, 170, 173
Hyman, J. S., 15

Ice, P., 91–92
Inaba, K., 164
Ingram, R., 183–185
Isbell, C. L., 46–47

Jackson-Boothby, C., 5–6
Jacobs, L. F., 15
James, S., 162

Jarrat, D., 36
Jeffcoat, N. K., 17
Jonassen, D., 18
Jones, P., 92, 154
Jones, S. J., 6
Joyner, D. A., 46–47, 49
Joyner, S. A., 63

Kahn, P., 135
Kegan, R., 120
Kelly-Reid., J. E., 30
Kelm, K., 135
Kezar, A., 9, 106–107
Kift, S., 155
King, K. P., 167
Kirkpatrick, D. L., 18
Kirkpatrick, J. D., 18
Kivunja, C., 62
Knowles, M., 93–94
Koenig, S., 21
Kolhe, P., 47
Kop, R., 61, 63
Kozinsky, S., 81
Kromrey, J. D., 17
Kruger, K., 36, 64
Kuh, G. D., 74, 80–81, 123

Lack, K., 15
Lackie, R. J., 20, 22
Lam, L., 164
Lamarche, K., 16
Lamb, J., 134, 149
Lane, P., 34
Larsen, N., 47
Larson, L. R., 93
Lautenbach, D., 182
Lederman, D., 30
Lee, E., 134
Lee, J. J., 63
LeGore, C., 128
Lehan, T. J., 135
Leonard, M., 126–127
Lewiecki-Wilson, C., 181
Littman, M. L., 47
Locke, L. A., 164, 169, 175
Loeb, S., 19

Love, P., 127
Lovelace, M. D., 93
Loveland, E., 78
Lunde, R., 166
Lynn, L., 166
Lyons, B., 183

Magda, A. J., 14, 104
Majewski, D., 40
Maldonado, J., 74, 118
Mangal, A., 47
Mann, F. B., 30
Marathe, M., 46
Marra, R., 18
Martin, T., 76
Maslow, A. H., 123
Maxam, S., 127
Mazer, J. P., 82
McCallister, K. C., 21
McCarthy, J., 127
McCracken, H., 5
McCrudden, M., 163, 165, 175
McGuire, Am., 182
Mcmahon, M., 60
McPherson, M., 14
Meece, J. L., 151
Meehan, C., 67
Melkers, J., 44
Meyer, K. A., 6
Michelau, D. K., 34
Miller, C., 92
Miller, D., 128
Miller, P. T., 47
Milman, N. B., 7
Montañez, M., 18
Moody, J., 89
Moore, J., 18
Moss, G. S., 93
Motteram, G., 165, 170, 173
Muller, K., 32–33
Mupinga, D. M., 16
Murali, G., 47

NACADA, 32, 125
National Center for Education Statistics, 4, 14, 30, 89, 162

National Science Board, 162
Nelson, K., 155
Newton, D., 104
Nichols, M., 148, 151
Nora, R. T., 16
Norwood, A., 76
Nygren, T., 15

Ohrablo, S., 126–127
Okimoto, H., 91
Olive, J., 162, 166
Oliver, J., 183
Omar, N. D., 93
Ooms, A., 18
Open SUNY, 8, 30–36, 40
Orellana, M. L., 165
Osorio, A., 164
Ou, C., 47

Packham, G., 92
Pagnattaro, M. A., 82
Pajares, F., 163, 166, 173
Pallais, A., 44
Parusheva, S., 67
Pascarella, E. T., 17
Pasquini, L. A., 126–127
Pate, J., 134
Paterson, J., 104
Pelletier, S., 22
Pérez, A., 165
Perez, T., 186–187
Perry, B., 16
Perry, W. G., 123
Peuler, M., 21
Peylo, C., 89
Phelps, J. T., 118, 128–129
Pifer, M. J., 168, 172, 175–176
Pintz, C., 7
Polepeddi, L., 47
Posey, L., 7
Poulin, R., 89
Prevost, L. B., 93
Price, M., 181
Priem, J., 167
Public Broadcasting Service, 182

Name Index

Radda, H., 165, 171
Radford, A. W., 5
Randall, J., 169
Rawlings, B., 151
Reid, I., 135
Reisser, L., 123
Rickes, P. C., 75–79, 82
Rigler Jr, K. L., 166–167
Rispinto, S., 166
Robbins, S., 126
Robinson, C., 151
Robinson, D. A. G., 17
Rockinson-Szapkiw, A.J., 165–167, 169
Rodriguez, M. C.,18
Ross, J., 135, 137, 139
Rovai, A. P., 93, 149, 153–155, 165
Rowntree, D., 94
Ryan, R. M., 63

Salinas, J., 165
Sanger, J., 38
Sasso, P. A., 74, 77, 84
Scalzo, K., 32
Schlossberg, N. K., 123
Schraw, G., 163, 165, 172
Schuh, J. H., 74, 80, 123
Schwehm, J., 34
Scottish Credit and Qualification Framework, 69
Scottish Social Services Council, 63
Seaman, J. E., 4, 14, 30, 89
Seemiller, C., 74, 76, 78–79, 81–82, 84
Shapiro, D., 90
Sharkey, M., 91
Shaw, M., 163, 165
Sheail, P., 135, 137, 139, 148, 151–152
Sherrill, J., 92
Shriner, M., 135
Siemens, G., 61
Simpson, O., 94
Smith, A. R., 135
Smith, B., 6
Smith, D., 32
Sotto, R. R., 126–127
Spaulding, L. S., 166
Starner, T., 47

Steele, G. E., 126–127
Steele, G., 126–127
Stillman, D., 78–79
Stillman, J., 78–79
Stone, C., 10, 168–169, 171
Strauss, W., 75–77
Sullivan, M. E., 164
Sundt, M., 162, 174
Surkes, M., 92
Swan, K., 162
Sweat, K., 166

Tacoli, C., 79
Tailor, C., 47
Taylor, E. S., 19
Terenzini, P. T., 17
Terras, K. L., 81
Thomas, A. G., 5
Thomas-Varcoe, C., 165, 167, 173
Throne, R., 166
Tinto, V., 74, 83, 93
Tobbell, J., 148
Toffner, G., 16
Tremblay, P., 21
Trifilo, J., 40
Twenge, J. M., 74, 77–78

U.S. Department of Education, 14, 89
U.S. Department of Education, National Center for Education Statistics, 14, 89
University Academic Success Programs, 10, 135

Verenikina, I., 154

Wahal, S., 47
Wakhungu, P., 90
Walker, J. T., 76
Walti, C., 5
Wang, Z., 21
Watkins, F., 135
Watts, S., 166
Weltzer-Ward, L., 166
Wenger, E., 8, 128
White, J., 76

Whitt, E. J., 74, 80
Williams, A., 76
Williamson, B., 183
Wilson, S., 90
Wood, T., 181
Wright, K., 7

Xue, Q., 47

Yang, S. C., 63
Yardi, P., 46

Yates, K. A., 164
Yaw, D. C., 16
Young, R., 63
Yukselturk, E., 165–166, 170, 173

Zammit, M., 148
Zapta, L. P., 5
Zawacki-Richter, O., 5
Zhao, W., 155
Zhou, P., 7
Zimmerman, B. J., 94

SUBJECT INDEX

Academic advising, 44, 47–48, 81–82, 126–127
   UD, 124–125
Academic Advising Programs (AAP), 125
Academic advisors, 81–82
Academic conduct, 156
Academic integrity, 8, 45, 53
Academic program directors, 96
Academic skills, 134–135, 158, 165
Academic support, 135, 148, 155–156 (*see also* Student support)
   in higher education, 148
Academic transitions roadmap (ATR), 10, 149, 152–153
Access, 188–189
Access course in English, 68–70
Accessibility, 9, 82, 167, 169, 181, 183
Accommodation, 5, 8, 11, 50, 181–182
Accreditation, 43, 96, 118
Adaptive courses, 90
Adaptive learning system (ALS), 90
Advising, 81, 89
   from cloud, 128–129
   professional standards for, 124–125
Affordable degrees at scale, 14
Alumni relations, 44, 48–49
Ambassador, 112–113
American postsecondary education institutions, 118
American Women's College (TAWC), 9, 88, 91–92
American Women's College of Bay Path University, The, 88, 90
Americans with Disabilities Act of 1990 (ADA), 11, 50, 181
Analytics, 91
Arizona State University (ASU), 135
Assistive technologies (ATs), 180
Associates degree (AA), 14

Asynchronous, 18
   advising, 75
   communication, 127
   email communication, 127
AT Lab, 187
Autonomy, 61, 63–64

BA Childhood Practice online program (BACP online program), 67–68
Baby Boomers, 75–76
Barriers, 6–7
Baxter Magolda's Epistemological Reflection Model, 126
Bay Path University, 88, 90
Best practices, 40
   and guidelines, 52–54
Blogs, 60, 66
Building commitment, 106–107
Business degrees, 5

Campus ecosystem, 15–17
Campus life model, 35–40
Campus networks, 107–108, 110
Campus Press, 69
Campus processes, 109–111
Campus services, 16
Campuses, 6–7, 9, 16, 30, 40, 73, 113
Career development, 44, 48
Carnegie Project on the Education Doctorate (CPED), 162
Case study, 61, 104
CAST, 183–184
Childhood practice program, 67–68
Cloud advising, 118, 128–129
Co-curricular programing, 74
Coach communication plan, 19
Coach-to-student ratio, 20
Coaches, 20, 90
Coaching, 82, 89

Collaborate/collaboration, 9, 96–97, 104–114
Collaborative learning formats, 83
Collective activities, 62
College degree, 14
College Reading and Learning Association (CRLA), 140
Commitment
  building, 106–107
  to collaboration, 107
  sustaining, 107–108
Communication, 106–107, 151–152
  plan, 110–11
Communities of inquiry, 8
Communities of practice, 8, 35
Community, 153–155
Community college system, 14
Community facilitation, 20
Community-building, 64
Computer science, 43, 45
Concierge, 20
Concierge model, 33–34
Connected learning, 61
Connectivism, 61–62
Connectivity, 16, 20, 65
Consistent interaction, 84
Council for the Advancement of Standards in Higher Education (CAS), 125
Course instructors, 92
Course travel or immersion experience, 84
Culture of collaboration, 106, 108, 113
Customer relationship management (CRM), 90

Data analytics of online students' behavior, 22
Data consistency, 95–96
Data infrastructure, 53, 90
Data warehouse, 91–92, 94
Data-driven intervention strategies, 92
Dean of Students' advocacy, 51
"Dear Colleague" guidance letters, 186–187

Departments, 9, 96–97, 100, 107, 113, 159, 186
Dependence, 129
Dependency, 124
Design, 6
Device dependent Gen Z, 78
Diagnosis, 187–188
Digital badging opportunities, 37
Digital engagement, 74
Digital environments, 74
  generational theory, 75–76
  implications for practice, 81–84
  student engagement in college, 80–81
  student generations, 76–80
Digital library, 21
Digital natives, 76
Disability 1.0, 181
Disability 2.0, 181
Disability 3.0, 180–181
Disability accommodations, 50–51
Dissertation, 137
Distance learners, 148
Distance learning, 31–32
Distributed knowledge, 61
Diversity, 61
  of online experiences, 162–163
DIY, 79
Doctoral degree, 162
Doctoral education, 173
Doctoral programs, 10
Doctoral students, 175
Dragon Naturally Speaking, 188
Driven, 79
Dynamic Student Development Metatheodel (DSDM), 9, 119
  conceptual framework, 119–124
  constructs, 119–121
  implications for practice, 126–129
  integration, 121
  stages, 124
  theoretical foundations, 122

Early alert monitoring and interventions, 34–35
Echo generation, 77
Ecosystem, 7, 15

Subject Index

Educational institutions, 11
Educational technology, 48, 190 (*see also* Higher education)
Educator coaches, 91
Employment of online graduate students, 139–142
Engagement, 15, 91, 104–105
  opportunities checklist, 26–27
Equity, 188–189
Esports teams, 39

Face to face (F2F), 152
Facebook, 127
Faculty/staff site visits, 83
Family Educational Rights and Privacy Act (FERPA), 16, 22
Fee equity checklist, 27
Feedback, 163
Focus actions, 97–98
FOMO, 79
"Food pantry" outreach, 39
Formal collaborative programs, 111–114
Fresher's Week, 154
Fund for the Improvement of Postsecondary Education (FIPSE), 88
Fundamental attribution error of higher education, 118

Gen X, 76
Gender, 46
General Teaching Council for Scotland (GTCS), 68
Generation, 75
Generation Z, 74–75
  intersection of, 79–80
  students, 78–79
Generational theory, 75–76
Genetic Information Non-discrimination Act of 2008 (GINA), 182
George Kuh's seamless change model, 105
Google Hangout, 127
Grade point averages (GPAs), 92, 139

Graduate and Professional Student Association (GPSA), 135
Graduate Launch (GL), 21
Graduate students, 135
Graduate Writing Tutors (GWTs), 136, 141
Greatest generation, 76
Growth, learning, and development (GLD), 119–120

Health Insurance Portability and Accountability Act (HIPAA), 22
Helicopter parents, 76–77
HelpDesk, 30, 33
Heutagogy, 62–63
"High-tech, high-touch" practices, 90–91
Higher education, 4, 74
  provision of academic support in, 148
  student support in, 5–6
Higher English, 68
Hyper-Custom, 79

Implementing commitment, 109–111
In-person residency, 83
Inclusion, 11
Inclusive language checklist, 26
Independence, 124
Induction, 155
Informal peer support, 148
Instant messaging (IM), 127
Institutional readiness (IR), 31
Institutional Review Board (IRB), 22, 140
Instructional designers, 96
Interactivity, 61
Interdependence, 124
International English Language Testing System Academic test (IELTS-Academic), 45
Intrusive advising, 34
Intrusive success coaching (*see* Proactive success coaching)

Kairos, 181
Key performance indicators (KPIs), 19
Kezar's collaboration model, 9, 105
  analysis of initiatives using, 108–114
  building commitment, 106–107
  commitment to collaboration, 107
  sustaining commitment, 107–108
Knowledge acquisition, 61
Knowledge–Motivation–Skills human performance model, 175
KnowledgePath, 90
Kuh's theory of student engagement, 80

Language, 7, 16, 69
Learner attrition, 60
Learner autonomy, 63
Learner motivation, 68
Learning, 4, 22, 32
Learning Academic Skills Support (LASS), 153
Learning communities, 62
Learning environments, 11, 128
Learning management system (LMS), 30, 50, 90, 128, 137, 165
Library services, 17
Life cycles, 75
Listserv, 37
Literacy, 11, 68, 189
Live meeting collaborative document platform, 93

Massive open online course (MOOC), 46
Master of Science in Computer Science (MSCS), 44
  program demographics, 45–46
  program requirements, 45
  program-level structures, 47–50
  student experience, 46–47
  university-level structures, 50–54
Master of Science program (MSc program), 148
Masters, 148
Me Generation, 79
Medical *vs.* social model of disability, 182–183

Mental effort, 163–164, 166
Messaging, 47
Metatheodel, 119
Metis, 181
Millennial students, 76–77
Millennials, 73–76
  intersection of, 79–80
Mixed-method approach, 148
Modalities, 46
Motivation, 151–152, 163–164
  issues, 170, 173
Multiple modalities checklist, 26

NACADA, 32
National Center for Education Statistics (NCES), 4, 162
Networked learning activities, 62
Networks and partners, 98–99

On-campus program, 44–45
One-Day-a-Week Saturday Program, 88
Online, 162–163
Online courses, 5
Online Dissertation Writing Camp, 137–139
Online distance learners (ODL), 148
Online doctoral students, 175
Online education, 4, 30
Online graduate program, 43
Online graduate students, 134
  (*see also* Postgraduate online distance students)
  areas for program growth and future research, 143–144
  employment of, 139–142
  limitations, 143
  recommendations for practitioners, 144–145
Online graduate writing centers, 135–137
Online instruction, 14
Online learners
  building learning communities, 62
  challenge of connecting with, 60
  heutagogy, 62–63
  literature review and theoretical framework, 61–62

Subject Index

motivation, 63–65
rationale for choice of case studies, 64–70
Online learning, 14, 30, 104, 152, 172
   courses, 64
   environment, 60
Online Learning Consortium (OLC), 31
Online library services, 20–22
Online MSCS program, 45
Online orientation, 17–18
Online program, 88
Online Program Manager (OPM), 170
Online students, 4, 44, 104, 134
   barriers for providing services to, 6–7
   challenges, 104–105
   characteristics, 4–5
   engagement days, 39
   readiness, 34
   success coaching, 18–20
   support services, 15–22
   time and energy, 135
Online tutoring, 35
Online university programs, 104
Open SUNY, 31
   IR process, 31–32
   model, 8
   Open SUNY+ Program Designation, 32
   Open SUNY+ Signature Elements, 32–33, 40
Openness, 61
Optical character recognition (OCR), 188
Organizational factors, 164
Organizational issues, 166–169
Orientation, 7, 17–18, 90

Pathways to Success program, 113
Peer personality, 75
Peer support, 153
Performance coaches, 82
Personalized engagement, 90
Personalized learning environment, 9
Phase, 9, 75
Phigital, 79
Plagiarism, 156
Postgraduate online distance students, 148
   ATR, 152–153
   methodology, 149–151
   motivation and communication, 151–152
   transition into university, 153–157
   transition–during studies, 157–158
   transitioning out of university, 158–159
Predictive analytics, 91–92
   for online student success, 22
Private university, 104
Private virtual map, 155
Proactive advising (*see* Intrusive advising)
Proactive faculty support, 94
Proactive success coaching, 18
Process, 105
Professional doctoral program, 162
Professional Graduate Diploma in Education (PGDE), 68
Professional learning, 60
Professional standards for advising, 124–125
Program-level structures, 47 (*see also* University-level structures)
   academic advising, 47–48
   alumni relations, 48–49
   career development, 48
   student employment, 49–50
Programatic learning, 84
Programs, 6, 17
Public Broadcasting Service (PBS), 182

Quality Scorecard, 31

Realistic, 79
Reasonable accommodation, 181–182, 187
Relatedness, 63
Remote learning, 88
Response timeliness checklist, 26
Retention, 9, 145
   risk triggers/predictive analytics, 20

Roadmap, 149
RooSuccess, 37

Self-determination, 63, 70
Self-efficacy, 163–164, 166
Sense of belonging, 74
Signature elements evolution to support student success, 32
    24/7 support, 33
    concierge model, 33–34
    early alert monitoring and interventions, 34–35
    online student readiness, 34
    online tutoring, 35
Significant other (SO), 120
Silent Generation, 76
Social communities, 37
Social engagement, 64
Social media, 60
Social model of disability, 182–183
Social networks, 148
Social Online Universal Learning (SOUL), 9, 88
    communities, 90
    elements, 88–90
    infrastructure supporting, 90–91
    lessons learned, 95–99
Stakeholder groups, 164
Starfish, 35
State University of New York (SUNY), 8
    history of SUNY online learning, 30–31
    Open SUNY IR process, 31–32
    system, 30
Strategic plan, 106–107, 109
Student Academic Support Scale (SASS), 152
Student advising, 19
Student advocacy, 51
Student affairs, 6, 15, 171
Student conflict resolution, 51–52
Student development, 119
Student employment, 44, 49–50
Student engagement, 6, 8, 31, 135
    building community, 93–94
    in college, 80–81
    data-informed interventions, 92
    faculty early alert, 94
    fostering relationships in online classroom, 94–95
    optimizing technology for, 82
    predictive analytics, 91–92
    wrap-around support framework for, 91
Student experience, 10, 14, 19, 84, 153
Student generations, 75–76
    Gen Z students, 78–79
    intersection of Millennials and Gen Z, 79–80
    millennial students, 76–77
Student Government Association (SGA), 37
Student information system (SIS), 91
Student involvement theory, 134
Student preparedness, 34
Student retention, 163
Student services, 15, 32
Student success, 32–35
Student support, 16, 170
    in higher education, 5–6
    needs checklist, 26
    signature elements evolution to support student success, 32–35
Students' expectations, 63
Substantive interaction, 84
Success, 7, 15, 22
Summits, 110
SUNY Canton case study on engaging online students in campus life, 35
    assessing student interest in campus life, 36
    assessment, 39
    implementing online student engagement framework, 37–39
    steps, 39–40
SUNY Excels, 31
    framework, 33

Subject Index

SUNY Learning Network (SLN), 30
Supplemental Instruction (SI), 143
Support, 134, 148
   mechanisms and programs, 17
   online library services, 20–22
   online orientation, 17–18
   online student success coaching, 18–20
   predictive analytics for online student success, 22
Supports, services, interventions, and programs (SSIPs), 119–121
Sustaining commitment, 111–114
Synchronous, 18
   communication, 127
   sessions, 15

Task value, 163–164, 166
Teacher education program, 65–67
Teacher–student relationship, 15
Teaching Qualification in Further Education (TQFE), 65–67
Technical support, 33
Technology, 74, 93
   advising, 126–127
Test of English as a Foreign Language (TOEFL), 45
Text-to-speech (TTS), 186
Tinto's theory of student departure, 74
Town hall, 7, 106–107, 109, 114
Tracking communication for seamless support, 19
Training, 6, 22, 142, 164
Transforming, 14–15
Transitions, 149, 151
   shock, 155
Transparency, 81
Tutoring, 34–35
24/7 Online Student Listserv, 37
24/7 support, 33

UK Higher Education Academy Retention Grants Briefing Program, 151
Underrepresented minorities, 46
Unified university vision, 108–109
Universal design (UD), 124
   in academic advising, 124–125
Universal design, 125
Universal Design for Instruction (UDforI), 125
Universal design for learning (UDL), 9, 91, 125, 180, 183–187
   case study, 189–190
Universal Design in Education (UDE), 124
Universal Design in Higher Education (UDHE), 125
Universal Design of Instruction (UDI), 125
Universal Instructional Design (UID), 125
Universally Designed Teaching (UDT), 125
University Academic Success Programs (UASP), 135
University ambassadors, 112
University campuses, 15
University-level structures, 50
   disability accommodations, 50–51
   student advocacy, 51
   student conflict resolution, 51–52
US Professional Doctoral Degree, 162
US-based professional doctoral programs
   conceptual framework, 163–164
   context for online, 162–163
   factors influencing online doctoral degree completion, 164–175
   themes/lessons, 175–176

Varsity Esports teams, 39
Virtual academic gaming, 82
Virtual Assistive Technology Lab (VAT Lab), 181
   case study, 189–190
   at SUNY Empire, 187–188
Virtual book clubs and scavenger hunts with library and tutoring resources, 38
Virtual career fairs, 38

Virtual clothing fairs, 38
Virtual Learning Communities (VLCs), 90, 93
Virtual learning environments (VLEs), 60, 152
Virtual private network (VPN), 187
Virtual student IDs, 38
Virtual Student Union, 17
Virtual study abroad fairs, 38
Visual literacy, 82

We Generation, 79
Webinars, 60, 66
Weconomist, 79
Welcome and finals stress relief care packets, 37–38
Welcome Week, 154
Wraparound supports, 92
Writing, 135
   camp, 137–139
   center, 136, 141

www.ingramcontent.com/pod-product-compliance
Lightning Source LLC
LaVergne TN
LVHW012249070526
838201LV00092B/165